BLACK MIXED-RACE MEN: TRANSATLANTICITY, HYBRIDITY AND 'POST-RACIAL' RESILIENCE

BLACK MIXED-RACE MEN: TRANSATLANTICITY, HYBRIDITY AND 'POST-RACIAL' RESILIENCE

CRITICAL MIXED RACE STUDIES

Edited by Shirley Anne Tate, Leeds Beckett University, UK

This series adopts a critical, interdisciplinary perspective to the study of mixed race. It will showcase ground-breaking research in this rapidly emerging field to publish work from early career researchers as well as established scholars. The series will publish short books, monographs and edited collections on a range of topics in relation to mixed race studies and include work from disciplines across the Humanities and Social Sciences including Sociology, History, Anthropology, Psychology, Philosophy, History, Literature, Postcolonial/Decolonial Studies and Cultural Studies.

Forthcoming Titles:

Shirley Anne Tate, *Decolonizing Sambo: Transculturation, Fungibility and Mixed Race Futurity*

Paul Ian Campbell, *Identity Politics, 'Mixed-Race' and Local Football in 21st Century Britain: Mix and Match*

BLACK MIXED-RACE MEN: TRANSATLANTICITY, HYBRIDITY AND 'POST-RACIAL' RESILIENCE

BY

REMI JOSEPH-SALISBURY
Leeds Beckett University, UK

emerald
PUBLISHING

United Kingdom – North America – Japan – India – Malaysia – China

Emerald Publishing Limited
Howard House, Wagon Lane, Bingley BD16 1WA, UK

First edition 2018

Copyright © 2018 Emerald Publishing Limited

Reprints and permissions service
Contact: permissions@emeraldinsight.com

British Library Cataloguing in Publication Data
A catalogue record for this book is available from the British Library

ISBN: 978-1-78756-532-6 (Print)
ISBN: 978-1-78756-531-9 (Online)
ISBN: 978-1-78756-533-3 (Epub)
ISBN: 978-1-78756-534-0 (Paperback)

INVESTOR IN PEOPLE

CRITICAL MIXED RACE STUDIES

Edited by Shirley Anne Tate, Leeds Beckett University, UK

This series adopts a critical, interdisciplinary perspective to the study of mixed race. It will showcase ground-breaking research in this rapidly emerging field to publish work from early career researchers as well as established scholars. The series will publish short books, monographs and edited collections on a range of topics in relation to mixed race studies and include work from disciplines across the Humanities and Social Sciences including Sociology, History, Anthropology, Psychology, Philosophy, History, Literature, Postcolonial/Decolonial Studies and Cultural Studies.

Forthcoming Titles:

Shirley Anne Tate, *Decolonizing Sambo: Transculturation, Fungibility and Mixed Race Futurity*

Paul Ian Campbell, *Identity Politics, 'Mixed-Race' and Local Football in 21st Century Britain: Mix and Match*

BLACK MIXED-RACE MEN: TRANSATLANTICITY, HYBRIDITY AND 'POST-RACIAL' RESILIENCE

BY

REMI JOSEPH-SALISBURY
Leeds Beckett University, UK

emerald
PUBLISHING

United Kingdom – North America – Japan – India – Malaysia – China

Emerald Publishing Limited
Howard House, Wagon Lane, Bingley BD16 1WA, UK

First edition 2018

Reprints and permissions service
Contact: permissions@emeraldinsight.com

British Library Cataloguing in Publication Data
A catalogue record for this book is available from the British Library

ISBN: 978-1-78756-532-6 (Print)
ISBN: 978-1-78756-531-9 (Online)
ISBN: 978-1-78756-533-3 (Epub)
ISBN: 978-1-78756-534-0 (Paperback)

INVESTOR IN PEOPLE

Acknowledgements

Thank you to my family, friends and colleagues who have supported me in the writing of my PhD, and this book. Thank you especially to Ian and Shirley for their meticulous guidance, and to Laura for her unwavering support and confidence.

A special thank you to the experts: the Black mixed-race men themselves.

Contents

Introduction

Excuse me
standing on one leg
I'm half-caste.

Explain yuself
wha yu mean
when yu say half-caste
yu mean when Picasso
mix red an green
is a half-caste canvas?
explain yuself
wha yu mean
when yu say half-caste
yu mean when light an shadow
mix in de sky
is a half-caste weather?
well in dat case
england weather
nearly always half-caste
in fact some o dem cloud
half-caste till dem overcast
so spiteful dem don't want de sun pass
ah rass?
explain yuself
wha yu mean
when yu say half-caste
yu mean tchaikovsky
sit down at dah piano
an mix a black key
wid a white key
is a half-caste symphony?

Explain yuself
wha yu mean
Ah listening to yu wid de keen
half of mih ear
Ah looking at yu wid de keen
half of mih eye
an when I'm introduced to yu
I'm sure you'll understand
why I offer yu half-a-hand
an when I sleep at night
I close half-a-eye
consequently when I dream
I dream half-a-dream
an when moon begin to glow
I half-caste human being
cast half-a-shadow
but yu must come back tomorrow
wid de whole of yu eye
an de whole of yu ear
an de whole of yu mind.

an I will tell yu
de other half
of my story.

John Agard (2004, pp. 11–13)

Growing up as a young Black mixed-race man, John Agard's poem *Half-caste* sparked a rare moment of interest and inspiration in an otherwise mundane, whitewashed and Eurocentric schooling experience. It was not solely the curricular recognition of Black mixed-race identities that spoke to me but the very words of the poem resonated as profoundly with me then as they do today. Those words initiated a journey of self-discovery that culminates in, as far as there is ever a culmination of such a journey, the completion of this book.

Agard's poem evokes so many memories as it returns me to those moments in my life where I felt the heightened saliency of my racial identity; the pride I felt as I wore my first Nigeria replica football shirt and the anger and hurt that soon followed as an older white boy intentionally mispronounced the name on the shirt: 'Nigg-er-ee-ya'. This was his attempt to wound and degrade through racial epithet. I'm reminded of the mixture of pride and alienation I felt as, in 2002, whilst I was at high school, the national football teams of England and Nigeria faced each other in the World Cup of that year. As I sat in the dining hall with my peers, crowded around a small screen watching the game, my allegiances became the subject of fierce debate. Those around me asserted variously that I should support England, that I cannot support England, that I should support Nigeria, that I cannot support Nigeria, and ultimately, that I cannot possibly have allegiances with both sides. 'Are you related to the players?' was one particularly banal, yet loaded, question. Luckily, as the teams played out a boring goal-less draw, I did not have a chance to find out how my peers might have reacted had the game contained more action. What did become clear from this encounter, however, was that my peers sought to have some control over who and what I could be. They sought to erase the totality of my identity in order to situate me neatly within the Black/white racial dichotomy. My *difference* from my white peers was neither exclusively positive nor exclusively negative but certainly subject to my manipulation and modification. As I will discuss more fully later in this introduction, by engaging with theories of performativity and hybridity, much of my endeavour in this book is to understand these processes of negotiation, manipulation and modification. For now, let us return to my school days.

A year or two after the incident surrounding the Nigeria/England game, the racial disharmony in the school manifest in lunchtime football games as the white boys and the South Asian boys formed two opposing teams in racially charged, physically and verbally aggressive, games. My body, a disruption to the school yard's white/non-white dichotomy, was literally and metaphorically dragged from side-to-side. As each side made the case for my inclusion on their team, it became clear that I was not readily identifiable as a member of the team of white boys nor was I undisputedly part of the team of South Asian boys. As a member of the team of white boys argued, I was 'part white'. As the opposing team responded, I was 'not white'. Whilst at once, both sides seemingly had a case, this was an instance in which I not only became aware of my hypervisibility but also of the desire of others to position me within the predefined racial dichotomy of white and Black or white and non-white. It was through instances such as this — as well as a plethora of experiences where race was less explicit but no less present — that I became aware of the acute need to take some control over my identification. As I now recall my last day of high school, I know that it was such a desire to self-define that led me and my friends to emblazon our shirts with a bold scrawling of 'nigga'. Although I now occupy a place in which, even with the 'reclaimed' spelling, I refuse to reappropriate a term with such an injurious past, this was an act of defiance that encapsulated our desire for self-definition and my demonstrative refusal to be wounded by the racist interpellation of my white interlocutors. Agard's poem returns me to each of these moments as I make sense of the person I am today.

In the first instance, John Agard's poem manifests as a form of resistance to the, now largely outdated, limiting and pathological label of 'half-caste' (Ali, 2003; Fatimilehin, 1999). In my early years, half-caste represented common parlance used to describe people like me. Indeed, there was a time when I too would describe myself in this way. Agard's work taught me not only that language is important but that it is possible to resist the ascription of labels and identities; we should be defined in our own terms and not by those terms imposed by (white) others. Terminologically, half-caste has its origins in British colonialism and imperialism and was, more latterly, 'used in Britain as a derogatory racial category associated with the moral condemnation of "miscegenation"' (Aspinall, 2013, p. 503). The opposition to the descriptor, so powerfully conveyed by John Agard, is echoed by Peter Aspinall's (2009) findings that half-caste is deemed the most offensive term among mixed-race people. As one respondent to his research reasoned, 'it portrays the notion that I am only half a person' (Aspinall, 2009, p. 7). This is the message Agard so strongly imparts as he encourages his interlocutors to engage with 'de other half' of his story. Of course, the battle over terminology that Agard engages in, although itself an important intervention, is emblematic of much larger struggles.

As he somewhat sarcastically interrogates his interlocutors, Agard makes a mockery of the societal pressures that seek to render the mixed-race population less than whole. In so doing, Agard evocatively resists the erasure and fragmentation of the totality of his identity and lived experience. It is this, his totality, which is at stake. Through his words, Agard demonstrates resiliency as he refuses to become the pathological 'half-caste' of the white imaginary. As he playfully evokes imagery of world renowned art, classical music and nature, Agard troubles the pathological and moves towards a positive reinterpretation of what it might mean to be 'half-caste'. As he encourages his interlocutor to return with the 'whole of yu mind', the critique is shifted firmly to the white other who is unable or unwilling to recognise the totality of Agard's identity and his wholeness as human. In these remarks, Agard captures something of my own journey, and the journeys of the Black mixed-race men in this study, as I and they strive to constitute whole, complex and multiplicitous identities of our own making. That Agard does all of this in an Afro-Guyanese creole is demonstrative of a refusal to succumb to the pressures of white supremacy and a pride in one's Blackness that I see as reflective not only of my own experiences but of the Black mixed-race men's accounts that unfold in the pages that follow. This book continues in the tradition of John Agard's half-caste and offers a corrective to the pervasive pathological myths that surround understandings of the lives of Black mixed-race men. In offering this corrective, *I argue that through the ceaseless process of hybridisation (read as culture), and the utilisation of various forms of cultural capital, Black mixed-race men develop the 'post-racial' resilience to withstand threats of identity erasure.* Before I return to explicate the theoretical framework that will underpin this argument, I want to offer two notes: first, a note on the use of terminology and second, a note on the discursive history of Black mixedness. So, why the descriptor 'Black mixed-race'?

I use the term *Black mixed-race* not to override or delegitimise often complex and nuanced self-identifications but to 'capture a certain phenomenological experience' (Botts, 2016, p. 8). As this book demonstrates, Blackness and mixedness represent the two predominant racial identity discourses at play in the experiences and identifications of Black mixed-race men. The participants in the study draw heavily upon discourses of Blackness and mixedness as they make sense of their lived experiences. Several of the men articulated a sense of Black mixed-race 'duality'. In Chapter 2, I explore more fully the fluid, varied and complex self-identifications of the study's participants.

Given that this book is about Black mixed-race men, and thus about race more broadly, I use race terminology throughout. Whilst the use of such terms is integral to the scope and nature of the book, it is worth acknowledging – as so many have done before me – that race has 'little meaning in biology' and has been heavily discredited by geneticists, anthropologists and biologists (Khanna, 2011a, p. ix). Race is therefore taken as a social construction that is incredibly (socially) significant in structuring our society and in shaping the lives of Black mixed-race men. Thus, the descriptors used – Black, white, mixed-race, Black mixed-race, mono-racial,[1] multiracial and more – to describe *social*

---

[1] I use the term mono-racial much in the same way I use mixed-race: not to refer to a mythological mono-racial identity but to denote those who are socially constructed as being of a single race only.

phenomena (Root, 1996; Winant, 1994). If we are to understand the lives of Black mixed-race men, we must understand the historical construction of mixedness. Before setting out the theoretical framework that underpins the book, I offer this brief history as a basis from which we might do so.

A (Very Brief) History of Discourses on Black Mixedness

Mixed-race people have been subject to pathologisation and conceptual violence for centuries (Henriques, 1975). Emerging out of racist fears of miscegenation, pseudo-scientific mythology offered an early discourse on mixedness (Alibhai-Brown & Montague, 1992; Tizard & Phoenix, 2002). As those in power sought to maintain the white supremacist racial order, mixed-race children came to be seen as the embodiment of the dilution, contamination and degeneration of superior white blood (see for example: Grant, 1916). Due to the scientific dominance of polygenic ideas, it was speculated that mixed-race children would suffer from biological and genetic problems (Provine, 1973).

A robust discrediting of eugenicist-thinking did not engender the erosion of pathologies of mixedness but merely saw the ideas morph and take on new forms. Pseudo-scientific genetics came to gradually be displaced by pseudo-psychological, cultural and sociological pathologies of mixedness.[2] This discourse, spanning the Atlantic, posited that, caught between two communities, mixed-race individuals were destined for psychological maladjustment and identity confusion (Fletcher, 1930; Stonequist, 1937). Such ideas continue to hold some credence in popular discourse (Ali, 2007; Aspinall & Song, 2013; Joseph, 2012; Spickard, 2001). So prevalent is this discourse that in 2006, Trevor Phillips, then Chair of the Commission for Equality and Human Rights, described mixed-race children as growing up 'marooned between communities' and being particularly susceptible to 'identity stripping' (Caballero, Edwards, & Smith, 2008, p. 51). As recently as 2016, an academic article in the *British Medical Journal* cited identity confusion as a potential explanation for 'behavioural problems' among mixed-race youth (Zilanawala, Sacker, & Kelly, 2016).

---

[2]East and Jones' (1919) work *Inbreeding and Outbreeding: Their Genetics and Sociological Significance* captures this shift as it encompasses influence from both the former and the latter discourses.

Attempts to respond to this discourse have suggested that rather than marginally positioned, mixed-race people are in fact liminally positioned and are able to move freely between 'mono-racial' groups (Caballero, 2004; Daniel, Kina, Dariotis, & Fojas, 2014; Rockquemore, Brunsma, & Delgado, 2009). This discourse quickly slips into a 'post-racial' romanticisation of mixedness that positions the mixed-race population as 'a nice coffee coloured solution to all our problems in time' (Alibhai-Brown & Montague, 1992, p. 128). Barack Obama, Jessica Ennis-Hill and Meghan Markle are just a few of the many prominent mixed-race figures that have been co-opted as the face of a 'post-racial' utopia (Donnor & Brown, 2011; Ford, Jolley, Katwala, & Mehta, 2012; Jolivétte, 2012).

This is not only the historical context that is denied by 'post-racial' logic, a point I will come to later, but it is also the historical context that continues to shape the lived experiences of Black mixed-race men. A glance to history points to a number of Transatlantic continuities that make a focus on both the UK and the USA particularly interesting. Given their interlinked migratory histories (Morning, 2012), the countries are both shaped by the legacy of a Black/white racial dichotomy and of viewing mixedness 'as an illegitimate state outside the either/or binary' (Caballero, 2004, p. 12). The two countries are still shaped by the residual impact of transatlantic slavery and the imposition of white superiority and Black inferiority (Caballero, 2004). White supremacy is at the core of the structure of each country and both countries exhibit the 'post-racial' conditions that are integral to my analysis in this book.

The relationality between the two contexts is evident in the parallels between two early sociological works on mixedness: the Fletcher report in the UK (Fletcher, 1930) and the marginal man thesis in the USA (Stonequist, 1937); both of which posit that the mixed-race population are marginal and pathological. Scholars like Platt (2012) have since observed the cross-pollination of analysis with perhaps a UK reliance on US literature. Although somewhat different in nature, the parallels between the USA's 2000 and UK's 2001 inclusion of mixed-race options on their respective national censuses also hints at a Transatlanticity of mixedness. Finally, research from Warikoo (2011) who looks at youth culture in UK and US schools finds remarkable similarities between the two contexts.

It is in these relational contexts that Black mixed-race men's identities are formed (Goldberg, 2009) and as has been intimated already, in both contexts, attempts to disrupt this discourse — and challenge the pathological marginalisation of mixedness — are burgeoning. As I seek to speak back to the pathologisation of mixedness, this is the entry point for this book. The framework that follows aims to facilitate our moving beyond these vacuous and unsubstantiated discourses of pathologisation and romanticisation (Joseph, 2012) and to develop a Critical (Mixed) Race Theory of Black mixed-race men's 'post-racial' resilience.

Critical (Mixed) Race Theory, Performativity and Hybridity: Towards a Theory of Post-Racial Resilience (PRR)

In this book I draw upon insights from interviews I conducted with 28 Black mixed-race men: 14 from the UK and 14 from the USA. Through these accounts, I aim to develop a Critical (Mixed) Race Theory of PRR based on Transatlantic data drawn from Black mixed-race men. Theories of performativity and hybridity are integral to the underpinning of such a project. At this point, I will first briefly outline the usefulness of Critical Race Theory (CRT) before going on to discuss performativity and hybridity.

In *The Erotic Life of Racism*, Sharon Patricia Holland (2012, p. 3) argues that 'for scholars of critical race theory, "racism" is almost always articulated as an everyday occurrence, as pedestrian rather than spectacular'. It is the everydayness of racism that is evident in the personal experiences I recounted earlier, as well as in John Agard's poem at the opening of this book. Like Agard and myself, the accounts of the Black mixed-race men in this study highlight the normalcy, the inevitability and the incessancy of racism (Bell, 1993). It is for this reason that I take a firm grounding in CRT (Delgado & Stefancic, 2012; Hylton, 2012). Such a grounding engenders an 'understanding that everyday racism defines race, interprets it, and decrees what the personal and institutional work of race will be' (Holland, 2012, p. 3). Recognising that mixedness means that race manifests in particular ways, and that this has not always been recognised in studies of race and ethnicity, leads me to complicate CRT through emphasising the particularities of mixedness: this gives us Critical (Mixed) Race Theory (C(M)RT) as the theoretical, epistemological and ontological grounding for the book.

Specifically, though, my primary interest in this book lies in the ways in which Black mixed-race men respond to and engage in this work of race. Therefore, CRT's emphasis on exploring phenomena from the perspective of the racially marginalised (Hylton, 2012; Warmington, 2012) provides an befitting theoretical and methodological framework for a C(M)RT exploration of the lived experiences, and particularly the identification processes, of Black mixed-race men. Given this focus on identification, I draw heavily on performativity and hybridity as central components in the study's theoretical framework.

Race and gender are not pre-existing or inherent facts but are performative; they are made intelligible, and therefore brought into being, through discourse (Ali, 2003; Butler, 1997, 1999, 2011; Byrne, 2000; Salih, 2007; Tate, 2005, 2012, 2015; Youdell, 2000). It is through the continued reiteration and repetition of discursive acts that gender and race come to exist (Butler, 2011; Byrne, 2000; Tate, 2005, 2012). In this sense, race and gender are something that people *do*, rather than something that people *are* (Lawler, 2014). In the *doing* of identity and as the accounts throughout this book make clear, race and gender are inseparable. That is, race is always gendered, and gender is always raced (Ali, 2003). The two are inextricably bound up in the process of identification and negotiation of identities: thus, it is impossible to think of one without thinking of the other (Byrne, 2000; Pateman & Mills, 2007; Tate, 2005). The participants in this study are never just Black mixed-race nor are they ever just men, they are always *Black mixed-race men* located in a raced and gendered society (Pateman & Mills, 2007). As I show throughout this book, Black mixed-race men are simultaneously constituted by discourse and active in the constitution and reconstitution of discourse. However, without historical and contextual citationality, identifications are not intelligible (Youdell, 2000). Given the need for contextual citationality, in this book, I consider how Black mixed-race men performatively *do* their raced and gendered identities in the context of the discursive constraints of white supremacy and a Black/white dichotomy that threatens the erasure and fragmentation of complex and multiplicitous identities. Hybridity theory is integral to this endeavour, but first, let me say something about the Black/white racial dichotomy (Jones, 2015; Spell, 2017).

Writing at the turn of the twentieth century, and inspiring the establishment of CRT, WEB Du Bois (1903, p. 9) noted that '[t]he problem of the twentieth century is the problem of the color line'. Well into the twenty-first century, and despite the mystification of the 'post-racial', his prognosis continues to ring true. The Black/white dichotomy that characterises both UK and US society has played and continues to play a fundamental role in shaping the lives and experiences of all, specifically Black mixed-race men (Jones, 2015; Patel, 2009; Spell, 2017). This colour line, characterised by the polarisation of Black and white, has been essential to the maintenance of white supremacy (Dalmage, 2000).

Black mixed-race populations have historically posed a unique problem to the maintenance of the colour line (Caballero, 2004). Thus, in the USA, the legal and moral principle of the one-drop rule dictated that Black mixed-race individuals were to be considered as Black; such classification was integral to the maintenance of white supremacy (Khanna, 2011a; Zack, 1994). Whilst the legal manifestations of the one-drop rule have long since been abolished, the moral and socio-cultural legacies persist in terms of racialisation and identification (Townsend, Markus, & Bergsieker, 2009). Similarly, given the abiding impact of UK enslavement colonies, and the influence of US ideas, manifestations of the one-drop rule are prevalent in the UK too (Aspinall & Song, 2013). The one-drop rule therefore represents a significant factor impacting upon the lives, experiences and identities of Black mixed-race men. The prevailing thought has been that since society designates Black mixed-race men Black status, they should understand their identity as Black (Tizard & Phoenix, 2002; Townsend et al., 2009). Such thinking seeks to avoid the purported threat of marginalisation and confusion of languishing on the colour line (Cross Jr, 1971, 2001; Nakashima, 1992; Patel, 2009; Tutwiler, 2016). It is through hybridity, I want to argue, that Black mixed-race men come to resist the pressures of this racial dichotomy.

In order to explicate what is meant by hybridity, an example may be apt. In 1997, following his ascent to golfing stardom, Tiger Woods, appearing on the Oprah Winfrey show, was asked about his racial identity. He answered with the following,

> Growing up, I came up with this name: I'm a 'Cablinasian',
> Ca, Caucasian; bl, Black; in, Indian; Asian. I'm just who I
> am. Whoever you see in front of you.

This quote represents an attempt on the part of Woods to resist what he sees as the threat of identity erasure. For Woods, as his interlocutors interpellate him as African American, they attempt to fragment his totality. It is in understanding how Woods — like the Black mixed-race men in this study — responds and resists, that the concept of hybridity, as theorised by Homi Bhabha (1990, 1996, 2012) and others (Ali, 2003; Ifekwunigwe, 1999; Tate, 2005) proves revealing.

In his utterance, his refusal of his interpellation, Tiger Woods rejects the Black/white dichotomy and acts to open up what Bhabha describes as a 'third space' in which identities and meanings are negotiated and reworked through processes of hybridisation (Alexander, 1996;

Bhabha, 1990; Tate, 2005). In so doing, he brings forth 'possibilities of and for multiplicity' (Ali, 2003, p. 12). For Homi Bhabha (1990, p. 211), 'identification is a process of identifying with and through another object'. This is what is apparent in Tiger Woods' account. Whilst his imbrication in discourse is inescapable, he 'puts together the traces of other meanings of discourses' and thus opens up a third space to create a new identification (Bhabha, 1990); *Cablinasian.* This is an identification that is neither entirely bound by any of its constitutive discourses nor is it entirely bereft of their meanings. The only language that Tiger Woods has to constitute his new identity is that of identities that are already discursively intelligible. To put it another way, his identification is a 'yoking together' of that which is already known (Bhabha, 1990, p. 212). In this book, I argue that Black mixed-race men's identities are always in a process of hybridity (Tate, 2005) as they, like Tiger Woods, draw upon, *speak back* to, and refashion competing discourses in the *bricolage* like assemblage of new and complex identities (Hall, 1990, 1996).

The enunciation of Woods also offers a reminder that identities are not constituted in abstraction from the social world but are always developed and negotiated interactionally between people (Butler, 1990; Goffman, 1990; Khanna, 2011a; Mead, 1934; Tate, 2005; Youdell, 2004). This is what he alludes to when, after describing his self-conception, he acknowledges the gaze of the other; he is 'whoever you see in front of you'. Perhaps even Woods himself could not have fully grasped just how resonant those words would be. Whilst his identification was celebrated by many as a beacon of 'post-racial' and multiracial futures (Cashmore, 2008; Kamiya, 1997; Kennedy, 2012), for others, particularly African Americans, Woods was a 'traitor' and a 'sell out' (Pitts Jr, 1997). For many African Americans, Woods' identification was out of keeping with the realities of race in America. As his critics argued, regardless of how Tiger chooses to identify, he would continue to be racialised as Black and face the kind of anti-Black racism he had already experienced in his golfing career (Pitts Jr, 1997). Thus, as one critic puts it, 'the desire to be biracial seems more than anything else a desire to escape being black' (Pitts Jr, 1997, no pag.). It is in the midst of this apparent racial-firestorm, as he seeks to resist the erasure of his totality, that Woods must find the resilience to resist being torn asunder (Kennedy, 2012).

As I demonstrate throughout this book, hybridity is not just about the emergence of mixed-race as an identity category (or the kind of nomenclatural representation that Woods strives for), important though this may be, but about the reformation and refashioning of existing identity signifiers – how Black mixed-race men engage with the perpetual mutation of racial meanings (Joseph, 2012). For instance, whilst Barack Obama identifies as an African American Black man (Roberts & Baker, 2010), his identification is not necessarily indicative of a rejection of aspects of an identity that is both complex and multiplicitous. Identifying as Black does not represent his conscription to a narrowly defined and homogenous Black identity but a reimagining and rearticulation of what constitutes that Black identity. The work of Shirley Anne Tate (2005, p. 1) is useful here as she shows that such hybrid Black identities are constituted as social actors who occupy the position of 'an-other Black'. This is a suturing and refashioning of discourses of *the Black same* (homogenous Blackness) that opens up a third space of hybridity in which Barack Obama may be a Black man despite the attribution of light skin femininity (Cooper, 2009), without the erasure of his experiences of having a white mother and without invalidating his claims to a mixed-race identity (Obama, 2004). This is the configuration of a Black identity that subverts the narrowly defined regulatory ideal of Blackness (Tate, 2005). Describing himself – and being described – variously as mixed-race, Black and African American, Obama's racial identity is always in flux, always in process and never fixed (Khanna, 2011a). This is reflective of the experiences of Black mixed-race men who refuse to be bound by identity categories and refuse the erasure of the totality of the self as a Black mixed-race man (Korgen, 1998). The agonistic struggle to recognise sameness and difference – a ceaseless process of hybridity – was captured in the study by Carl, a US participant. Talking about Black mixed-race men, he notes, 'we have similar experiences. We all have our uniqueness. We branch off somewhere'. It is at this point of 'branching off' that the third space of hybridity is located. As I will go on to show, in their hybridisation, Black mixed-race men draw upon discourses including race, ethnicity, culture, ancestral nationality, class and masculinity.

Again, heeding Agard's warning, it should be noted that terminologically hybridity has antecedents in the aforementioned discourse of scientific racism. Denoting impurity and racial contamination, hybridity is something of a loaded discourse (Caballero, 2004; Ifekwunigwe, 1999; Werbner & Modood, 2005). Whilst not being uncritical of discursive meanings, I draw upon work from scholars like Suki Ali (2003) and Shirley Anne Tate (2005) who have paved the way to theorise beyond hybridity as pathology to consider hybridity as strength. We know that identification is not merely volitional but is a process that occurs in the context of socioracial norms and structures. Having briefly touched upon the interlocking conditions of white supremacy and the Black/ white racial dichotomy already, as I continue to lay the groundwork for understanding the accounts of the men in this study, it is important here that I discuss the interlocking epochal conditions of the 'post-racial'.

The 'Post-Racial'

In 2008, the election of a Black mixed-race man to the presidency of the USA signalled, for many, the transition into a 'post-racial' era (Donnor & Brown, 2011; Howard & Flennaugh, 2011; Lentin, 2016; Tutwiler, 2016; Wise, 2013). For post-racialists, this is an era in which race is no longer a determinant of life chances and thus no longer shapes the lived experiences of Black mixed-race men (Critcher & Risen, 2014; López, 2010; Wise, 2013). The 'post-racial' 'encourages whites to believe racism is a thing of the past' (Bell, 1993, p. 6). 'After all, a Black man in the White House must signal the end of race and racism' (Leonardo, 2013, p. 600). Under these 'post-racial' conditions, it is commonly held that 'racism belongs to a bygone era and that remaining racist attitudes and behaviours are the preserve of unbalanced or uneducated individuals' (Lentin, 2016, p. 34). Since Obama's election, this logic has come to be hegemonic, transcending the political spectrum (Lentin, 2016). We see the reiteration of the logic in the discourses that surround the marriage of Meghan Markle – a Black mixed-race woman – to the UK's Prince Harry. The supposed entry into a 'post-racial' epoch is not only signified by Obama's election or Meghan's marriage into the royal family, but, as authors like Passel, Wang, and Taylor (2010) have asserted, increasing rates of intermarriage are taken to signal the cessation of the social significance of race (Tutwiler, 2016). Thus, whether symbolised by Obama's election, the royal wedding, or increasing rates of intermarriage, Black mixed-race men are in many ways central to the celebration of 'post-race'.

In this book, I draw upon 'post-racial' theory – particularly as it is conceptualised by David Theo Goldberg (2015)[3] – as a lens that brings forth possibilities to see beyond romanticised ideas about the end of race. Through this lens, we avoid mistaking the individual 'successes' of

---

[3]Valluvan (2016, p. 2241) has suggested that Goldberg's work offers 'probably the definitive theoretical account of the putatively 'post-racial' present'.

one man, for the end of racism. So too, we see that far from signalling the end of race, the very notion of racial intermarriage 'reinforces and perpetuates ordinary ideas about physical race as natural entities' (Zack, 1994, p. 40). This framework enables us to see that the 'post-racial' is not the end of racism but its latest iteration (Bojadžijev, 2016; Valluvan, 2016): post-raciality is a refurbishing of racism in order 'to remake inequality' (Benjamin, 2016, p. 2227). Or, as Goldberg (2016, p. 2279) puts it, the post-racial is the latest iteration in racisms' 'self-renewal for the sake of preserving and extending [white] power'. So what are the conditions of the 'post-racial'?

As Goldberg (2015, p. 6) sets out in his seminal work *Are we all post-racial yet?*, in this 'post-racial' epoch, 'the enduring conditions made and marked by the racial continue to structure society. This is so regardless of the fact that its various explicit manifestations may now be rejected, rendered implicit, silenced or denied' (also see Goldberg, 2016; Benjamin, 2016; Valluvan, 2016). 'Post-racialism', therefore, is little more than the denial of the structural, the 'burying alive', as Goldberg (2015, p. 78) might put it, of the histories and conditions of race (Goldberg, 2016, p. 2278). The 'post-racial' is not the removal of but the mystification of the racial conditions − including Black/white dichotomised white supremacy − that shape society (Pateman & Mills, 2007). This mystification of the racial belies the lived experiences of those, like the men in this study, for whom 'race remains an underlying and salient component in their lives' (Donnor & Brown, 2011, p. 1; Howard & Flennaugh, 2011; Tutwiler, 2016). As will become clear throughout this book, in spite of pervasive 'post-racial' ideology, for the men in this study, as Donnor and Brown (2011, p. 2) have observed elsewhere, 'being "Black" and "male" irrespective of societal position recapitulates the historically and ideologically informed racial imaginary of Black male deviance and criminality'. To return to Goldberg (2015, p. 24) once more, 'far from being the end of racisms, then, "post-raciality" represents rather a certain way of thinking about race, and implicitly of racist expression' (Goldberg, 2015, p. 24).

As Derrick Bell (1993, p. 3), the early and leading proponent of CRT (Delgado & Stefancic, 2012), asserts, often '[w]hat we designate as "racial progress" is not a solution to the problem. It is a regeneration of the problem in a particularly perverse form'. The 'post-racial' turn is the very embodiment of Bell's warning. Whilst the 'post-racial' is celebrated by many, those who continue to live lives shaped by racism are stripped of the requisite tools and language 'to identify, compre-hend, or condemn' it (Goldberg, 2015, p. 82, 2016). Racisms are reduced to individualised expressions bereft of historical context. To extend Bonilla-Silva's concept of racism without racists, in this sense we may talk of *racisms without racism* (Bonilla-Silva, 2006; Goldberg, 2015). Let us look at an example. Commenting on the tenure of President Obama as the first Black president, Bill Clinton remarked that 'we are all mixed-race people'. Whilst Clinton's comments were made with reference to the science of the Human Genome Project, the comments preclude the realities of the way race permeates US society. In applying this colour-blind logic, Clinton threatens to erase the lived experiences of Barack Obama and what it means to be the first Black president in a society defined by race. Moreover, as I have argued elsewhere, in so doing, he acts to deny his own white privilege,

> To deny race – to state blithely that 'we are all mixed race' and therefore seen as and treated as equals – is to be complicit in the maintenance of the racial hierarchies that operate at all levels of US society. These racial hierarchies provide immeasurable advantages to white Americans like Bill Clinton. (Joseph-Salisbury, 2016a)

At a similar time to Bill Clinton's comments, Meryl Streep threatened to destabilise and invalidate criticisms of the #whiteout at the Oscars film awards. Rather than recognising the underrepresentation of racial minorities on screen, Streep proclaimed 'we're all Africans, really' (Joseph-Salisbury, 2016a). It is difficult to imagine how such logic would ever bring about racial equality on screen or in society. In actuality, such logic acts only to maintain inequitable racial conditions: this is the 'post-racial' at work. Whilst examples abound, these two examples attest to the importance of a C(M)RT perspective as a combative to 'post-racial' thought.

It is in CRT's recognition of the normalisation of racism (Bell, 1993; Delgado & Stefancic, 2012; Hylton, 2012) that the understanding takes on particular utility for theorising in 'post-racial' contexts. C(M)RT provides a framework that is illuminatory for the aims of this book. As I go on to argue, whilst the 'post-racial' threatens the erasure of their lived experiences (Tutwiler, 2016), the Black mixed-race men in this study are acutely aware of their racialisation and the ubiquity of systemic and institutional racism. Moreover, as I demonstrate throughout, Black mixed-race men refuse the erasure of their identities and experiences. It is through the cultivation of what I refer to as *'post-racial' resilience* that this is achieved. So, what is invoked by the concept of 'post-racial' resilience?

'Post-Racial' Resilience (PRR)

Let us first consider resilience in relative abstraction, before returning to place it in the particular context of the 'post-racial'. Etymologically, resilience presupposes *a something* that must be withstood – a threat to which one must remain resilient. For Black mixed-race men, these threats are posed by racial and racist worlds that are underpinned by systemic and systematic white supremacy. Characterised by the persistence of a Black/white racial dichotomy, these racial structures govern a white gaze (Yancy, 2017) that threatens to fragment and erase Black mixed-race men's identities. According to the Oxford Dictionary (2015, no pag.), resilience is a noun with two usages:

1. *The capacity to recover quickly from difficulties: toughness.*
2. *The ability of a substance or object to spring back into shape: elasticity.*

In each definition, there is a ubiquitous presence: that to which one must respond. In the first, the response is framed as *recovery*. In the second, *springing back into shape*. As I have suggested, in the lives of Black mixed-race men, the ubiquitous presence to which one must respond manifests in *systemic Black/white dichotomised white supremacy* and the racism that maintains it. Of course, this racism takes on many forms. If we adapt that first definition, we might see resilience as, *the capacity to recover quickly from racist and racialised difficulties; toughness.* Given the unnamed 'substance or object', the second definition requires a little more translation for our purposes. Let us take this substance to be a sense of self. Thus, our definition becomes: *the ability of one's sense of self to remain in or spring back into shape, amidst threats that are deniable; elasticity.* Lamont et al.'s (2013, p. 14) work on social resilience advances this definition as the authors refer to the creative processes through 'which people assemble a variety of tools, including collective resources and new images of themselves, to sustain their well-being'. From Lamont et al.'s definition we begin to see resilience as describing a highly active and combative set of processes. Not only is resilience about the ability to 'spring back', but also, in some instances, the ability to 'sustain' shape entirely. Lamont, Welburn, and Fleming (2013) also show us that resilience draws upon a range of 'tools', and, as I show throughout this book, this is certainly true in the case of Black mixed-race men.

Now we have a sense of what is invoked through the social concept of resilience, let us return to think about the context of the 'post-racial'. The 'post-racial' deniability and apparent invisibility of race and racism (Goldberg, 2015; Palmer, 2016) complicate the threats that Black mixed-race men face. This complication requires forms of resilience that are characteristically different from those of the past. Thus, although representative of a 'long continuum of risk faced and survived' (Bell, 1993, p. 196), PRR is characteristically different from the forms of resilience that have characterised Black communities since the inception of slavery. Evident in resistance to the pressures of slave masters, the systems of transatlantic slavery, colonialism and imperialism, resilience has been a fundamental and enduring component in the experiences of Black communities. However, for much of history, the threats to resilience – the oppressor and system of oppression – were more clearly identifiable and recognisable than they are today. As African American communities resisted and fought Jim Crow (Gellman, 2012), and Black British communities fought the racism that pervaded the school and criminal justice system (Warmington, 2014), the threat of individual and systemic racisms were much more clearly identifiable. Assertions of Black pride were made in the face of, and in response to, this endemic and identifiable racism that degraded Blackness.

The 'post-racial' renders 'racially inspired or inflected injustices more difficult, even impossible to discern' (Goldberg, 2015, p. 67) and so 'post-racial' resilience must be cultivated whilst the language to identify and condemn the threat is taken away. These new forms of resilience are what I invoke through the concept of PRR. Let us add in Lamont et al.'s insight, and our understanding of the mutating racial conditions, our definition of 'post-racial' resilience becomes:

1. *The capacity to withstand and/or recover quickly from racist and racialised difficulties that are denied; toughness against the invisible.*
2. *The ability of one's sense of self to remain in or spring back into shape, amidst threats that are deniable: elasticity.*

It is this, I argue, that Black mixed-race men take up through PRR. Conceptualising PRR allows us to turn the figure of the marginal and confused Black mixed-race man on its head. Thus, the interventions I make here are as political as they are theoretical. 'Resilience shifts attention from risk and vulnerability to something more positive and prospective on analysing the capacity of people... to anticipate, persist with, adapt and minimise the damage caused by change, risk and adversity' (DeVerteuil, 2015, p. 8). In order to more fully understand the PRR of Black mixed-race men, an understanding of the intersection of gender is important. The participants in the study therefore are never just Black mixed-race nor are they ever just men; they are always *Black mixed-race men*. This brings us to theories of hegemonic masculinity.

Hegemonic Masculinity

Hegemonic masculinity does not refer to 'an entity that can be grasped by hand or discovered under a powerful microscope' (Whitehead, 2002, p. 34) nor should masculinity be thought of as natural, innate, or biological (Halberstam, 1998). Rather, masculinities are, in a sense, illusory social constructs brought into being through the performative repetition of acts and defined by relations to femininity and other masculinities. Masculine acts maintain the patriarchal social power structure; that is, the collective dominance of men over women (Connell & Messerschmidt, 2005). Thus, masculinity becomes about 'power and legitimacy and privilege' in a patriarchal social structure (Halberstam, 1998, p. 2). Whilst differentials of race, class, gender, sexuality and disability ensure individuals are all distinctly located, it would be a misnomer to assume that hegemonic masculinity was just about the experiences of white middle-class straight men. Whilst this may be the group who have historically been best placed to access 'traditional' forms of social power, hegemonic masculinity is perhaps best understood as a (white supremacist) discursive ideal that, whether accepted or rejected, shapes the lives of all and produces a multiplicity of masculinities (Connell & Messerschmidt, 2005; Whitehead, 2002). Hegemonic masculinity is far from a fixed entity or imposed diktat. Rather, as will be shown, its contours are fluid and malleable sites for contestation and negotiation (Connell & Messerschmidt, 2005; Halberstam, 1998; Whitehead, 2002).

Research on race and masculinity has acknowledged that differing positionalities to white supremacist power structures mean that racially minoritised men experience masculinity differently to white men and to other racially minoritised groups (Alexander, 1996; de Boise, 2015; Pateman & Mills, 2007). This acknowledgement has engendered a proliferation of research considering the way Black men constitute masculine identities (Hall, 1995; hooks, 2004; Lemelle Jr, 2010; Mac an Ghaill, 1994b; Mirza, 1999; Mutua, 2006; Sewell, 1997). However, despite a burgeoning research interest in *Critical Mixed Race Studies* (Daniel, 2014; Daniel et al., 2014; Small & King-O'Riain, 2014), such consideration of the way mixed-race men generally, and Black mixed-race men in particular, constitute masculine identities remains a stark omission from the literature (for some exceptions, see Joseph-Salisbury, forthcoming; Newman, 2017; Sims and Joseph-Salisbury, forthcoming). Whilst research has shown Black mixed-race men are likely to form peer groups with Black men (Tikly, Caballero, Haynes, & Hill, 2004; Tizard & Phoenix, 2002), and oftentimes identify as and with Black men (Morning, 2012), the ready assumption that Black mixed-race men experience masculinity in the same way as Black men is unsubstantiated. Research showing that Black communities and peer groups are governed by ideals of racial authenticity suggest that Black mixed-race men's masculinity may be constituted in contexts that, although similar, are somewhat different from Black men (Harris & Khanna, 2010; Tate, 2005). Stephen Whitehead (2002, p. 5) observed that '[t]he more we delve into men and masculinities, the more is revealed of the complex dynamics of difference, subjectivity, power and identity'. By centring the experiences of Black mixed-race men, this book contributes to the endeavour of de-centring of the white male middle-class body and to representing the heterogeneity of racialised men (Halberstam, 1998).

Conclusion and Outline of the Book

In this introduction, I have set out the theoretical framework for the development of a Critical (Mixed) Race Theory of PRR. I have shown that such a framework necessarily draws upon theories of performativity and hybridity in order to explicate the ways in which Black mixed-race men negotiate their identities. They do so in the face of racial and racist conditions that − despite 'post-racial' obfuscation − threaten to limit who and what they can be. In the next chapter of the book − *Black mixed-race male multiplicities: the third space of hybridity* − I return to consider theories of performativity and hybridity in more depth. In doing so, I show how Black mixed-race men resist identity erasure as they name and articulate complex and multiplicitous identities. Drawing upon a range of competing discourses, Black mixed-race men perpetually refashion new identifications as they strive to capture the totality of their lived and racialised experiences.

I take these themes forward into Chapter 3 − *Constituting and Performing Black Mixed-Race Masculinities*. It is here that I turn to look more directly at the intersection of gender, specifically masculinity. I show that Black mixed-race men are not duped by 'post-racial' mythology. In fact, they are ever conscious of the continued significance of race. At the intersection of gender, Black mixed-race men grapple with a range of seemingly contradictory and competing racist stereotypes: from the desirable mixed-race man (Newman, 2017), to the hypersexual Black monster (Yancy, 2017), to the effeminate light skin (Black, 2015). Black mixed-race men must grapple with the knowledge that they may in one instance be overdetermined as the 'Black monster' (Yancy, 2017) who embodies 'excessive masculinity' (Halberstam, 1998, p. 2), whilst in the very next instance be interpellated as the effeminate light-skinned Black man (Black, 2015; Hall, 1995) who embodies 'insufficient masculinity' (Halberstam, 1998, p. 2). Not mere victims of stereotyping, however, I show that Black mixed-race men exercise their PRR in two steps. First, a sense of double consciousness allows Black mixed-race men to see through the 'post-racial' in order to understand the racial processes that threaten to shape their lives. Second, a fluid sense of self sees them resist, modify, and even manipulate existing discourses and stereotypes. Oftentimes, PRR is exercised at the quotidian level, specifically through racial symbolism.

Whilst Shirley Anne Tate (2005) has shown how hybridity occurs at the quotidian level of speech, Prudence Carter has shown how Black youth masterfully draw upon 'dominant' and 'non-dominant' forms of cultural capital as they negotiate their identities. Synthesizing this work with Gans' (1979) and Khanna's (2011b) work, on *ethnic* and *racial symbolisms*, helps to further build the framework for understanding Black mixed-race men's PRR. Thus, in Chapter 4, I draw upon this work as I consider how *dress-styles*, *speech-styles*, *hair-styles* and *music-styles* represent important forms of cultural capital that Black mixed-race men utilise as symbols of race, culture, ethnicity and identity. I argue that Black mixed-race men draw upon sophisticated repertoires of *racial symbolism* as they ceaselessly negotiate their positionalities. Given the 'post-racialism' that pervades US and UK societies, styles become metonymic for race and act as a determinant factor in relationships and identification. For Black mixed-race men, racial symbolism is often used to display and negotiate racial authenticity and thus becomes a factor in the governmentality of Blackness, an important component of Black mixed-race men's PRR.

As the definitions discussed earlier make clear that PRR implies a threat against which one must remain resilient. This threat is manifest in the framework I have built thus far and the underpinnings that lie throughout the book. I have suggested that these threats are posed primarily by structures of white supremacy and a Black/white racial dichotomy. As I move through the book to focus more closely on the quotidian, in Chapter 5, the theoretical concept of racial micro-aggressions allows me to capture the everyday, seemingly innocuous experiences of racism that Black mixed-race men face (Pierce, 1988). Conceptually, microaggressions offer a response to the 'post-racial' 'changing face' of racism (Sue, 2010), and a framework for understanding how seemingly mundane interactions metacommunicate white supremacist, anti-Black, and Black/white dichotomised ideologies (Pérez Huber & Solórzano, 2015). It has been widely noted that, despite their apparent innocuousness, microaggressions, represent a real threat to the lives of racially minoritised people. So, how do Black mixed-race men respond?

I use Chapter 5 to demonstrate that Black mixed-race men face multifarious microaggressions that are predicated on their mixedness and on their Blackness. Through processes of hybridity, Black mixed-race men cultivate the PRR that allows them to resist racist interpellation and identity erasure. Where many psychological studies have focused on the aggressor of microaggressions, the C(M)RT-informed approach of this book means that the experiences of Black mixed-race men on the receiving end of microaggressions are placed at the centre of analysis.

Continuing the focus on social interaction, in Chapter 6 I consider how Black mixed-race men's friendships and peer groups influence and are influenced by Black mixed-race men's identities. Given that existing research has found Black mixed-race men often form school peer groups with Black boys/men (Tikly et al., 2004), the chapter considers the functionality and governmentality of Black masculine peer groups for Black mixed-race men: peer groups can strengthen Black mixed-race men's PRR in relation to external threats. Internally, I argue that Black mixed-race men engage in identity work that allows them not only to negotiate their own positionalities in the peer group but also the boundaries of those peer groups: the ability to do so is an essential component of the men's PRR. Recognising the heterogeneity of the ways in which Black mixed-race men engage with friendships, in this chapter I also consider how Black mixed-race men's fluid sense of self enables them to subvert and redefine the racial segregation of peer groups in order to form friendships with white peers and to move between racial peer groups.

In the concluding chapter, I draw upon each of the preceding chapters and return to consider how Black mixed-race men cultivate and access PRR in order to resist identity erasure and fragmentation. I argue that resisting the 'post-racial', and seeing one's identity as unfixed, fluid and contextual, allows Black mixed-race men to engage in a perpetual process of hybridity. As they shift through a range of forms of cultural capital, it is in the third space of hybridity that Black mixed-race men find their PRR. I hope that what I have set out in this chapter provides a basis from which we can begin to think through how Black mixed-race men enact PRR. Let us begin.

Chapter 1

Multiplicitous Black Mixed-Race Men and 'Post-Racial' Resilience: Double Consciousness, Hybridity and the Threat of Racial Mismatch

Introduction

In this chapter, I build upon and develop the theorisations on *'post-racial'* resilience (PRR) that I began to map out in the book's introduction. As I develop an understanding of how Black mixed-race men negotiate their racial identities, I more fully illustrate the processes that are invoked through the concept of *'post-racial'* resilience (PRR). In the book's introduction, I defined PRR as:

1. *The capacity to withstand and/or recover quickly from racist and racialised difficulties that are denied: toughness against the invisible.*
2. *The ability of one's sense of self to remain in or spring back into shape, amidst threats that are deniable: elasticity.*

These are the definitions I explicate more fully in this chapter. As I explore the way Black mixed-race men utilise PRR and negotiate their racial identities, the chapter is divided into three sections. The first two sections theorise key interrelated components of the men's PRR: *double consciousness* and *hybridity*. Through a consideration of *racial mismatches*,[1] the third section shows the threats Black mixed-race men face and how they utilise PRR to respond. Let us first consider double consciousness.

---

[1]Those instances where Black mixed-race men felt their racial identities were misread.

'Post-Racial' Double Consciousness: White Supremacy, the White Gaze and (the Absence of) White Privilege

Double consciousness describes a 'sense of always looking at one's self through the eyes of others' (Du Bois, 1994, p. 2), or, as Yancy (2017) might put it, seeing one's self through *the white gaze*. This has been a defining feature of the Black experience in the USA (Du Bois, 1994, p. 2; Yancy, 2017) and in the UK (Gilroy, 1993; Tate, 2005). To invoke the white gaze is to see a distortion of one's self (Du Bois, 1994). Whilst encountering this distortion threatens one's sense of identity, it would be a misnomer to see this as totalising or absolute. To draw on George Yancy (2017), to see and know the Black monster of the white gaze, does not mean one need become that Black monster. Nor does it mean that one becomes bound or fixed by the white gaze. Indeed, as I show in the next section, through processes of hybridity, Black mixed-race men are able to hold fluid, complex and multiplicitous identities. This allows Black mixed-race men to resist the threat of erasure. As they come to know the white gaze to be governed by a racist episteme, the men recognise its imposition to be untrue. This criticality brings about possibilities for double consciousness to be utilised as a site of strength, rather than weakness: a component of PRR. In a world underpinned by white supremacy, the ability to see how one is constructed through the white gaze has been integral to Black resistance, resilience and survival (Yancy, 2017). In our 'post-racial' epoch, this criticality takes on a new urgency: in order to understand the racist structures governing the white gaze, one must reject the pervasive 'post-racial' ideology that renders those very structures invisible: thus, what we have is a sense of 'post-racial' double consciousness. As we will see, those structures are maintained through a Black/white racial dichotomy that means there is also a necessary particularity and specificity to Black mixed-race men's sense of double consciousness.

Having described double consciousness, let me now make things more tangible. Here, I draw upon the accounts of the Black mixed-race men in the study, in order to illustrate how double consciousness manifests as a fundamental component of PRR.

We begin with Leon, a UK participant from a working-class background in Manchester. Whilst maintaining contact with his Black father and Black family, Leon grew up living with his white mother and white sister (who had a different father) in a predominantly white area. He also attended a predominantly white school. As we discussed identity, it became clear that Leon saw race as fundamentally constitutive to his sense of identity. Not only this, but in understanding his racialised positionality, Leon drew upon his double consciousness to invoke the white gaze,

> Say if there were any racist political parties came in, and they'd try to categorize you, you'd always say I'm Black, you know, I'm not white. They'd always put me in the Black, if there was a political party against Black people or different, you know, anyone that's not English, they'd put me in the, even though I am, you know, English.

Here Leon draws upon the gaze of a hypothetical racist political party not in a literal sense but as a metaphor. Perhaps the metaphor of a political party acts as a stand in for the much more diffuse capillaries of white power that characterises the society in which Leon lives (Tate, 2013). He rejects the 'post-racial' script and sets the tone for a discussion in which the ubiquity of race is salient. There are several points of note in Leon's account. Leon shows his sense that Black and white constitute the only identity options: two poles in a racially dichotomised structure (Ifekwunigwe, 2004). Perhaps it is through channelling the white gaze that Leon is best able to articulate his experiences of racialisation: through the white gaze, mixedness does not emerge as an identity option. Nevertheless, Leon's initial identification in the interview was as mixed-race, and throughout the interview, he moved relatively freely between Black and mixed-race identifications. Thus, whilst recognising how he may be interpellated is an important component of his PRR, he is not bound by a white gaze that threatens to limit who he can be. Indeed, PRR is not just identifying the white gaze but is also resistance to its message: *PRR is remaining in shape.* Consider in the first sentence how Leon uses 'you' to position himself as part of a general Black 'I'. As his interlocutors try to categorise him, Leon takes back control and says 'I'm Black'. Put another way, Leon interpellates himself in resistance to the racist white gaze: his invocation of the white gaze allows him to emphasise the centrality of Blackness to his sense of self. Here, we begin to see an inversion of the one-drop rule and a commitment to affirmative Black politics (Senna, 1998) that was prevalent among many participants.

In the introduction to her seminal edited collection on *Black British Feminism*, Heidi Mirza (1997, p. 3) describes being Black in Britain as,

> ... a state of 'becoming' (racialized); a process of consciousness, when colour becomes the defining factor about

who you are. Located through your 'otherness' a 'conscious coalition' emerges; a self-consciously constructed
space where identity is not inscribed by a natural identification but by political kinship. Now living submerged by
whiteness, physical difference becomes a defining issue, a
signifier, a mark of whether or not you belong. Thus, to be
black in Britain is to share a common structural location;
a racial location.

There are clear parallels between those processes that Mirza describes
and the articulations of Leon (UK). Through the white gaze, mixedness
is erased in order to maintain a Black/white racial dichotomy. It is this
to which Leon alludes. Notice, Leon's 'consciousness' comes through
his understanding of the white gaze; his double consciousness. It is
through this that he becomes aware of his 'otherness' (Du Bois, 1994)
and, as Mirza (1997, p. 3) suggests, a 'conscious coalition' emerges.
Living, as he does, 'submerged by whiteness', Leon's identity is 'not
inscribed' but is based upon a 'common structural location'. Through
this 'racial location', a sense of 'political kinship' develops that sees
Leon identify with Blackness.

Notice, too, that it is Blackness *in Britain* that Mirza refers to. To be
Black in Britain is to be racially located as 'other'. In the popular imaginary, Blackness is in contrast to Britain: to be Black is not to be *truly*
British. This brings us to another point of interest in Leon's account.
Through oppositional binaries (Derrida, 1981; Lawler, 2014), there is a
clear associative slippage from 'Black', to 'not white', to 'not English'.
He is Black, he is not white. He is Black, he is not English. Leon reminds
us that race and nation, or, whiteness and Englishness, are inextricably
bound (Gilroy, 1993). It is worth recognising that this is perhaps a reality
particularly prevalent in Britain where the much more recent large Black
migration continues to construct Black Britons as foreigners (Caballero,
2004). However, note that Leon does not accept the 'largely unspoken
racial connotations' (Parekh, 2000, p. 38) that 'you can be either one or
the other... but not both' (Mirza, 1997, p. 3). As he affirms 'I am, you
know, English', Leon troubles the discursive synonymy of whiteness and
Englishness. He speaks back to and rejects discourses that try to limit his
identity. In so doing, Leon creates a third space for the negotiation and
emergence of new identities (Bhabha, 1990; Hall, 1996). In this third
space, he is Black *and* English. Leon's utterance is subversive and counterhegemonic as he not only reconstitutes his own identity, but he threatens to redefine Englishness: 'belonging and unbelonging is a question of

negotiations that can undergo a number of shifts in the course of a given situation' (Pettersson, 2013, p. 417). This is what Leon shows us. Whilst I will return to discuss hybridity more fully in the next section, it suffices to observe here how double consciousness facilitates positive hybrid identifications. We see Leon's PRR in action as he rejects 'post-racial' logic and speaks back to the white gaze in order to position himself as something new.

To varying extents, Leon's sense of double consciousness was representative of all of the Black mixed-race men in the study. Demonstrating the Transatlantic continuities in the double consciousness of Black mixed-race men, these parallels are particularly apparent in the account of Tayo (USA). Tayo comes from a lower middle-class background and was raised by his white mother. Like Leon, he grew up in a predominantly white area and attended a predominantly white school. Here he discusses how he feels the white gaze and structural white supremacy impact upon his sense of identity,

> ... it's not like I don't identify, or I don't recognize my Caucasian heritage, ethnicity, whatever. I more so identify with African Americans because, okay, well one reason is because... I believe there is a set of privileges that sole-Caucasians – *or not even necessarily full because in the example of George Zimmerman he's half Hispanic, half Caucasian but he benefits from the privilege* – I believe there is a set of privileges that people of Caucasian heritage can take advantage of and I don't take advantage of that. I don't have the opportunity to. I'm perceived as a minority and that's what I identify as anyway. And there are institutionalized systems of racism and prejudice that I am victim of and there are systems of prejudices that apply to African Americans as disadvantages that African Americans face and these are the things that I identify with, and these are the things that are important to me, and these are issues that if I identified as purely Caucasian, I wouldn't be able to have part, well as much of a part of it. So, I believe that because these things apply partly to me they apply wholly. (Tayo, US)

As Tayo describes structural and institutional racisms that privilege whites (McIntosh, 1990), he – like Leon (UK) – rejects 'post-racial' logic. This – the first move in Tayo's PRR – allows Tayo to better understand and articulate his racialised positionality. That is, he is somebody rendered outside of those white privileges. As he further articulates the particularities of his experiences of racialisation, Tayo draws a comparison with George Zimmerman. This is Tayo's hybridity-of-the-everyday (Tate, 2005). This speech act allows Tayo to complicate the mixed-race category. Through his articulation of double consciousness, Tayo shows that his experience of racialisation and racism are different from Zimmerman. As Tayo suggests, as a mixed Hispanic-white man, after shooting and killing Trayvon Martin, Zimmerman was able to access white privilege. He was imbued with temporary or 'honorary' whiteness and white privilege (Hopkins, 2013): this is an assertion supported by wider literature that suggests Hispanics and Latinos can often be read as white (Lopez, 2003). Charles Mills (1997) and Eduardo Bonilla-Silva (2004) have both highlighted the elasticity of whiteness for certain groups: this is what we see here. There is evidence to suggest that Black mixed-race men are far more likely to identify and be identified with the race of their minority parent (Black) than men from other mixed-race groups and Black mixed-race women (Aspinall & Song, 2013; Rockquemore & Laszloffy, 2005; Davenport, 2016; Sims, 2016; Sims & Joseph-Salisbury, forthcoming). Like Leon, it is through double consciousness — his sense of seeing through the white gaze — that Tayo recognises the particularities of his racial location. Also like Leon, rather than Blackness being an imposition, this is something he actively affirms ('that's what I identify as *anyway*'). Blackness is important to Tayo, it is something he actively wants to be a part of. He is part of, as Mirza (1997) puts it, a conscious coalition. In *Mulatto Millennium*, Danzy Senna (1998, p. 16) illustrates how many Black mixed-race people invert the one-drop rule in opposition to the white gaze,

> You told us all along that we had to call ourselves black because of this so-called one drop. Now that we don't have to anymore, we choose to. Because black is beautiful. Because black is not a burden, but a privilege.

Notice how Senna — like Tayo (USA) and Leon (UK) — turns the imposition of Blackness on its head. The power of the white gaze is nullified as Senna claims Blackness with pride ('we choose to')! When Blackness is claimed, rather than imposed, something of its essence is transformed: it becomes positive rather than negative. To be affirmative about one's Blackness is constitutive of, and constituted by, PRR.

Returning specifically to Tayo's account, notice his assertion that he recognises his Caucasian heritage and ethnicity: whilst his sense of double consciousness engenders an acknowledgement that he is read as a Black man; this is not restrictive. By drawing upon notions of heritage and ethnicity, he is able to constitute a multiplicitous, fluid and hybrid identification that refuses erasure and fragmentation. His is a Blackness that also allows him to recognize his 'Caucasian heritage [and] ethnicity'. This sense of fluidity – or elasticity to draw back upon those definitions developed in the introduction – as a component of PRR, was apparent in another account from Reece (UK).

Coming from a lower middle-class background, Reece was raised by his Black mother and white father in a racially diverse area of London. Here he invokes the white gaze,

> I'm accepting of the fact that you know society and a white individual is going to view me as Black and it don't often mean, in its initial instance that the consequences of that are problematic but you know, I walk down the street and if you identify me as a proud mixed-race man or a proud Black man, I'm happy either way.

In understanding his identity and positionality, Reece (UK) draws upon the white interpellator. In a white supremacist society, the white subject is always, already interpellated as the norm who is in a position to interpellate the Other (Yancy, 2017). Seemingly rejecting any 'post-racial' persuasions that we are beyond race, he recognises how the white gaze interpellates him as Black. This is an astute observation that is historically and contemporarily grounded and perhaps constituted through what Yancy (2017) terms an *episteme of Blackness*.[2] As Tate (2005, p. 85) puts it, for 'whiteness Blackness is undifferentiated'. To know this is to be doubly conscious. To be doubly conscious is to understand one's racial location. To understand one's racial location is essential to Black mixed-race men's PRR. Notice, again, however, that Reece (UK) does not merely accept the white gazer as the purveyor of truth. Through an interview, Reece self-identified as 'Black', 'mixed-race' and, most often, as 'Black mixed-race'. As in Leon's account earlier, and as for so many of the participants, knowing that the white gaze would not

---

[2]Episteme of Blackness describes a way of knowing that is cultivated through lived experiences of Blackness, collectively and intergenerationally.

see mixedness did not foreclose a mixed-race identification for Reece. He does not necessarily see the consequences of the white gaze as inherently 'problematic'. The fluidity in his identifications allows him to remain *resilient* to the threat of fragmentation. To think metaphorically, a hammer would more easily destroy a fixed, rigid and brittle substance than it would a fluid and transformable one. On first reading of Reece's account, it might appear that he makes a concession as, in part, he allows the white gaze to identify him racially. It is not only his having cultivated pride in mixedness *and* Blackness that allows Reece to take this position, but importantly, he wants this pride to be recognised. It is in insisting on being seen as 'proud' that Reece subverts and speaks back to a white gaze that too often tries to pathologise Black mixed-race men. If his counterhegemonic pride is recognised, Reece is happy. In a similar vein to the positive affirmations of Leon and Tayo, this is Reece's hybridity-of-the-everyday. Double consciousness is a fundamental component of Black mixed-race men's PRR. An understanding of the threat one faces is essential to the cultivation of resilience. Contemporarily, this requires a rejection of the dominant ideology: the 'post-racial'. Double consciousness can inform one's sense of self. As I have shown in this section, this double consciousness can lead Black mixed-race men to hold multiplicitous and fluid *post-racially resilient identities*. In these identities, Black mixed-race men often express pride and positivity that, in white supremacist societies, is counter-hegemonic. Double consciousness is conducive to hybridity. Let us now turn to consider identifications through hybridity-of-the-everyday more closely.

Fluidity, Multiplicity and Hybridity-of-the-Everyday

In the introduction and in the last section, I began to discuss hybridity. I argued that identities are constituted through, within and across discourse. Identities are historically located and constituted through repetition and reiteration (Butler, 1990; Youdell, 2000). Identities are not fixed or static. They are made and remade through interaction and negotiation. As Stuart Hall (1996, p. 17) explains,

> … identities are never unified and, in late modern times, increasingly fragmented and fractured; never singular but multiply constructed across different often intersecting and antagonistic, discourses, practices and positions.

This is the context in which Black mixed-race men's identities are formed. For Black mixed-race men, it is conceivable that Hall's words are intensified by the historical, structural and ideological dichotomisation of Black and white (Brunsma & Rockquemore, 2001; Ifekwunigwe, 2004). This dichotomy is perhaps productive of the pervasive and widespread stereotypes that imagine mixed-race people as confused, fragmented and marginal. As Mengel (2001, p. 101) argues,

> The most common designation imposed on mixed race people of all ancestries is the inference that they are fragmented beings ... in a race conscious society, [this] serves to reinforce the ideology that the mixed race individual is somehow less than a whole person.

Through the lens of hybridity-of-the-everyday, in this section, I argue that Black mixed-race men remain resilient against these threats of fracture, fragmentation and erasure. In so doing, Black mixed-race men draw upon multiple discourses to produce fluid, complex and multiplicitous identities. This is their refusal of, perhaps resilience against, a white gaze that always overdetermines who and what Black mixed-race men can be (hooks, 2004).

Let us recall the earlier definition of resilience: *the ability of one's sense of self to remain in or spring back into, shape amidst threats that are deniable; elasticity.* If Black mixed-race men hold fluid and multiply constructed identities, they are better able to *spring back into shape*. It is, in part, the *elasticity* of their identities that allows them to be resilient against 'fracture and fragmentation' (Hall, 1996): *elasticity is resilience.*

According to Homi Bhabha (1990, p. 211), identification involves 'a process of identifying with and through another object'. These processes of identification open up 'possibilities of and for multiplicity', as one may draw upon multiple discourses in order to fashion and refashion an identification (Ali, 2003, p. 12). To put it another way, in what Bhabha (1990) calls the 'third space', new identities are produced from a bricolage-like assemblage of existing discourses. These new identifications are neither entirely bereft of, nor entirely bound by, the meanings of those discourses that constitute it. Perhaps to put it more plainly, hybrid identities are a 'yoking together' of that which is already known (Bhabha, 1990, p. 212). For Shirley Anne Tate (2005), this constant making and remaking of identity through discourse occurs at the quotidian level: that is, *hybridity-of-the-every-day.* To constitute hybrid identities is to be *resilient* to the threat of erasure. These identities emerge out of 'the special stress that grows with the effort involved in trying to face (at least) two ways at once' (Gilroy, 1993, p. 3). Recall earlier how Tayo (USA) engaged in speech acts that constituted him as a Black man who also has Caucasian heritage and ethnicity. It is in this sense that Tayo comes to occupy the position of *an-other Black*. Recall too, how he invoked the figure of George Zimmerman to disrupt and complicate the homogeni-sation of mixed-race groups: he is *different from the mixed-race same:* he is *an-other mixed-race*. As Bhabha (1984, p. 126) might puts it, he is 'almost the same, but not quite'. This — informed by his double consciousness — is his hybridity-of-the-everyday.

Let us look at another example of this hybridity-of-the-everyday in action. Trent (UK) was raised in the UK by his African American mother. He described his background as relatively middle-class and attended a predominantly white school. Here Trent talks about his identity,

> I would say I'm definitely proud of being Black, and I would say I was Black mixed-race, obviously ... I called myself mixed for a long time. You know, then like in year nine, I think I was like fifteen, fourteen and I was like, no I'm Black mixed and then slowly started to capitalize the Black ... fourteen, fifteen is when I started like openly saying I'm a Black mixed person in Britain.

Notice how pride re-emerges here as it did in the accounts earlier. This pride frames Blackness positively: it is *not* the pathological Blackness of the white gaze. Trent speaks back to the limits of iden-tity categories: he refuses to be Black *or* mixed-race, as officialdom so often dictates. He is Black *and* mixed-race: he is *Black mixed-race*. This is a hybrid identification produced through the assemblage of its constitutive parts. This identification challenges the 'limitations of existing boundaries' (Meredith, 1998, p. 3) and 'initiates new signs of identity' (Bhabha, 2012, p. 1). Notice how Trent's identification evolves and mutates over time. He moves through identity categories (first mixed, then Black) before producing his own hybrid identifica-tion (Black mixed-race). As he capitalises the B in Black, Trent draws on discourses of political Blackness and, again, Black pride (Tharps, 2014). This is an identification that is in opposition to white suprem-acy and to the pathological Black of the white gaze (who should feel shame rather than pride). Pride contributes to PRR.

Finally, Trent asserts that he is a Black mixed-race person *in Britain*. Perhaps, given his mother's African American heritage, Trent believes that his racialised experiences might be shaped by his national context. Indeed, elsewhere in interview, as he engaged in 'identity work' (Khanna & Johnson, 2010) to distinguish himself from discourses of the *Black same*, Trent spoke of his African American and European heritage: 'I always try and heighten the fact that I'm a dual citizen cos I think it helps to derive where my Blackness comes from'. This hybridity-of-the-everyday was Trent's striving for a multiplicitous and nuanced identity that could not be confined by the hollow Black figure of the white imaginary. According to Trent, this was important because of 'differences in upbringing and cultural references'. Thus, through discourses of culture, Trent is able to complicate Blackness, make distinctions between himself and his peers, and reflect the multiplicity of his identity. 'We cannot speak for very long, with any exactness, about "one experience, one identity"', said Stuart Hall (1990, p. 225). As he complicates race through culture, Trent shows the resonance of Hall's observation. Further affirming Hall's words, Trent also spoke of his queer identity. In so doing, he added complexity and dimensionality to his identity: the intersection of sexuality complicates his multiplicitous identity (I return to discuss this more fully in the next chapter). Tate (2005, p. 138) observes that 'to name oneself, is at one and the same time to locate oneself politically, socially, intellectually, philosophically, culturally, 'racially' and emotionally'. Indeed, 'to name oneself' can be an act of defiance: a refusal to be named by the white gaze. As Trent names his multiplicitous identity, he refuses to be reduced to a Black monolith. In a 'post-racial' (Black/white dichotomised) white supremacist structure, to insist upon the multiplicity of one's identity requires one to be *resilient* and resistant. Trent's insistence on multiplicity is his PRR in action.

In relation to Blackness, the 'totalizing narrative of homogeneity' (Tate, 2005, p. 153) was generally challenged and disrupted by participants on both sides of the Atlantic. This identity work allowed Black mixed-race men to produce hybrid identifications that refused fragmentation and erasure. Take Erik (USA), for instance. Erik grew up with his middle-class Black African mother. He spent some of his young life in Ghana, where he attended an international school. He spent the latter years of his adolescence in a rural and white area of Pennsylvania. He commuted to a racially mixed school. Asked about his identification with Blackness, Erik (USA) argued,

> ...Yeah. I'm Black. I feel like here the word Black encompasses a lot more than just, like, alright, alright, so this is how I've noticed recently it's broken down. Especially through social media and other stuff but within the Black community there is like a distinction between the two; there are light skins and there are dark skins.

Erik complicates what is invoked through the descriptor 'Black'. It 'encompasses a lot more', he argues. Perhaps this is Erik's challenge to a white gaze that sees Blackness as undifferentiated (Tate, 2005). This might also be a challenge to the essentialist discourses of 'racial purity' and 'dark skin' that define the mythical norm of Blackness (Harris & Khanna, 2010; Tate, 2005). Erik moves through oppositional binaries (Derrida, 1981) as he first identifies as Black (not white), before identifying as 'light skin' (not dark skin): he is a light-skin member of the Black community. Notice that this is not a rejection of Blackness but a *speaking back* in order to redefine that Blackness. Through the assemblage of multiple discourses, Erik produces his identification: this is Erik's hybridity-of-the-everyday. The discourses that Erik is able to draw upon become components in his PRR. To be clear, Erik's speech act operates on at least two interrelated levels: to complicate Blackness as an identity category and to complicate his own identification (in relation to, through, and in resistance to that category). This hybrid identity work was a recurrent theme in interviewee accounts. Take Calvin for example: Calvin grew up in an upper-middle-class family with his white mother and Black father. He attended a predominantly white school in a white Conservative area. We enter the conversation as Calvin responds to a question I ask about how and why he identifies as Black and mixed-race,

> ... 'cos I have an experience like I do have the white culture in me, like my Mum's side they're German and then I do have my Dad's like African American culture and his France culture. So, I'm definitely mixed-race in that aspect and then I'm obviously, I'm African American based on like complexion and everything like that.

As Calvin draws upon multiple discourses to constitute a hybrid identification, this is his resistance to the common mixed-race designation of fragmentation, fracture and erasure (Mengel, 2001). Calvin argues that he has white cultural influences from his Mum's side and African American and French culture from his Dad's side. Notice how quickly nation, culture and race become entwined. Not only does Calvin understand his maternal culture through race (white culture) but the different cultures of his parents lead him to identify as mixed-*race*. We see then that this identification is multiply constructed for Calvin. That is, his identification as mixed-race is about far more than race. As he goes on to identify as 'African American based on complexion', he opens up a third space for a multiplicitous and hybrid identity: an identity that refuses to be fixed or bound by descriptors. Given the aforementioned suggestion that Black mixed-race men are more likely to identify (and be identified) as Black than their female counterparts, it is conceivable that gender impacts upon this identification (Joseph-Salisbury, forthcoming-a). In this speech act, Calvin's identity is constructed across the multiplicities of race, ethnicity, nationality and culture. Indeed, as Calvin references his Mother's German nationality and Father's French nationality, he further complicates his identification. Growing up in America, Calvin knows that German nationality complicates his mother's whiteness just as French nationality complicates his father's Blackness. As I asked him specifically about his reference to his French heritage, Calvin explained,

> ... they were immigrants from France so I'm not like the African slaves that got brought to America, I'm part of the African slaves that got taken to France and then they immigrated over here to America. So, in terms of identity, or racial identity, I would look at myself as African American mostly just because that's my culture, most of my culture lies, and my cultural influence.

Calvin engages in this identity work as he complicates homogenous notions of Blackness. He does so through discourses of ancestry, nationality and culture. Although Blackness manifests as (and is understood as) a common and unifying identity, there are multiple identities within Blackness. Blackness is heterogeneous: this is what Calvin tells us. Calvin's identity work adds another layer of complexity and multiplicity to his identity and creates a space in which he can articulate the particularities of his racial location in relation to his African American peers. As he makes reference to history and suggests this history impacts upon his present, he shows a racial consciousness that speaks back to the ideology of 'post-racial' white supremacy. Calvin suggests that despite his ancestral heritage, his primary 'racial identity' is African American. He attributes this to his immersion in African

American culture. In this, we see the tangling of race, nation, culture and ancestry again. That is, despite different ancestral national histories, a shared sense of culture leads Calvin to an African American racial (and perhaps ethnic) identification. Of course, this is an identification not at odds with his earlier mixed-race identification but one that is mutually constitutive: possible only through a multiplicitous sense of self. The ability to identify with complexity and multiplicity demonstrates Calvin's PRR; his resilience to withstand fragmentation. In turn, his multiplicity and fluidity acts to bolsters his PRR to withstand threats to his identity.

Like Calvin, Derrick (USA) assembled his multiplicitous identity in bricolage-like fashion, from a range of intersecting discourses (Roth, 2008). Derrick grew up with his white mother and Black mixed-race brother Will (also a participant, we'll meet later). They lived in a predominantly Black, working-class, de-facto segregated area of Baltimore. Derrick attended a predominantly white Quaker school. During the interview, Derrick observed how others identify him 'as Black or African American solely'. As in the accounts in the previous section, this is Derrick's sense of double consciousness; his seeing himself through the eyes of the (white) other. Given the way he is interpellated by others, Derrick argues that he has 'experiences of being a Black man in America'. At this point, Derrick identifies himself as part of the *Black masculine same*. That is, he has common experiences with other Black men in America. We might think back here to Tayo's (USA) account of being subject to systems of 'racism and prejudice' as a Black man. With that identity work done, Derrick (USA) engages in a speech act that complicates that identification,

> I think it was different because of the fact that I got a lot of different realms of exposure. So, when I go to my Dad's house, my Dad is Jamaican and Scottish and Puerto Rican, so I would get Hispanic parts on my Dad's side and cultural things from my Dad. Like the food, dance, music, stuff like that. And on my Mum's side, I would get spirituality, religion and the food, like Southern Black food from her. So, it was very different, it was cool though.

Having already identified himself through the racial discourse of Blackness, Derrick now draws upon intersecting and antagonistic discourses to position himself as *different from that Black same*. Through nationality and culture, Derrick is able to capture an assemblage of 'common historical experiences and shared cultural codes', in order to constitute his mixed-race self (Hall, 1990, p. 223). Through the common cultural tropes of 'food, dance, music... spirituality and religion', Reece's identity is 'subjected to a creative process of restructuring that draws selectively and strategically' from each, in order to 'open up new alternatives and meanings' (Soja, 1996, p. 5). This is Derrick's hybridity-of-the-everyday. From this multiplicitous identity, Derrick is able to cultivate the PRR to resist being torn asunder. Derrick sees his multiplicity not as fragmentation or as weakness but as strength: in his words, it is 'cool'. He goes on to talk about his identification with mixedness,

> For me it allows me to have a sound identity to the point where I can identify with a lot of different things and really have those be a part of my identity, and me to learn about different things. So, before I was growing up I was like okay, I'm just Black, whatever. And those were like the traits that were associated with me and those were the things that I was taught to be important. But now identifying as a mixed male, it's something that allows me to get to know white culture, well everybody knows white culture 'cos it's America[3], but Black culture, Hispanic culture, Native American culture. It allows me to be a lot more and to learn a lot more about where my family came from and how I am now. (Derrick, US)

For Derrick, it is *mixedness* that allows him to identify in a way that reflects the totality of his lived experience. He feels more able to identify with and through the multiple cultural influences within his family. Derrick argues that identifying as '*just* Black' in his early years proved to be restrictive. The emphasis on '*just*' is significant here. Perhaps Derrick proscribes to (or feels constrained by) a narrow definition of Blackness: to identify as *just* anything is to occlude the multiplicities of identity or to restrict the elasticity so integral to PRR. As the preceding accounts have shown, no Blackness is *just* Blackness. Rather, it is always multiplicity constructed across intersecting and antagonistic discourses. However, the structures of white supremacy always threaten to

---

[3]Derrick here notes the pervasiveness of whiteness and the impact this has on his identification (Tate, 2005); as he notes, 'everybody knows white culture'.

limit Blackness. For Derrick, mixedness offers the fluidity and multiplicity to 'be a lot more': this, he argues, offers a 'sound identity'. This multiplicity means that it is perfectly possible for Derrick to recognise his racialisation as a 'Black man in America' and identify in ways that resist and complicate this ascription. This is Derrick's hybridity-of-the-everyday. It is in this bricolage of identity that Derrick finds the PRR to resist erasure and fragmentation. Derrick shows us something important about PRR: it is cultivated over time and is informed by an awareness of his positionality in a racially stratified society: this awareness is in resistance to 'post-racial' ideology. Whilst Derrick identifies primarily through mixedness, others, like Reggie, identified primarily through Blackness.

Reggie (USA) grew up with his white mother and Black father in a working-class area he described as 'rough'. He recalls interactions with his parents who always taught him, 'okay, yeah you have a bunch of different races [...but] you're Black. That is that'. Through hybridity, this speech act serves at least two functions. First, the recognition of various racial ancestries is resistance to the erasure of multiplicity. Second, much like Derrick, there is recognition that one will be racialised as a Black man. This is his family's resistance to the 'post-racial'. Through this identity work, Reggie becomes an-other Black who has 'a bunch of different races'. The two positions are not mutually exclusive: this is Reggie's hybridity. As Reggie identifies primarily through Blackness, and Derrick primarily through mixedness, taking the two accounts side by side can be particularly revealing. Most immediately, we see the heterogeneity in the ways that Black mixed-race men understand and articulate their identities (Brunsma & Rockquemore, 2001; Williams, 2011). Despite using different identity categories, we also see great parallels in what the men say. Thus, we begin to see more clearly that identity discourses are merely vessels. It is through these vessels that Black mixed-race men produce identifications that move far beyond the 'limitations of existing boundaries' (Meredith, 1998, p. 2). As in Reece's account earlier, many of the men saw a fluidity between Blackness and mixedness. That is, they both operate as vessels through which Black mixed-race men can identify. This is articulated clearly by Luke (UK).

Coming from a working-class background, Luke grew up living with his Black father and white mother in a white working-class area outside of Manchester. When asked how he identified, Luke's (UK) response was representative of several, he answered, 'well mixed-race or Black. Either or, it's not an issue for me. Like people say Black mixed-race, people say Black; they're all the same thing, innit really, to me'. This fluidity, what Reece (UK) termed a 'duality', becomes an important component of PRR. It is perhaps this that gives Black mixed-race men the resilience to withstand the supposed threat of 'racial mismatches'. Aspinall and Song's (2013) work has challenged the axiomatic assumption that these mismatches are always inherently problematic for the individual: The accounts of the majority of participants in this study add support to that challenge. Jamal (UK) came from a middle-class background and spent time living with both of his separated parents. Whilst he is identified as mixed-race, on being identified by others as Black, he said, 'I'm proud of my Black heritage and would like it to be appreciated so therefore it doesn't bother me as I'm glad my differences are recognized at least in some form'. Notice the theme of pride emerges again here: In white supremacist conditions, Black pride is defiant. Pride becomes an *affective* response to the white gaze. The combination of pride and fluidity allows Jamal to remain resilient against the threat of racial mismatch. I now turn to consider more closely how PRR is enacted when identities are placed under threat from *racial mismatch*.

The Threat of Racial Mismatch

As I have begun to show, identification occurs at the everyday level through social interaction. More specifically, according to Jenkins (2014), identification occurs through dialectics of the internal (self-definition) and the external (definition by others) (also see Aspinall & Song, 2013; Nagel, 1994). Harris and Sim (2002) observed a further layer of complexity to this process: as they suggested, *expressed* identities could be considered partially distinct from both the internal and external. External identifications are largely and primarily determined by physical appearance, and this is true in relation to race and ethnicity (Brunsma & Rockquemore, 2001; Rondilla & Spickard, 2007). As I have suggested, the majority of participants in this study felt they were most frequently identified as Black and/or mixed-race, often interchangeably: this was rarely deemed problematic. However, there were some instances when external identifications fell outside of these categories, and this posed a potential threat to the individual.[4] In this

---

[4]Many of these incidents can be understood through the theoretical lens of racial microaggressions. This is the focus of Chapter 5.

section, I consider the implications of those incidents and how Black mixed-race men cultivate the PRR to respond.

Let us begin with Bradley (USA). Bradley grew up with his Black African mother. He described the family unit as upper middle-class. They spent time living in various African countries and in New York. In New York, he attended a racially diverse school. Here Bradley recalls his experiences of racial mismatches,

> I've been called a lot of things, the majority I would say is Spanish, or Dominican, just cos I lived in New York and that I guess I look in that aspect, in colour, skin tone, but then as soon as I start talking, I guess it's completely different and I always end up explaining my story and my background, in terms of where I'm from. I'm very, very patriotic to my country. I always preach about my country. It's my country first and then the US, and I always make that a standpoint when I meet anyone.

Bradley first highlights the importance of locality and context in processes of racialisation (Brunsma, 2006; Sims, 2016). This awareness is antithetical to 'post-racial' logic. Bradley reasons that New York's high Hispanic population (Bonilla-Silva, 2004) means that his racially ambiguous appearance ('colour, skin tone') often engenders incongruence between his internal and external identifications. Perhaps a response to a momentary 'crisis in racial meaning' (Omi & Winant, 1994, p. 59) reflective of a dominant racial imaginary that erases mixed identities; this form of misidentification is one that 'mixed-race people who live in the United States contend with' regularly (Sims, 2016, p. 9). Demonstrating his agency and PRR, this interpellation is not merely accepted by Bradley but is something he resists and challenges. Whilst physical appearance is the primary determinant of the way one is identified by others, it is not the only determinant: Bradley engages in identity work that reconstitutes his identity. He does this by 'explaining [his] story', his 'background' and by talking about his 'country'. It is through these performative acts that Bradley negotiates his identity. In the first instance, double consciousness allows Bradley to recognise how he is *misread*. Drawing upon discourses of nationality, he is then able to engage in speech acts that produce a hybridity-of-the-everyday. He is *an-other Black* who is Swazi. Later in the interview Bradley noted that 'through the cultural aspect of the United States, I consider myself African American now'. Moving through discourses race, nationality and culture, Bradley conveys the multiplicity and elasticity of his identity. Notice that again, as in several accounts in this chapter, pride (this time, articulated through patriotism) is present. This is an important affective component of Bradley's PRR.

Whilst Bradley's skin-tone (and locality) means he was regularly interpellated as Hispanic, there were three participants in the study who reported regularly being interpellated as white (or not Black) due to their light skin-tone: Brendon (USA), Claude (UK) and Isaac (USA). First, Brendon (USA): from a working-class background, Brendon grew up with his white mother in a white area. He attended a white school where he was one of the only three non-white students. In this extract from the interview, he recalls how he expresses his frustrations at being misidentified,

> My entire life I was forced to be white and I could never really tell, or let out, or even like express or fully, I don't know. Sometimes I couldn't even validate that I was Black, I couldn't even be Black I was just white. So, I don't know; couldn't even consider myself as Black ... I even, I got it from family once but that is what it is ... can I just be my own thing? Can I not be put on a label? Can I yeah, just be mixed? (Brendon, US)

Brendon's account really underlines the power and the threat of the white gaze. It is this gaze that has the power to limit who and what Brendon can be. He conveys his sense of frustration and fragmentation as he is unable to 'validate' or 'express' the totality ('fully') of his identity. As Brendon argues that he could not consider himself Black, the role of the internal-external dialectic is evident here. That is, his inability to produce a performance that sees him identified as Black (externally) impacts upon his (internal) sense of self. In turn, his sense of self impacts upon his performances, and the dialectic becomes apparent. As he went on to tell me, performative Blackness was met 'with weird faces ... so it stopped'. The 'post-racial' myth is shattered here as there are demonstrable racialised expectations constraining Brendon's identification with Blackness. The persistence of the Black/ white racial dichotomy is also starkly apparent as Brendon reasons his inability to validate Blackness means he is 'just white'. Brendon shows his desire to move beyond these discursive constraints as he asks to be his 'own thing', 'not be put on a label' and 'just be mixed'. This is perhaps Brendon's attempt to hybridise beyond those categories and beyond the gaze of the other.

Let us now look to the UK and consider the account of Claude. Claude grew up with his white mother. He came from a working-class background and went to a predominantly white school. Talking about his identity, and how it is perceived by others, Claude suggested, 'the colour of my skin comes into it quite a lot as well cos I'm really pale'. He recalled frequently being told 'you're not mixed-race, you're white'. According to Linda Alcoff (1999, p. 31), 'when mythic bloodlines which are thought to determine identity fail to match the visible markers used by identity discourses to signify race, one often encounters these odd responses'. Here Claude shares his recollection of one particularly memorable experience,

> It made me quite angry. It made me quite horrible to people as well, because it's like I don't have anything to say like that about you so why are you doing it to me? Especially when I met new people. I was in a maths class... and we were given sheets, and we were asked to sign them and one of the boxes was your ethnicity and I was sat next to this girl and she goes 'you're not mixed-race' and this was like at fourteen. I was like 'yeah I am' and she was, just like, insistent that I wasn't. This girl that I'd just met, cos the schools had just merged, and she was, I don't even know her second name you know what I mean? I'd just sat next to her today. She was like insistent that I weren't.

Notice the impact this identity erasure has on Claude. It makes him feel 'angry' and act 'horribly'. This has very real implications for Claude. He feels a sense of powerlessness as he does not 'have anything to say' to his interlocutor. As a white subject, Claude's interlocutor is always already named. White supremacy imbues the privilege to question the identities of racialised others. Despite the supposed 'post-racial' turn, this account shows that racial borders are still subject to close surveillance. As Claude's skin-tone renders him outside of the regulatory ideal of mixedness, his attempt to leave whiteness is censured (Youdell, 2000). Song and Aspinall (2012, p. 131) talk about the implications of incidents such as the one Claude recalls. Speaking of their study of mixed-race identity in Britain, they state,

> [Some] respondents encountered outright incredulity (and sometimes hostility) when they claimed their minority ancestries. Because they felt a very strong attachment to

their minority backgrounds, scepticism about their minority ancestry was often painful.

These incidents certainly can be understood as microaggressions. I return to that discussion later in Chapter 5. For now, however, my primary concern is to consider how Black mixed-race men respond to these incidents that Song and Aspinall argue can be so 'painful'. Returning to Claude's (UK) accounts can offer insight here,

> After a certain point, I kind of just said like 'whatever, cool, you say that'. Like, 'whatever, not bothered', but there as certain times where I'd like challenge it, like where I'd really make a big deal about it. Especially where people would say 'why do you think you're Black?', 'How do you think you're a colour?' That's what I'd say to them and it proper like stumped them because they didn't know what to say. Usually it was probably just something to say in front of their mates, to try and make somebody look silly. I got it a lot, 'why do you think you're Black?' [Laughs]. That's bad.

Claude first suggests that his ability to respond to his interlocutors is something that developed 'after a point'. As I have suggested, PRR is something that is developed and cultivated over time. Claude shows his ability to draw upon a range of tactics as he responds to his interlocutor. In so doing, he shows not only the agency of Black mixed-race men but also the ability to read a situation and respond accordingly. Claude shows an acute awareness of the racism governing his interlocutor's episteme. In so doing, Claude shows his *racial literacy*[5] (Twine, 2010) that is resistant to 'post-racial' logic. This is an important component in Claude's PRR. From his position of racial literacy, Claude is then able to exercise his resilience. In some instances, this involves Claude performing ambivalence ('whatever, you say that... not bothered'). This is an act of defiance that sees Claude refuse to be fractured and fragmented by his interlocutor. On other occasions, Claude decides to 'challenge it'. These challenges come from a position of resilience, strength and racial literacy. This position allows Claude to identify the threat, reject

---

[5]A set of practices to identify, respond to, and counter forms of everyday racism. Racial literacy takes on a particular urgency in 'post-racial' times.

it and speak back to it. Claude's racial literacy allows him to shift the power imbalance as he outwits his interlocutor in order to 'leave them stumped'. As he positions Blackness as 'a colour', rather than a race, Claude draws upon social constructionist discourse in order to invalidate his interlocutor's biologically essentialist discourse. It is through PRR that Claude is able to offer an effective rebuttal: this rebuttal renders the threat of his interlocutor impotent. In turn, that invalidation acts to strengthen Claude's PRR. Underpinning Claude's arguments is his contention that Blackness 'goes a lot further than the colour of your skin'. This rejection of Blackness conceptualised through *politics of skin* allows Claude to open up a *third space* in which definitions of Blackness can be negotiated. Thus, we see how hybridity-of-the-everyday becomes a component in Claude's PRR.

In order to strengthen his resilience, Claude developed a knowledge of 'heritage' and Black history,

> I kind of like had to know a little bit more about, just heritage and stuff, you know?... once I started to learn about me and like, I already knew, so it affected me less and less.

Note that this is a direct response ('had to') to the threat of (and experiences of) racial mismatch. Knowledge of his heritage and Black history (racial literacy) allow him to perform and validate his Blackness. The development of racial literacy helps to strengthen Claude's resilience, and the threats affect him 'less and less'. Through discourses of heritage and Black history, Claude transgresses and subverts discourses of dark skin as authentic Blackness (Tate, 2005). In so doing, and in the words of Stuart Hall (1996, p. 14), he is able to 'fashion stylize, produce and perform' his identity, 'in a constant agonistic process of struggling with, resisting, negotiating and accommodating the normative rules' of Blackness. As the interview went on, Claude asserted that he knew far more about African history than his African born peers. In so doing, Claude draws upon a critique of others in order to produce a positive character reference for himself. Through this speech act, Claude reiterates his deconstruction of discourses of dark skin authenticity and reconstruction of Blackness through discourses of consciousness. This is Claude's third space in which, as Nikki Khanna (2010, p. 115) observes, 'white phenotypic characteristics may not preclude a Black identity'.

On the other side of the Atlantic, Black skin as a marker of authenticity was a key theme in the accounts of Isaac (US). Isaac comes from a middle-class background and was raised by his white mother in a suburban predominantly white area. Here he talks about his experiences interacting with Black and white peers,

> I'd love to be more Black because sometimes people who are Black look at me and they're like 'oh what does this kid know? He don't know nothing; He's got white skin' but then when I start talking they're like, 'okay, this guy knows wassup. He knows what he's talking about'. And the white kids don't see that. The white kids just be like, 'whatever. We're white.' And they don't see, you know, they don't see the struggle that I have to live with just because of how I look. The Black kids only hear that I'm a quarter Black and that I have these issues and they be like 'I get where you're coming from. No, you're not Black... but you know, you're not like all white people. Like, you know that times are tough. Not all white people know what it's like to be a Black person and like you, you know. Not completely but you know how it is.

For Isaac, the Black community's governmentality of the borders of Blackness means his light skin restricts his ability to interact with his Black peers. He is, as Tate (2005, p. 152) puts it, rendered outside of Blackness due to 'the exclusionary practices of a Black politics of the skin'. As he conveys his wish to 'be more Black', notice how Isaac himself is imbricated in biological essentialism mediated by a Black politics of the skin. As Isaac argues, not unlike Claude, his rendering outside of the contours of Blackness is not totalising. When he 'starts talking' his ability to performatively demonstrate a level of Black cultural capital (Carter, 2003) (that he 'knows wassup') means that he at least partially, though 'not completely', challenges and modifies these borders: this is the elasticity of Isaac's PRR. In demonstrating that 'he knows times are tough' Isaac debunks the 'post-racial' and opens up a third space. In this space, Isaac's identity becomes one in which, despite appearing to be phenotypically white, his performances show he is 'not like all white people'. Demonstrating his sense of *multiple consciousness*, Isaac contrasts this experience with that of his interactions with white peers who he argues 'don't see the struggle' he experiences; they are perhaps duped by the 'post-racial'. It appears that Isaac recognises an invocation of the one-drop rule as his Black peers only need to hear that he is 'a quarter Black' to form a sense of fictive kinship. Whilst biological essentialism is deployed again here, the pervasiveness of skin as a marker of race ensures that Isaac's ability to identify with his Black peers is never more than partial. Skin tone may not be the only factor impacting upon Isaac's ability to identify with Black people. Later in the interview, he spoke about his early childhood years,

> When I was first in kindergarten or middle school, up until I got through to high school, I saw myself as a white kid. Even when my Mum would be like 'Isaac, you know, you're part Black'. I'd be like 'I know' but I hung out with other white kids. I never really bothered to learn or hang out with Black kids.

This second account might lead us to another interpretation of his partial alienation from his Black peers. This is not to say that skin-tone is not significant, as Isaac (US) initially suggests, but to recognise that skin-tone might coalesce with other factors. Having been schooled in a predominantly white environment with only white friends and white family, Isaac understands his (internal) racial identity as white. Perhaps, in part, Isaac's socialisation in whiteness leads him to produce performatives associated with whiteness. Or, put another way, he does not know how to perform Blackness. Isaac conveys to us that Blackness is something to be learned and acquired (Harris & Khanna, 2010; Khanna, 2004, 2010). Blackness is performative (Alexander, 1996): this is something Isaac 'never really bothered to learn'. I noted earlier that identities are constituted through dialectics of the internal and external. Through this frame, we might see Isaac's light skin-tone and his performatives as interactive and dialectical. Perhaps Isaac's light skin-tone means others interact with him as white, and this leads him to identify as white and perform whiteness. His performative whiteness then means he is identified by others as white: thus, this becomes an iterative and cyclical process. Multiple factors become entanglabled in the constitution of identities. Let us consider another example of this: The reader may recall the accounts of Trent (UK) who spoke earlier about the necessity of emphasising his African American heritage, as a Black mixed-race man in Britain. He suggested that cultural 'upbringing' and references marked him as different from his Black British peers. However, first attributing those differences to his mixedness, this was an awareness developed over time. This is what Trent conveys here,

> I put that to my white, my mixedness, rather than my different Blackness. So, I thought it was cos I've got some

white in me that I'm not getting these cultural references and then actually I realized that it was like, more to do with like where our Blackness comes from. Like, but, the young thirteen-year-old me didn't look at it with that much nuance.

As in Isaac's (USA) accounts above, Trent (UK) shows that the multiply constitutive nature of identities can make it difficult for social actors to understand how those identities impact upon social interactions and racial locations. Of course, to understand his experiences with 'nuance' requires Trent to reject the logic of the 'post-racial'. His racial literacy allows him to better understand his positionality, and this becomes an important component in his PRR. The accounts of Trent (UK) and Isaac (USA) show us at least three things. First, we see that there are multiple factors that may impact upon how one is read by others. Second, those factors are not always readily distinguishable. Third, we begin to see more clearly that Blackness is about more than phenotype: Blackness is performative.

So far, I have spoken of racial mismatch in terms of a phenotypical misreading of a person's racial identity. However, recognising Blackness as performative opens up other possibilities for racial mismatch. I want to now turn to consider racial mismatch from another angle. What happens when a person's performance does not match the way they are identified by others? Here I want to look at the accounts of two participants: Max (UK) and Jake (UK). Max (UK) came from a lower working-class background and grew up with his white mother, white stepfather and white stepsister. He attended a predominantly white school. Here he discusses the way he is identified by others,

> Once they get to know me, they'll say oh he's the whitest Black person I've ever met. [RJS: what does that mean?] Not quite sure. I think it means that I'm not stereotypically Black. I don't, I don't know. I don't act like a Black person, or speak like I'm from a really urban area, I suppose.

Max shows us that there are certain performances that are associated with Blackness. Whilst he might initially be read as Black or Black mixed-race based on phenotype, the way he acts and speaks is seen to be incongruent with this reading. It is this incongruence that leads his interlocutors to draw upon discourses of biological essentialism (Black skin) and cultural essentialism (white speech and acts) to produce the seemingly paradoxical notion of being 'the whitest Black person'. Max's racial identity is understood through an assemblage of that which is already known: this is a hybridity-of-the-everyday. This identification is perhaps constrained by narrow and monolithic stereotypes of Blackness that threaten to limit who and what Black mixed-race men can be. As Isaac attributes his interpellation to not being 'from a really urban area', Isaac shows the discursive inseparability of Blackness, urbanity and poverty (Collins, 2004; Harris & Khanna, 2010). To be Black and not poor (urban being a metonym for Black and poor) is to be a contradiction in discourse or to contradict that discourse. Miri Song (2003, p. 8) observes this contradiction as she argues that 'a person may take on "white" middle-class culture and it is that aspect that can cause rejection on the basis of authenticity from black communities'. In the next chapter, I will return to consider the governmentality of Black peer groups more closely. For now, let us look more closely at this notion of Black performativity.

Jake (UK) comes from a middle-class background. He grew up living with his white mother and had sustained contact with his Black father. In the following account, he discusses how he understands his identity in relation to how he is identified by others,

> If we're going to go on stereotypical personal characteristics attributed to looks then you could say that I see myself as typically white whilst others may not see that, based on looks alone, but then I don't quite believe the Oreo-effect of having such 'white' attributes meaning that I am any way less of the POC [Person of Colour] that I am, so really it would be going against that for me to say that I see myself as a *whiter version* of how other people see me, despite that being the best way to crudely define it.

Jake understands his (internal) racial identity as 'typically white'. However, as he invokes the white gaze, this is complicated by Jake's awareness of the external (the way he is viewed by others). As he attempts to articulate his sense of identity, Jake engages in multiple speech acts to express his frustration at the limitations of the discourses available to him. To recognise and resist these limitations is demonstrative of Jake's PRR, his pushing back against constraints. In the first instance, Jake critiques what he refers to as 'the Oreo-effect'. Oreo — a biscuit that is black on the outside and white on the inside — is often used pejoratively to describe individuals who are phenotypically Black but are perceived to perform whiteness. (Note the parallels with Max's account). This is a notion that Jake does not 'quite believe in'. As he suggests '"white" attributes' (perhaps *white habitus*) do not render him 'any way less' a 'person of colour', he speaks back to discourse. This is Jake's hybridity-of-the-everyday. In his summation, Jake offers an identification he believes is intelligible through discourse: 'a whiter version of how other people' see him. However, he caveats this identification as 'the best way to crudely define it'. According to the Oxford English Dictionary Online (2015), crudely means 'rudimentary or makeshift'. Thus, Jake shows us that this identification underdetermines his totality. He is more than the limits of those constitutive discourses. To recognise, withstand, resist and speak back to the limitations of racial discourses is Jake's PRR.

Whilst Jake (UK) is now demonstrably proud to be a 'person of colour', as he recalls, this was not always the case. Talking about his racial identity, he argued, 'I hated it. I just wanted to be white. I went home and I was like I wanna be white. I wanna be white'. A similar experience was recalled by Max (UK). Despite performing whiteness, and an expressed desire to be white, Jake's (and Max's) phenotype precluded a white identity. Surveillance of the borders of whiteness is integral to the maintenance of white supremacy, and this renders Jake outside of those borders. Jake's inability to identify volitionally shatters the myth of the 'post-racial'. Perhaps this recollection reveals the potential impact of external identifications on Black mixed-race men's sense of identity. Jake now recognises himself as somebody with 'white attributes' who is also no way 'less a person of colour'. This is a hybridity-of-the-everyday that reflects the multiplicity of his identity. This identity emerges through resistance to fragmentation and erasure. It is indicative of Black mixed-race men's PRR. Emerging through PRR, this identification then acts to bolster that PRR: Jake's multiplicitous sense of self means he is better able to withstand future threats of erasure. *Racial mismatches* show us very tangible manifestations of those threats to which Black mixed-race men must remain resilient. I will return to look at instances like these in Chapter 5. For now, it suffices to say that by holding fluid and multiplicitous identities, and rejecting the 'post-racial', Black mixed-race men are generally able to cultivate the PRR to resist erasure and fragmentation.

Conclusion

In worlds underpinned by white supremacy – and maintained through the persistence of a Black/white racial dichotomy – it is through PRR that Black mixed-race men resist being torn asunder. At the beginning of this chapter, I suggested that PRR describes *the capacity to withstand and/or recover quickly from racist and racialised difficulties that are denied: toughness against the invisible.* I also suggested that PRR is *the ability of one's sense of self to remain in or spring back into shape, amidst threats that are deniable: elasticity.* Throughout this chapter, I provided illustrations for those definitions as I first showed integral components of PRR and then showed how PRR is enacted in the face of threats.

Double consciousness describes Black mixed-race men's sense of seeing themselves through the 'eyes of others' (Du Bois, 1994, p. 2). This seeing is a rejection of the 'post-racial' that enables Black mixed-race men to better understand their positionality in racial and racist structures. This understanding can be vital in overcoming barriers and avoiding threats. Oftentimes, double consciousness led the men to recognise that white interlocutors saw them as mono-racially Black: often based on negative Black stereotypes. Knowing the white gaze to be governed by a racist episteme allowed the men to remain resilient against the threat of internalising the pathological figment of the white imaginary. Many of the men expressed a sense of pride in Blackness that was defiant and acted to nullify any threat posed by the white gaze. Thus, double consciousness and Black pride strengthened Black mixed-race men's PRR. Alongside this Black pride was a sense of fluidity, multiplicity and hybridity that allows Black mixed-race men's identities to remain intact even when under threat.

If double consciousness enables Black mixed-race men to identify threats, hybridity emerges as a response to those threats. In societies underpinned by white supremacy, and maintained through the dichotomisation of Black and white, Black mixed-race men are unsurprisingly faced with near-ubiquitous threats of fragmentation and erasure. Moreover, as Blackness is reduced to stereotype and pathology, the need to resist can be seen to take on particular intensity for Black mixed-race men. To hold a multiplicitous and fluid sense of self is an important component in Black mixed-race men's PRR: particularly, offering the *elasticity* to *spring back into shape.* As Black mixed-race men produce hybrid identifications that draw upon multiple intersecting discourses of race, ethnicity, culture, nationality and ancestry, they demonstrate an acute awareness of their nuanced positionality in white supremacist structures. They refuse to be bound by a white gaze. To see one's identity as fluid, multiplicitous, and hybrid is both a cause and consequence of PRR.

In the final section, I looked at some tangible instances in which Black mixed-race men's identities came under threat: *racial mismatches*. Here I showed that threats of erasure are very real in the lives of Black mixed-race men, particularly those who are misidentified as white. Nevertheless, I showed how Black mixed-race men deploy a range of discursive strategies as they negotiate their identities. Particularly, I showed how those men misread as white spoke back to Black politics of skin to demonstrate the multiple lines upon which racial identities are constructed. Conversely, I showed how those men who were seen to perform whiteness despite a phenotypic appearance of Blackness or mixedness rejected the racial essentialism of performances: this is perhaps the 'springing back into shape' of PRR. Whilst almost all of the men cultivated the PRR to resist threats of erasure, the accounts of Brendon in this section testify to the very real negative impact that racial mismatch can have.

This chapter has shown how double consciousness and hybridity-of-the-everyday are mutually constitutive components in Black mixed-race men's PRR. This double consciousness takes on a particular urgency as it requires Black mixed-race men to reject 'post-racial' ideology. As Black mixed-race men repeatedly engage in this rejection, the accounts in this section attest to the adage, 'who feels it, knows it'. Throughout, and again demonstrative of rejections of the 'post-racial', Black mixed-race men showed forms of racial literacy that supported the cultivation of their identities (Twine, 2010). Evident in several accounts, 'pride' represents another noteworthy component of Black mixed-race men's PRR. To be proud of Blackness and mixedness is antithetical to white supremacy and requires one to speak back to racial ideologies. This therefore becomes both cause and consequence of Black mixed-race men's PRR.

Building upon this chapter, in the next chapter, I further develop an understanding of PRR as I consider how Black mixed-race men cultivate identities in relation to the intersections of race and gender.

Chapter 2

Constituting and Performing Black Mixed-Race Masculinities: Hybridising the Exotic, the Black Monster and the 'Light-Skin Softie'

Introduction

Whilst Critical Mixed Race Studies (CMRS) is burgeoning as an academic field (Daniel, 2014; Daniel et al., 2014), relatively scant attention has been paid to disaggregated and intersectional analyses of mixedness. Similarly, whilst Critical Studies of Men and Masculinities (CSMM, see Hearn, 2004) has been complicated by efforts to understand a diverse range of racialised masculinities (Edwards, 2006), the focus has too often situated Black men as a homogenous and undifferentiated group (note the parallels with the white gaze discussed in the previous chapter). That is to say, whilst much of the CSMM literature is increasingly intersectional, this is based on a flawed and occlusive assumption of Blackness as a stable and homogenous axis. Taking gender, like race, to be performative (Alexander, 2003; Butler, 1990) and recognising the inseparability of race and gender (Collins, 2004; Davis, 2011; hooks, 2004), in this chapter, I bring CSMM and CMRS into conversation in order to trouble the assumed heterogeneity of Black masculinities. In focusing on the intersection of race and gender, I consider the particular ways in which Black mixed-race men's PRR is cultivated. In so doing, I offer analyses that advance both CMRS and CSMM and strengthen our understandings of Black masculine mixed-race identities.

As the participants spoke of their interpellation as mono-racially Black (Tikly et al., 2004; Tizard & Phoenix, 2002), the accounts in the previous chapter supported the notion that *under the white gaze, Blackness is undifferentiated* (Tate, 2005). Mixedness undergoes a process of erasure that acts to maintain the Black/white racial dichotomy and, in turn, white supremacy (Vest, 2016). It is in this context – as Blackness is homogenised and reduced to a monolithic stereotype – that Black mixed-race men's masculinities are constituted. To be clear, as I will show, the white gaze consistently interpellates Black mixed-race men as *the Black monster*. As George Yancy (2017) describes, the Black monster – a historically and contemporarily constructed figment of the white imaginary – is violent, criminal, unintellectual and hyper-heterosexual (also see, Donnor & Brown, 2011). As Heidi Mirza (1999, p. 137) puts it, 'unthinkingly in our everyday discourse, we have come to associate black men with absent fathers, violent deaths, drugs and crime'. Near-hegemonic as this discourse is, it would be an ahistorical misnomer to see this as absolute. The historical construction of the Black man as physically strong and sexually potent is simultaneously evocative of 'admiration and fear' (Collins, 2004, p. 153; Fanon, 2008). In this chapter, I show how Black mixed-race men are implicated by discourses of monstrosity and sexual attractiveness. I also show that, to a certain extent, mixedness and/or light skin intersects to produce particular outcomes for Black mixed-race men.

bell hooks (2004, p. x) suggests that 'stereotypes about the nature of black masculinity continue to overdetermine the identities black males are allowed to fashion for themselves'. Whilst this is certainly true, in this chapter, I argue that Black mixed-race men often have the PRR to resist and challenge these constraints. Indeed, Black mixed-race men seem to be acutely aware of the apparent dichotomy between admiration and fear. Not only that, but through hybridity-of-the-everyday, Black mixed-race men demonstrate an ability to modify, manipulate, and speak back to those apparently dichotomised discourses.

In the first section, I consider how heterosexual attractiveness becomes an important component in Black mixed-race men's PRR. In the second section, I consider how Black mixed-race men utilise PRR as they respond to discourses of the Black monster.

'Girls Love Mixed-Race Guys'

As Butler (1990) and others (Halberstam, 1998; Pascoe, 2011) have shown, gender proves to be performative. That is, gender comes to be through the repetition of acts and the construction of social (gender) norms. Fundamental to the construction of gender is what Judith Butler (1990) calls *the heterosexual matrix*. Put more plainly, gender is constituted through a desiring of the opposite sex (Lloyd, 2007; Preves, 2003). Straight Masculinity is performed through heterosexuality: a desiring of women and a concomitant desire to be desired by women (Pascoe, 2011). Discourses of Black hyper-heterosexuality perhaps intensify these connections for Black mixed-race men. As Patricia Hill Collins (2004,

p. 151) puts it, sexual prowess grows in importance as a marker of Black masculinity. It is through the (racialised) heterosexual matrix that Black mixed-race men often make sense of their position in schools and in society more broadly. Following on from the preceding chapter, double consciousness is a returning theme in discussions of masculinity. The following is an account from Leon (UK),

> ... in year ten when Chris Brown and Black artists came out and girls sort of fell in love with Chris Brown ... Drake ... Kanye, Jay-Z, I feel like, that's when I felt a change. I feel like girls from [town], white girls, or from [borough], took more of an interest in me being Black once they sort of heard the music and stuff like that. I think up until then I don't think there was as much attention, even with guys, I don't think there was as much attention until they sort of started getting inspired from Black artists, you know? I don't know why its music, it's not really, it's just music. That was the reason. They started to look up to; they started trying to dress like Chris Brown; all these different people.

Notice that the gaze invoked is the white *female* gaze. As the heterosexual matrix intersects with white supremacy, it is the white female who is Leon's arbiter. Leon suggests that the white girls at his school desired a number of famous Black male music artists. This is unsurprising given the impact of Black art forms on British society (Chambers, 2016). As hooks (2004, p. 155) argues, 'popular culture has made the black male body and presence stand for the apex of "cool"'. Leon believes that the presence of Black and Black mixed-race men in popular culture meant that those white girls 'took more of an interest' in him. This offered validation for his performative Black masculinity. According to Alexander (1996), the ability to attract women is an integral component in the constitution of Black straight masculinity (also see, Lemelle Jr, 2010). Given the fundamentality of the heterosexual matrix, the validation of the white female transcends the peer group and is evident as a form of homosocial capital; 'even with guys'.

Leon conveys his sense that there is something particular about the emergence of the wave of Black artists in his account. In actuality, those Black male artists were preceded by popular Black male artists who were also preceded by a wave of popular Black male artists. To be clear, Black men have long since been represented in popular culture. Rather than a distinct cultural moment, perhaps the particular development Leon seeks to pinpoint is attributable to the stage of schooling and adolescence. It is conceivable, and has been argued, that 'year ten' is merely the age at which gendered and sexualised identities become most pronounced in the school (Mac an Ghaill, 1988).

Suki Ali (2003, p. 45) found that her participants 'often use popular culture' as they explore 'discourses of 'race' and ethnicity and gender'. It might be the case that Leon's reference to popular culture is merely a speech act that allows him to convey a positive representation of his identity and positionality without performing the stereotype of the *egotistical Black mixed-race man* (Newman, 2017). In a heteronormative and patriarchal context, this positive reference is achieved through positioning one's self as heterosexual and heterosexually desirable (Connell, 2005). Perhaps Leon uses popular culture as a way to articulate his positionality.

Leon's (UK) account demonstrates how the ability to elicit the attraction of white women might be seen as a form of Black masculine cultural capital (Carter, 2005). In resisting racism and social exclusion, this capital can be seen to support Black mixed-race men's PRR. Lamar, a participant in my previous research with Black mixed-race men in the UK (see Joseph-Salisbury, 2013), demonstrated how this translated into a form of capital,

> ... not to be big headed but I was quite popular with the girls and that kind of helped a little bit as well, so that kind of increased my popularity at school ... So that I wasn't too bad with the ladies, kind of thing, that helped and I think I felt more comfortable with it, so I got invited [to social events] more.

Somewhat more explicitly than Leon, with the predication 'not to be big headed', this account shows a discernible desire to resist being read as an *egotistical Black mixed-race man* (Newman, 2017). As Lamar identifies himself in opposition to that stereotype, this might be interpreted as a hybridity-of-the-everyday: he is *another-Black mixed-race man who is not egotistical*. Double consciousness is evident here too as Lamar pays attention to how he may be read. Much like Leon, Lamar links his 'popularity at school' to his ability to attract girls, particularly white girls (Pascoe, 2011). Lamar's account reemphasises the fundamental impact of the racialised heterosexual matrix as it means he is 'invited [to social events] more'. Lamar's suggestion that the cultural capital accrued through his ability to attract girls (Pascoe, 2011) enables him to feel 'more comfortable' might easily be understood through the frame of PRR. *PRR is the ability to remain comfortable in the face of threats to one's sense of identity or wellbeing: the ability to attract girls bolsters PRR.*

In the previous chapter, I showed that, in their early years, there were two participants who spoke of wanting to be white – Max (UK) and Jake (UK). This was a desire that dissipated as Max and Jake got older. Put another way, remembering that resilience is cultivated and strengthened over time, as Max and Jake cultivated greater levels of PRR they cultivated multiplicitous identities beyond whiteness. In the following account, Max (UK) discusses how the capital accrued through attracting girls bolstered his PRR,

> Something just clicked in my head where I was like actu-
> ally, I'm not bothered. I am who I am. Maybe it was when
> I started getting more of an interest in girls, and girls
> started getting more of an interest in me cos I was mixed-
> race. I was like, actually, this is a good thing.

Max suggests that eliciting the interest of girls – at a time when the heterosexual matrix is particularly central to the negotiation of position-alities in the school (when he also 'started getting more of an interest' in them) (hooks, 2004; Warikoo, 2011) – is what enabled him to view his 'mixed-race' identity as a 'good thing'. At this point, he had cultivated the PRR to declare 'I am who I am'. To borrow Lamar's words from the previous account, the accrued racialised masculine capital made Max 'more comfortable'. This was a sentiment shared by many of the participants, one of whom was Zak.

Zak (UK) grew up in a working-class family with his white mother and Black father. He went to a predominantly white school. Speaking about his mixedness he said 'it feels like I'm unique. Like always in school I was the only mixed-race, and all the girls like love it. I used to get all the girls'. Zak's account supports Pascoe's (2011, p. 92) observation that 'getting girls' is integral to the acquisition of 'masculine capi-tal'. As I have suggested, given the stereotypical discourses surrounding Black masculinity, this is perhaps particularly pronounced for Black and Black mixed-race men (Alexander, 1996; hooks, 2004). Through his access to this racialised masculine capital, Zak was able to generate a sense of pride. Pride was a theme running through much of the last chapter, and it is an affect underlining all of the accounts in this section.

This should not come as a surprise, according to Scheff (1990), pride and its antithesis, shame, are the most prevalent of human emotions. In white supremacist conditions, shame haunts Blackness (Tate, 2017). Put another way, the ubiquitous degradation of Blackness threatens to affect shame upon the Black body. Of course, in so doing, it also has the potential to imbue whiteness, as the antithesis of Blackness, with pride. Under the 'post-racial', it does so in ways that are unremarkable (Tate, 2017). In order to cultivate a sense of pride, Black mixed-race men must remain resilient to the threat of degradation, a threat that is obscured by the 'post-racial'. It is through PRR that Black mixed-race men are able to do so. In turn, that sense of pride becomes an affective component in Black mixed-race men's PRR. Pride might be defined as *consciousness of one's own dignity*. This consciousness allows Black mixed-race men to reject erasure and fragmentation of that dignity.

There was certainly a sense that Black masculine identities were valorised across the heterosexual matrix, and that the white gaze saw Blackness as undifferentiated. That said, returning to Max (UK) can reveal something more about Black mixed-race men and the hetero-sexual matrix. Max (UK) argued, 'it's easier to get girls when you're mixed-race than when you're proper Black'. Notwithstanding Max's inadvertent association between mono-raciality and authentic Blackness, his was a sense shared by a small number of participants who felt their mixedness left them particularly well positioned to access this racialised masculine capital. This idea certainly has some credence: the work of Jennifer Patrice Sims (2012) has shown that mixed-race attractiveness is a popularly held notion: of her sample, Sims (2012) found that those who had mixed Black and white parentage rated themselves more highly in terms of attractiveness. Those findings support a small-scale study by Lewis (2010) in which she found that mixed-race individuals were rated as more attractive by Black and white people. Although Lewis (2010) dubiously attributed this to the 'biological phenomenon' of 'heterosis (or 'hybrid vigour')', the study was reported in the popular press (BBC News, 2010; Hope, 2010) and therefore seemingly became part of popu-lar discourses on mixedness.

Notwithstanding the disproportionate female focus, the white supremacist cultural economy of skin shade has been well documented (Hunter, 2007; Tate, 2017). Intentionally or otherwise, this is what Max perpetuates. Research from Curington, Lin, and Lundquist (2015, p. 783) responds to the limited focus on men and supports Max's sense that Black mixed-race men may be positioned as more desirable than mono-racial Black men (although less desirable than white men) (also see, Newman, 2017; Uzogara et al., 2014). It is conceivable therefore that proximity to whiteness through white heritage of light skin makes this form of racialised masculine capital more accessible to Black mixed-race men. Recall that in the preceding chapter, in an attempt to articulate the particularities of his racial positionality, Erik (UK) drew distinctions between light skin and dark skin Black people. In this account, Erik recalls a particular instance in order to illustrate that distinction at the intersection of gender,

> This one kid who was with me who's also lighter complexion but still mixed like me, so we call him a light skin, like I'm a light skin as well but one of my darker friends said like 'it must be nice to be a light skin' cos he just like walked up to some girl, he's six-two has light skin and just walked up to some white girl and said, 'Shawty, you got a fat ass!' and she was like 'what?' And obviously, him as like a dark skin, I guess you could call him, but he couldn't pull that same thing off. So, he said 'it must be nice to be a light skin'.

Notice that it is again the gaze of the white woman that is the arbiter: this is the *white supremacist heterosexual matrix*. For Erik, it is the 'light skin' of his peer, and subsequently himself, that means, unlike his 'dark skin' friend, he is able to engage in heterosexual predatory 'rituals' of '"getting girls"' (Pascoe, 2011, p. 92). I have suggested that the white gaze's ignorance to the heterogeneity of Blackness means that, like their assumed mono-racial peers, Black mixed-race men are consistently interpellated as the hypersexual, criminal and predatory Black monster (Yancy, 2017). Whilst accounts elsewhere have attested to this observation, this understanding is complicated by Erik's account. Erik suggests that his dark-skinned friend 'couldn't pull that same thing off': owing to his darker skin, Erik's peer is interpellated as the Black monster. Erik's account suggests that light skin (and/or mixedness) might, in *some* situations, leave *some* Black mixed-race men less fixed by the imposition of the Black monster stereotype. Whilst this view was not articulated by the majority of participants, Margaret Hunter (2007, p. 312) has argued that unlike their darker skinned peers, 'light-skinned men are often feminized as pretty boys or sissies' (also see, Deutsch, 2008). Similarly, although talking about implications in the British context, Leona Nichole Black (2015) has observed a proliferation of Internet memes questioning and ridiculing the masculinity of light-skinned Black men.

Perhaps, therefore, Black mixed-race men are faced by two seemingly contradictory stereotypes: *The Black monster* and *the effeminate light skin*. Perhaps it is the coalescence of these stereotypes that makes it, as Max (UK) puts it, 'easier to get girls when you're mixed-race than when you're fully Black'. Whilst Blackness evokes 'admiration and fear', perhaps, *sometimes*, the intersecting discourse of *effeminate light skin* positions *some* Black mixed-race men as *the Black monster who is less fearsome*: Black enough to evoke some fear and be fetishised, light enough not to evoke *too much* fear (Newman, 2017). Thus, perhaps accessing this racialised masculine capital becomes something of a balancing act: a hybridising between competing discourses. With great eloquence, Erik continues to discuss what he sees as the logic underpinning Black mixed-race men's closer proximity to this form of capital,

> It's still like holding up this whiter skin colour on a pedestal, I guess. So, like you see that when you say 'must be nice to be a light skin', you're essentially saying it must be nice to be like that much closer to being white. But I don't think people think about it in that context.

Erik's analysis demonstrates a sense of racial literacy that is resistant to the logic of our 'post-racial' epoch. When he suggests that others do not 'think about it in that context', perhaps he is suggesting they are to some extent duped by the 'post-racial'. He is acutely aware of the pernicious workings of white supremacist ideology (Hunter, 2007) and the apparent privileges this imbues to him as a light-skinned Black man (Glenn, 2009). As a knower, Erik is able to resist and speak back to this logic: knowing is a component of Erik's PRR.

Whilst the sense that mixedness made Black mixed-race men especially covetable is an important one, it was not the majority perspective. Coming from a middle-class background, Nathan (UK) grew up living with his Black father and white mother. Here he discusses his experience of the heterosexual matrix,

> Mixed-race girls, I guess they just get attention from white guys and Black guys, sort of thing. Mixed-race guys, I think white girls just see as Black, and they would still, for some white people, Black is like no, I don't do. I'm talking about, I guess romance and relationships here. But for them, Black is like off the table, their parents wouldn't like it sort of thing. So, they're not even thinking about that.

Hinting at the heterogeneity of Black mixed-race men's experiences, Nathan articulates a perspective and experience somewhat different from Erik (USA). Nathan's views are consistent with earlier accounts that suggested under the white gaze, Blackness is undifferentiated. Placing the accounts side-by-side emphasises that Black mixed-race men's experiences can be diverse, contextual and situational. Much like Erik, Nathan invokes the white female gaze in order to convey something about his racialised and gendered positionality. Nathan (UK) is interpellated under a gaze that reduces him to a Black monolith that is 'off the table'. Nathan draws upon a comparison with Black mixed-race girls in order to suggest that, across the white supremacist heterosexual matrix ('talking about romance and relationships'), his interpellation is particular to the intersection of race and gender.

Certainly, there is evidence to suggest that Black mixed-race men's identities are more restricted than other groups: Black mixed-race men are more likely to identify and be identified with their minority (Black) parent than other mixed-race men from other minority backgrounds (Aspinall & Song, 2013; Brunsma & Rockquemore, 2001; Caballero, 2004). Research also suggests that in comparison to mixed-race men, mixed-race women experience more flexibility in the negotiation of their identities (Ho, Sidanius, Levin, & Mahazarin, 2011; Penner & Saperstein, 2013) and are more likely to identify as mixed-race (Davenport, 2016).

In a study of third-generation Mexican–Americans, Vasquez (2010, p. 45) found that 'women are afforded more "flexible ethnicity" than men' and whilst 'women are racialized through exotification', 'men are racialized as threats to safety'. Nathan's account suggests that this experience is extendable to Black mixed-race men. As he argues that 'their parents wouldn't like it', the myth of the 'proverbial white victim at the hands of the Black predator' is evoked (Yancy, 2008, p. 19). Nathan becomes the Black monster and the longstanding discourse of fear over interracial sex is reproduced (Tate, 2015a). Whilst the taboo of desire for Black mixed-race women's bodies is made more palatable through its combination with white femininity (Newman, 2017), Nathan suggests this observation is not readily transferrable to Black mixed-race men.

Perhaps demonstrating the Transatlanticity of these experiences, Tayo (USA) – who we met in Chapter 2 – concurred with the apparent impossibility of interracial dating as he argued 'white girls will laugh at your jokes but you're not gonna date them. You're still Black'. Tayo's account suggests that his Blackness allows him to play the role of comedian: white girls will laugh at his jokes. From Black slaves acting as jesters in order to entertain their slave masters to contemporary Black comedians, 'comedian' is an acceptable role for a Black man in white supremacist societies (Majors & Billson, 1993). However, the longstanding fear over interracial dating − even as it pertains to the child of an interracial relationship − means that the role of 'date' is not.

The experiences of Nathan and Erik are paralleled by those of a Black mixed-race man in Pascoe's (2011, p. 96) research who, given his racial identity, 'saw his options as somewhat limited'. In these instances, the capital of sexual attractiveness is constrained by the evocation of fear; the Black monster of the white gaze who is always a possible rapist (hooks, 2004; Yancy, 2017).

As the accounts in this section attest, the tension between admiration and fear − well documented in Black masculinity literature (Fanon, 2008; Collins, 2004; Mutua, 2006; Noguera, 2009) − appears to be at play through much of the experience of Black mixed-race men and was somewhat variable, situational and contextual. Earlier in this section Max spoke about his perception that it is easier for Black mixed-race men to 'get girls' than it is for Black men. However, he did go on to make the caveat that his popularity was rarely unconditional. Talking about whether others liked him he argued, 'some people did, some people saw me as a bit of a threat' (Max, UK). Theo (UK) − who also argued 'girls love mixed-race guys' − seemed to think this was a fairly common experience for Black mixed-race men,

> Sometimes you'd go to a white school and they'll be like 'ooh a Black guy, ooh we love Black guys, ooh' [mock feminine voice], or they might just be like, you know, 'who the fuck's this guy?

The sexual attractiveness of Black mixed-race men therefore is always precarious and situational; it is always haunted by its antithesis. An awareness of this ongoing tension between desire and fear means that Black mixed-race men are, to a certain extent, able to respond to these discourses and negotiate their positionalities. Indeed − as will be argued in the following subsection on toughness, and in the following two chapters − whilst in some instances, it is deemed necessary to downplay the role of the fearsome Black, in others accentuating the threat of Black masculinity may be utilised as a form of capital. In each circumstance, Black mixed-race men refuse to be rendered docile by discourse. Whether through the evocation of admiration or fear, it is through the manipulation of discourses and stereotypes that Black mixed-race men cultivate PRR.

The discussion thus far has focused on how Black mixed-race men cultivate racialised masculine identities across the heterosexual matrix. I have argued that the heterosexual (racialised) performative ritual of what Pascoe (2011) calls 'getting girls' – particularly *white girls*, in this case – is central to the constitution of Black mixed-race men's racialised masculine identities. This is perhaps unsurprising given that discourses on race are dominated by heterosexuality (McBride, 1998). The work of Fanon and others (Tate, 2015b; Yancy, 2017) has shown that it is under the gaze of white eyes that Black people come into being. Across the heterosexual matrix, perhaps this is what governs the interpellation of Black mixed-race men. However, what does this mean for Black mixed-race men who deviate from the supposed heterosexual norm?

'It's Always Important for Me to Highlight My Sexuality When Talking About My Race'

Connell (2005, p. 143) argues that 'patriarchal culture has a simple interpretation of gay men: they lack masculinity'. Whilst this certainly holds some demonstrable truth, I have also made the observations that discourses of Blackness overdetermine Black mixed-race men as hypermasculine, and that, in some cases, mixedness can see Black mixed-race men interpellated as less monstrous than their mono-racial Black peers. This suggests that Black mixed-race men who are not heterosexual constitute their identities across seemingly contradictory discourses of race, gender and sexuality.

The reader will recall Trent from the preceding chapter. There I argued that the intersection of sexuality complicates his multiplicitous identity. In the following account, Trent (UK) discusses the impact of being outed as gay at the age of 15,

> I was like one of the cool kids but I think onwards from fifteen, sixteen I couldn't separate it from my sexuality. And sometimes I wonder cos I was never bullied whereas the other gay kid in our school was bullied, like horribly. And sometimes I always wonder like was it the Blackness that saved me from getting bullied.

There is a lot to unpack here: the apparent discursive tensions are manifest in Trent's account. That Trent was positioned as one of the cool kids is no surprise. A plethora of research has demonstrated how Black men are positioned as 'cool' (Carter, 2005; hooks, 2004; Warikoo, 2011). Cultivated across the heterosexual matrix, Black masculine cool represents a form of cultural capital that bolsters Black mixed-race men's PRR (Majors & Billson, 1993). Given that heterosexual masculinity is so heavily predicated on attracting and being attracted to girls, the intersection of Trent's sexuality, his non-participation in rituals of 'getting girls', means that he became less able to access this capital. On one level, we might argue that the failure of Trent's masculine performance is intensified by the intersection of race. There was a sense, as one participant puts it, that 'Black boys are more interested in girls'. Thus, Trent's sexuality positions him further away from the racialised masculine expectations (Lemelle Jr, 2010). However, this was not the only way the interactions between these discourses manifested. Trent also suggested that it was perhaps his Blackness that 'saved' him from being bullied due to his homosexuality. Trent's imbrication in discourses of Black masculine toughness (Majors & Billson, 1993), or proximity to the Black monster, actually acts as a protective factor that protects him from the fate of 'the other gay kid'; 'getting bullied'. (I will discuss Black masculine toughness more fully in the next section.) In Trent's account, we see how his sexuality detracts from his Black masculine cool, whilst, simultaneously, his Blackness imbues him with the masculinity to resist homophobic bullying. Whilst perhaps somewhat reductive to the nuances of those intersections, it is certainly succinct to say that in Trent's case, *the apparent excesses of Black masculinity compensate for the apparent masculine deficiencies of homosexuality.* Trent continues to explicate this more fully,

> ... the time when Blackness was most in question was when I came out as gay and I was trying to think of why that was happening. Like why, did I suddenly feel less Black? And I feel like it's because, you know, the thing that was Black about me, the thing that I always was like now I'm gonna play my Black card, was when I wanted to act tough and fend off anybody. You know, I'd clump up together with the other Black boys in the year and we'd act hella tough and scare them, scare the white boys off, or scare them off so much that they'd wanna be friends with us, so we were accepted.

The presence of the Black monster is evident in this account as Trent equates 'playing his Black card' with acting 'hella tough' in order to 'scare the white boys off'. It becomes apparent through Trent's account that, in some contexts, the supposed pathological stereotype of the Black monster has utility for Black mixed-race men (I discuss this more fully in the next section). In Trent's case − in order to resist interpersonal racism and bullying, as well as to 'scare them off so much they'd wanna be friends with us' − the Black monster stereotype becomes a component of his PRR. Trent's account reminds us that Blackness is performative and that stereotypes can be manipulated for Black mixed-race men's own ends. As Majors and Billson (1993, p. 30) note of Black men in the USA, 'symbolic displays of toughness defend his identity and gain him respect: they can also promote camaraderie and solidarity among Black males'. The applicability of these words to Trent's experiences again attest to the Transatlanticity of the experiences of Black mixed-race men.

Trent also suggests that the revealing of his sexuality resulted in him feeling 'less Black'. Again, the account demonstrates the performative nature of Blackness and the ubiquity of the internal/external dialectic. It is not Trent's own sense of his sexuality that threatens his identity with erasure, rather it is an acute awareness of how others might identify him. Trent's account reminds us that it is through the racialised hetero-sexual matrix that masculinity is constituted. Trent's experiences are perhaps also impacted upon by longstanding notions that position all Black men as straight, and Black people as particularly homophobic (Holland, Cohen, Johnson, & Henderson, 2005; Nero, 2005). Trent's interpellation as gay restricts his ability to cultivate and perform Black masculine toughness. This is intensified given that masculine identities are so often cultivated and performed in groups (Majors & Billson, 1993; Pascoe, 2011). (I discuss friendships and peer groups more fully in Chapter 6.) Trent attributes his marginalisation from his Black peer group to the groups' need to maintain its masculine performance. As Trent put it, 'having a gay Black dude in there is really not gonna help that'. As a result, Trent 'slowly became more friends with more of the white girls'. When asked about this shift he explained, 'cos I was the gay kid now rather than the Black kid'. Trent is no longer the Black monster to be feared, he becomes the archetypal gay best friend. His sexuality renders Trent no longer fearsome: thus, there is a suggestion that the evocation of fear and (sexual) admiration are intertwined for Black mixed-race men. As Trent deviates from the heterosexual matrix, he is less fearsome.

In his attempts to understand the multiplicities of his identity, Trent returns us to the themes of the preceding chapter. In the following account, he articulates a sense of being faced with threats of erasure and fragmentation. This account advances understandings in the previous chapter, as we see these threats occurring at the intersection of race, gender and sexuality,

> I think one of the challenges we face as people of colour is that our humanity isn't seen in full and with that comes, you know, the ability to be, not just heterosexual, the ability to be fully something else and different and complex, and sexuality I think that's, I can't be that as a Black man. I can't be other things than just a Black man. So yeah, I think it's always important for me to highlight my sexuality when talking about my race as well.

In this account, Trent posits those threats of erasure as 'challenges'. That is, they are not absolute: There is opportunity to resist and speak back. Trent speaks back to discourses that homogenise Blackness through the construction of a mythical heterosexual Black monolith. Trent strives to be 'something else', to be 'different and complex'. Put another way, through a hybridity-of-the-everyday Trent resists a white gaze that refuses to see his 'humanity ... in full'. As he highlights his sexuality − an act he sees as important − he shows himself to be *an-other Black who is also gay*. This is Trent's 'elasticity', his maintaining shape despite the threat of erasure. This is Trent's PRR.

Trent's identity work is very much reminiscent of that of Audre Lorde, who, Alexander (1994, p. 696) argues, engages in processes of 'collaged self-construction' to resist the erasure of her multiplicitous Black queer identity. This bricolage-like identity work was also evident in the account of Jake (UK). We met Jake in the preceding chapter. Whilst he spoke decidedly less about how sexuality intersected with his identity, he did deem it important that, where possible, he expressed his identity as 'something more long-winded like a mixed-race, non-hetero, cis-male, young man'. The inference here is that Jake is always all of these things: like Trent, his identity is multiplicitously constructed 'across different often intersecting and antagonistic discourses, practices and positions' (Hall, 1996, p. 4). As Tate (2005, p. 100) puts it, these identities 'refuse any simple reduction to each other'. It is through hybridity that Jake and Trent are able to cultivate the PRR to resist erasure and fragmentation. In the preceding section of this chapter,

I showed how the ability to elicit the attraction of girls manifested as a form of cultural capital for Black mixed-race men. This capital bolsters Black mixed-race men's PRR. The accounts of Trent show that this capital is predicated on heterosexuality. Trent's account also showed that Black mixed-race men's masculinities are cultivated in relation to the Black monster and Black masculine toughness. It is this that I turn to in the next section.

The Endangerment of the Black Monster

The spectre of the Black monster looms large in the lives of Black mixed-race men. Too often, Black mixed-race men are interpellated as the criminal, deviant and hypersexual Black monster (Yancy, 2017). This is an underlying theme in the following account from Reece (UK),

> I have a younger sister, she's seventeen and until this day … my parents are still much more concerned whenever I leave the house than when she does and it's because you're a young man, a young boy, person of colour … you're a person of colour in a society that is still not really for you.

As Reece draws a comparison with his sister, he engages in a hybridity-of-the-everyday: he is *the same (race) but different (gender)* (Bhabha, 2012; Tate, 2005). Reece's account attests to the particularity of the intersection of gender and, in so doing, problematises a field of CMRS that has too often homogenised mixedness across gender. So, what is it that Reece's speech act reveals? Drawing upon his sense of double consciousness, Reece's account might be interpreted as his sense of being interpellated as the Black monster. As Donnor and Brown (2011, p. 2) put it, 'being "Black" [mixed-race] and "male" irrespective of societal position recapitulates the historically and ideologically informed racial imaginary of Black male deviance and criminality'. It is this racial imaginary that means Reece embodies, in the words of Coates (2015, p. 137), 'a body more fragile than any other'.

Reece (UK) is cognizant of all of this: he shows that the apparent threat posed by the Black monster acts to place Black mixed-race men under threat. Monsters pose a threat to society: they must be controlled. Think of Trayvon Martin: George Zimmerman saw a Black monster enter his gated community. In order to protect that community, George

Zimmerman felt that the Black monster needed to be controlled. In order to maintain control, George Zimmerman set out to kill that Black monster. But the Black monster does not exist. In actuality, George Zimmerman killed an innocent young man eating a bag of skittles (Yancy, 2017). Zimmerman's racist gaze did not see that man. It is not being seen, perhaps more accurately, being mistaken for the monster that so often endangers Black mixed-race men. Reece shows us that this sense of endangerment is etched into his family's consciousness who are only too aware that 'it is tradition to destroy the black body' (Coates, 2015, p. 103). This is no surprise: not only because of how African American experiences impact upon Black British consciousness but also because these forms of anti-Black racism manifest in the UK too.

The spectre of Stephen Lawrence looms large in British consciousness, particularly in Black British consciousness. The landmark case of the teenage Black man, murdered by white racists, brought at least two things into sharp focus. First, that racism places Black men in fatal danger. Second, institutional racism pervades the British police force (Hall, Grieve, & Savage, 2013) and therefore, by proxy, the British State are unwilling or unable to challenge the conditions that make such a callous racist attack possible. In sum, the case of Stephen Lawrence sent a message that, in Britain, Black men are endangered by racism. Stephen Lawrence was a reiteration of that which came before – for instance, in the 1969 death of David Oluwale (in the USA, think of the murder of Emmett Till – a story immortalised in US and UK history) – and that which would come after; the 2011 murder of Mark Duggan, for instance. This latter case is significant for a number of reasons. First, this latest reiteration pierced the consciousness of a new generation of Black youth. Second, occurring three years after Obama's election, for many Black communities this really put paid to any illusions of the 'post-racial'. Third, and most significantly for the context of this book, Mark Duggan's murder showed the ways in which the Black monster was readily applied to Black mixed-race men (Long & Joseph-Salisbury, 2018). Despite his white mother (and other family members) regularly being shown in the media, in the aftermath of his death, Duggan was near universally referred to as a Black man (Harker, 2011; Long & Joseph-Salisbury, 2018). This certainly offers some confirmation for the views expressed in the preceding chapter. Namely: *under the white gaze, Blackness is undifferentiated.* The aforementioned *episteme of Blackness* (Yancy, 2017) – a way of knowing, cultivated collectively, and intergenerationally – is cultivated in Black and Black mixed-race families like Reece's (Joseph-Salisbury, 2018a).

This episteme is cognizant of the ways in which the spectre of the Black monster endangers Black and Black mixed-race men. Reece continues,

> ... there is this element of masculinity being so linked to Black men and that's what often is why people in the States can justify the killing of them because Black kids aren't seen as kids. You know, Black kids are seen as young Black men at the age of twelve, and you know, are threatening.

It is, as Reece conveys, the white gaze's distorted way of seeing, at the particular intersection of race and gender, that places Black men under threat. It is this, he argues, that 'can justify the killing of Black kids'. Put another way: erasure endangers Black men. Reece's views are substantiated by psychological research (Goff, Jackson, Di Leone, Culotta, & DiTomasso, 2014), and have implications for Black boys in schooling (Brown & Donnor, 2011; Ladson Billings, 2011). Reece's account makes explicit reference to the intersection of gender: this is particularly about Black men, he argues: a view reiterated by Max (UK),

> I don't think that mixed-race girls have bad reputations at all ... all people ever say is that they're gorgeous ... I think all of the instant assumptions and prejudices are against males.

Max's claim is supported by a plethora of literature showing that Black women with lighter skin are regarded as more desirable than darker skinned Black women (Hill, 2002; Hunter, 2007; Matthews, 2007). Whilst later work from scholars like Newman (2017) has suggested that Black mixed-race men are also constructed as highly sexually desirable, as I have argued, this is perhaps always balanced by the spectre of the Black monster (Joseph-Salisbury, forthcoming-a).

Anton (UK) is a working-class Black mixed-race man who grew up living with his white mother. Here, he shares Max's conviction that, as a consequence of the intersection of race and gender, Black mixed-race men are seen as a threat,

> I think we're seen as more of a target in terms of fights. People wanna prove themselves to other guys ... we [Black mixed-race men] are definitely seen as more of a threat. I think that's where it starts.

Much like a slave who could run away or lead a revolt, Anton is a threat to the white supremacist order. His Black body is a threat to whiteness. As Anton argues, his endangerment is the starting point. From this starting point, Black mixed-race men must respond. Thus, it is perhaps the double conscious sense that stereotypes of Black masculinity place Black mixed-race men under threat that leads many of the men to engage in performances of toughness. This becomes a legitimate response. Let us now consider how we might see the Black monster as offering Black mixed-race men a source of cultural capital.

The Black Monster as a Source of Cultural Capital

> Some boys, through a desire to demonstrate masculinity, may in fact appreciate the hypermasculine stereotype's impartation of status among peers. (Warikoo, 2011, p. 79)

Several accounts in the current research support Warikoo's (2011) observation. To act tough can be a form of masculine capital that manipulates racist-gendered assumptions (Alexander, 1996). It is through 'post-racial' resilience that Black mixed-race men are able to utilise the Black monster against endangerment. Double consciousness enables the men to know the ways in which they may be constructed, and through a hybrid and fluid sense of their own identities, the men invert that stereotype for their own gain. That is, the stereotype becomes a source of capital that offers protection from racism and bullying. The reader may recall Trent's account earlier: as he spoke of acting 'hella tough', this is what he conveyed. In a context where 'appearing weak [can lead] to being bullied' (Warikoo, 2011, p. 20), performing toughness becomes an essential protective factor in the maintenance of Black mixed-race men's PRR. Warikoo (2011, p. 20) found that performances of toughness often 'prevented real, physical violence'. This is a conviction shared by Majors and Billson (1993, p. 290) who argue that performances of Black masculine toughness are usually nothing more than a 'façade to advertise the black male's willingness to resort to violence to resolve interpersonal conflict'. That it is a façade should not be a surprise, we know that the Black monster is a mere figment of the white imaginary.

That this need often be nothing more than a performance is something Trent was clearly cognizant of. As he reflected, '[b]eing at the time, quite masculine, white kids were scared of the Black masculine kids, so it didn't need any physical toughness'. Trent demonstrates the agentic nature of these performances when he recalled thinking, 'I'm gonna play up to this masculine side of me. That's gonna keep me safe today'. Notice the agency in Trent's account. His proximity to the Black monster is something he can 'play up' (and presumably 'play down') as he sees necessary.

Similarly, Max (UK) discusses how the cultivation of a tough masculine identity – characterised by a perceivable willingness and ability to fight (Majors & Billson, 1993) – bolstered his ability to withstand the threat of racist bullying,

> ... there was three people that did it consecutively and they never ever let up and they found out that I was a world champion kickboxer. They stopped then. They were like, they'd consider themselves to be close friends of mine now, they'd do like anything for me but up until that point every day it was always nigger, Paki, Black bastard, things like that.

For Max, his kickboxing achievements became a display of toughness, acting as a form of capital to bolster his PRR against threats of racism and unpopularity: others would 'do anything' for him. The reader may recall earlier that Trent (UK) spoke of how he (and his Black peers) scared white boys so much that they would want to be friends with him. As masculine toughness translates into popularity and friendships, the parallels with Max's account are striking. Perhaps this is indicative of the masculine nature of young men's homosociality.

Imbrication in Masculine Peer Cultures

The following accounts are demonstrative of Black mixed-race men's imbrication in masculine peer cultures. Take the following account from Reggie (USA) for instance,

> I always dealt with the bullying myself ... I never wanted to ... do those snitching things. You're not gonna snitch. You're not gonna do that. That's just a culture thing too. It's just like don't snitch ... you're tougher than that.

Reggie makes clear that as useful as it may be, toughness is not an entirely volitional performance. It is a consequence of a masculine peer culture (Warikoo, 2011) that necessitates the repetition of masculine norms. As I have suggested, discourses of Black hypermasculinity mean that, for Black mixed-race men, these norms are intensified at the intersection of race and gender (Majors & Billson, 1993; Peterson-Lewis & Bratton, 2004). Reggie argues that its 'a culture thing' that determines he 'dealt with the bullying' himself. To 'snitch' or to seek help would run counter to the masculine culture and to Reggie's masculine identity. He must therefore demonstrate that he is 'independent [and] always in control' (Majors & Billson, 1993, p. 29), or, in Reggie's words: 'tougher than that'. Reggie felt that the pressure to display one's toughness was something felt particularly by men, in contrast, he argued, 'girls definitely would get help'.

Reggie's account was echoed by several participants on both sides of the Atlantic. Take the following from Jermaine (USA) for example,

> ... like in my case if I were getting bullied, I wouldn't be the one to run home to Mum; I'd know how to handle it myself. You know not necessarily fight them or whatever but I'd go about it on my own and deal with it myself. If I needed to. If I needed help I could go about it, I guess you gotta feel for it and see. If you think they could handle it go ahead, I would do it. But if they're emotionally weak, you know, really like I guess soft, not independent.

Like Reggie, Jermaine suggests this is something that must be dealt with independently, without seeking help from outside of the peer culture (Majors & Billson, 1993). As Jermaine suggests that this is not 'necessarily' about fighting, he implies that he would resort to fighting but only if deemed necessary. Thus, Jermaine (USA) reflects the aforementioned idea that masculine culture often requires only displays of one's 'willingness to resort to violence' (Majors & Billson, 1993, p. 29). Jermaine also shows he is agentic to act in ways that are antithetical to his peer culture (Mancini, 1980). Aware that toughness is not always the best strategy, his responses are situational and contextual: 'you gotta feel for it and see', he argues. However, oftentimes, toughness is a virtue that allows Jermaine to avoid being 'emotionally weak', 'soft' and 'not independent'. To display any of those characteristics, Jermaine argues, would place him at risk of 'getting bullied'. Put plainly: Black masculine toughness becomes a component in Jermaine's PRR. Let us return to Reggie. Talking about his response to threats of bullying, he said,

> I'm not gonna let a bunch of guys clown me ... I'm not
> gonna let them demasculinize me because they're making
> fun of me and stuff like that.

The association Reggie makes here is simple but revealing. To be
made fun of is to be demasculinised. Thus, to be masculine is to resist
being made fun of. Thus, in order to resist being made fun of, one must
perform masculinity. It is Reggie's masculinity that allows him to resist
'being made fun of': masculinity maintains Reggie's PRR. Reggie (UK)
continues,

> You definitely have to have tough skin; you have to have
> thick skin. If you don't have thick skin you're gonna get
> eaten alive ... I just developed it from being bullied and
> criticized ... Home life helped; got toughened up a lot at
> home ... just learnt how to just become tough and I think
> that's where it lied with me.

Reggie's account here reminds us that masculine toughness is not
innate but is something that is developed over time. Toughness comes
as the consequence of the repetition of gender norms. In Reggie's case,
these norms are enacted through 'bullying, criticism and home life'. It is
this that leads Reggie to learn to develop 'thick skin' (Alexander, 1996).
If Reggie were not to learn to be masculine, he would 'get eaten alive'.
When asked a direct follow-up question on how his home life helped,
Reggie spoke of the racially literate approach of his parents (Joseph-
Salisbury, 2018a; Twine, 2010). To resist 'post-racial' mythology, and
be conscious of the ubiquity of racism, is what enables Reggie to resist
racism. As Reggie reflects, 'I think them instilling that in me at an
early age, especially early on, was really helpful'. Reggie's account
demonstrates how PRR generally, and toughness particularly, can be
cultivated and developed in Black mixed-race men's families (Joseph-
Salisbury, 2018a).

This sense that masculine toughness bolstered PRR was prevalent
among participants in both the UK and the USA. Talking about the
consequences of not performing toughness, Theo (UK) — a working-
class man raised with his white mother — reflected on the experiences of
his younger brother, Nico,

> He has a bit of a shit time at primary school because he's
> not like me; he won't defend himself ... he's quite

emotional; quite sensitive. So, you know, if someone says something, he'll take it to heart ... he's called Nico, so they've been calling him Niggerless Nico and he's taken it really badly.

Very quickly Nico's 'shit time' is attributed to his being 'emotional' and 'sensitive': that is, his inability to adequately perform masculinity. Theo implies that his brother should defend himself, perhaps by displaying toughness (Majors & Billson, 1993), but also, perhaps reiterating the points made by Jermaine and Reggie, he should not be – to use Jermaine's words – 'emotionally weak' (Majors & Billson, 1993). Whilst, for Nico, his inability to perform toughness leaves him susceptible to racist name-calling, this is a fate that Theo's masculine identity allows him to resist ('he's not like me'). Whilst certainly not always necessary, some of the men had experiences in which, in order to validate their toughness, they felt fighting was not only necessary but also fruitful.

Fighting

If we consider the experiences of Nico, alongside the experiences of Max (UK), we might begin to see the utility of one's ability to fight. Here Max reflects on how proving that he was able and willing to fight produced a discernible change in his experiences,

That's why I think it [racist bullying] stopped cos people knew if they said something I would fight back kind of thing.

It is not hard to see parallels here between Max and Nico. In his younger years, perhaps at an age similar to Nico, Max, like Nico, was the victim of racist bullying. Whilst Theo attributes the continuation of Nico's bullying to his unwillingness to 'defend himself', defending himself is exactly what stops Max from being bullied. Put another way, Max's account offers support for Theo's claim that masculine toughness is a solution for Nico's experiences of racist bullying. That is, fighting, as Theo and Max suggest, can be an important component in Black mixed-race men's PRR. This is a response shaped by, and manipulative of, masculine culture.

As Theo's interview went on, it became clear that his understanding of his younger brother's experiences was based on his own. Theo recalled an incident in which an older student had shouted at him: 'you Black cunt, fuck off back to your own country'. Encouraged by his older brother and his friends, Theo responded to his aggressor and this led to a fight. As Theo explains, having 'broke the guys nose ... that was pretty much the last fight I ever had ... I don't think I've had much racism since then either'. In this instance, for Theo, fighting became a necessary component in his PRR. As he goes on to argue, this was a very considered response,

> I was one of the youngest in the school ... at that time I had that 'don't let anybody disrespect you' kind of thing ... if you don't stick up for yourself, you're gonna get people going at you all the time.

Both Max and Theo's accounts make clear that willingness to fight is not a consequence of excessive aggression or an inability to resist becoming the Black monster but a considered response to the perpetual threat of white racism. Of course, this requires a rejection of 'post-racial' logic: this is PRR.

Theo's account also suggests that racialised masculinity is transmitted intergenerationally. It is his older brother who encouraged his response, and it is he that is critical of Nico's unwillingness to defend himself. This intergenerationality of fighting in response to racism is something that was abundantly evident in the following account from Leon (UK),

> ... as we got to the top of the hill the guy shouted 'Nigger' from the bottom ... I wasn't too bothered because I was only a baby, but my brother Marcus, Marcus drove back and he made me batter him, and this guy was only about my age, he was only young but that's what I do remember and that's when I first realized what racism was and that it's a serious matter. You know what I mean? I remember Marcus making me punch him and I was only young ... if he didn't make me hit that one boy for being racist then people would take advantage of that and then they would be racist to me because they know that I'd allow them to be racist, and that's why I wouldn't change anything, you know what I mean?

In this instance, Leon positions himself as too young to know the appropriate response to racist verbal assaults. It was his older brother that ensured Leon understood that violence was a proportionate response. It is in this instance that Leon comes to understand the seriousness of racism and the 'post-racial' is shattered. Not only this, but Leon comes to understand that violence is not just proportionate, but necessary; otherwise, he reasons, they would 'know that I'd allow them to be racist'. It is through this act that Leon first 'disavowed Black submission to the power/knowledge of white racist supremacy' and became aware of his ability to do so (Tate, 2005, p. 107). Like Trent, Max and Nico, Leon's PRR is cultivated through the guidance of his older brother. Demonstrating some Transatlantic consistency in Black mixed-race men's responses, Will shows how, in his case, resilience through toughness and fighting was also cultivated through the family. In the following account, Will (USA) recalls his learning one of his white peers had 'said the N-word',

> Mum always was like, 'if somebody hits you, hit them back'. That's the way that bullying culture works ... the way I reacted to those things had a lot to do with my gender ... as a Black man in America.

Again, Will's response is not attributable, as popular racist discourse may suggest, to hot-headedness or an inability to control one's emotions but is a considered response that is guided by his Mother's advice. By recalling and applying his Mother's advice in this instance, Will makes clear that he sees the use of a racial epithet as of a similar severity to a physical assault. Thus, he hits the perpetrator and in doing so offers some resilience for his withstanding the pressures of 'bullying culture'. Will argues that his resorting to violence as a response to racism has a lot to do with gender 'as a Black man in America' and thus reiterates that toughness is not only a particularly masculine phenomenon but one that is oftentimes amplified at the intersection of Blackness (Majors & Billson, 1993). So, what about the particular intersections of mixedness and light skin?

Light-Skin 'Softie'

Whilst the spectre of the Black monster certainly looms large in the lives of the Black mixed-race men, for some of the men, some of the time, a seemingly contradictory stereotype complicated their interpellation. Whilst I must reiterate that most of the men felt they were seen as part of a Black monolith, in a minority of cases there was a sense that stereotypes of the 'effeminate light skin' meant Black mixed-race men were seen as less masculine than their darker skinned mono-racial Black peers (Harvey, 1995). This was apparent for Jermaine (USA) who recalled having experienced 'some microaggressions ... in terms of being light-skinned or soft'. Reading softness as a metonym for femininity, there is a clear discursive association between light skin and femininity. Jermaine is light-skinned, and so, at least by his mono-racial peers, he is read as feminine. This is a clear reminder of a key contention of this book, particularly this chapter: *gender and race are inextricably bound and this has particular implications for Black mixed-race men.*

Again, demonstrative of the Transatlanticity of Black mixed-race men's experiences, Jermaine's (USA) sentiments were echoed in the UK context by Alex,

> It's nothing like to get upset about, I don't think. But mixed-race guys are always like seen as less masculine than Black boys, innit?! And like especially from the Black side. Like they'll see you as kind of whitewashed yeah. As in you don't understand certain things. And yeah, you're just soft basically. You're a softie.

It is apparent that dark skin manifests as a form of cultural capital within Black masculine peer groups. That is, dark skin is positioned as the regulatory ideal of Black masculinity (Tate, 2005). Positioned as outside of that regulatory ideal, Black mixed-race men are assumed to lack understanding of 'certain things'. That Alex follows that observation up with 'you're just soft basically' suggests that those 'things' that should be understood pertain to one's masculinity. According to Alex, for Black mixed-race men, to be less Black (phenotypically) is to be less masculine. Alex continues,

> ... from my experiences, a lot of mixed-race boys that take from their Black side, or are surrounded by Black males, [in order to] fit in, I feel like they do overcompensate. And they feel like they have to try extra hard, or come across extra hard just to be on the same level, or get the same level of respect. I feel like I was probably over-compensating a bit.

Alex suggests that 'mixed-race boys' may engage in hypermasculine performances as they seek to speak back to and renegotiate the boundaries of Black male peer groups. Toughness, or acting 'extra hard', is seen as a form of social capital that can counter the predominance of dark skin authenticity. In such cases, Black mixed-race men engage in hybridities-of-the-everyday that reconstitute them as *an-other tough Black man who is also light skin* whilst also showing themselves to be *different from the effeminate light skin same*. Alex's claim of over-compensatory behaviour reiterates findings from existing research (Tikly et al., 2004) and popular stereotypes. However, if we take seriously the suggestion that Black peer groups are regulated by a *mythical* norm (Harris & Khanna, 2010), a case I make in Chapter 6, then it becomes conceivable that almost all group members are striving to perform an identity that very few (if any) people actually possess. Alex (UK) felt it important to close this discussion by reasserting the following:

> ... there's less of that on the white side cos again, on the white side, if you're not white then you're Black. So, the same stereotypes attributed to Black boys, I found attributed to me.

Under the white gaze, Blackness is undifferentiated (Tate, 2005). For Alex, as a Black mixed-race man, it is necessary to have a sense of multiple consciousness. Whilst many of the men did, at times, perform toughness and manipulate the Black monster, this was far from always the case. Many of the men oftentimes actively sought to distance themselves from the Black monster.

Distancing One's Self from the Black Monster: Troubling Toughness and Fighting

As useful as the Black monster stereotype can be Black mixed-race men were also agentic in their rejection of that stereotype. Indeed, the men engaged in reflection that showed them unwilling to engage in 'uncritical acceptance of narrow life scripts' (hooks, 2004, p. 86). Rejecting the imposition of the Black monster stereotype involves a degree of double consciousness. This was demonstrated by Carl (USA) who suggested,

> If you don't know me and I waked down a hall way, you're going on the other side. Know what I mean? You're frightened a little bit. If it's in an alley way, you're

really scared if I'm walking down there with you. Know what I mean? But if it's a girl, no-one is afraid of a girl. No-one sees them as a threat.

Carl's account is strikingly reminiscent of George Yancy's (2017), particularly that which he terms 'the elevator effect'. Just like Yancy (2017), Carl describes the ways in which the white gaze overdetermines him in ways he knows to be untrue. Carl (USA) makes clear that his interpellation as a monstrous threat is particular to the intersection of race and gender: 'no-one is afraid of a girl'. Whist Carl is certainly conscious of the Black monster, he is 'capable of resisting the white gaze's entry into [his] own self-vision' (Yancy, 2008, p. 5). To know you're not the Black monster is one thing (double consciousness) but to engage in performances to distance yourself from that stereotype is something more (hybridity-of-the-everyday). These are elements of Black mixed-race men's PRR: *the ability of one's sense of self to remain in or spring back into shape, amidst threats that are deniable: elasticity.* Alex (UK) speaks to the second phase here:

> I feel like sometimes I accommodate for these people and their ignorance. Like if I see someone kind of suspicious of me, maybe my body language will change. I'll try and come across more-gentle and maybe be softer in the way that I speak, and things like that.

The reader might recall that earlier Alex spoke about adapting his performance within Black male peer groups. In that scenario, he spoke about acting 'extra hard'. Here, he speaks of the opposite: he attempts to 'come across more-gentle' and 'softer'. These 'acts of self-censorship' emerge out of a sense of double consciousness that rejects the 'postracial'. Alex's actions are indicative of a sense of agency, an awareness that he might manipulate his interpellation. As he attempts to distance himself from the Black monster, as Yancy (2008, p. 15) puts it, he pays 'almost neurotic attention to [his] body movements' to ensure he is 'not too tall, not too threatening'. This is reminiscent of Coates' (2015, p. 107–108) words to his son: 'my wish for you is that you feel no need to constrict yourself to make other people comfortable'. Coates is wishing for a transformation of the white supremacist conditions that mean Black men must always be conscious of the ways in which their bodies are read. However, whilst we struggle for these conditions, he will no doubt hope that his son shows the consciousness that keeps

Black men alive. Whilst the successes of Alex's attempts to distance himself from the Black monster may always be constrained by the pre-marking of his Black body, this is Alex's attempt to speak back to anti-Black discourses and position himself as different from the *Black-monster-same*. However, one might quite rightly ask the following question: rather than disrupting that discourse, do men like Alex in fact 'reinforce the prevailing racist imaginary while attempting to distance' themselves (Yancy, 2008, p. 17)?

Positioning himself as somebody who rejects those norms, Jamal (UK) spoke critically of the gendered expectations facing young men,

> I think boys are probably more likely to have a sense of macho bravado and try and be thick skinned about it, whilst it burns inside. Whereas girls, without generalizing, often vocalize their discomforts and will tackle the problem head on ... for boys I think it sinks in and just fuel their aggression, and they are more likely to retort similar things back, adding more vigour and thrust to the pre-existing banter/bullying culture. (Jamal, UK)

Alongside the accounts that preceded them, Jamal and Jake's accounts really underline the heterogeneity of Black mixed-race men's experiences and the utilisation of PRR. Whilst toughness and thick skin are so valued by many (Alexander, 1996), Jamal suggests those characteristics can have negative repercussions; 'it burns inside'. For Jamal, as they vocalise their concerns, feminine girls are able to avoid holding onto negative emotions. Conversely, the 'macho bravado' of masculine boys means the emotional suppression 'fuels aggression'. This aggression, Jamal suggests, feeds back into a dialectic loop between the individual and the wider peer group. Whilst group norms encourage the individual to produce a masculine performance that masculine performance validates and reaffirms the masculine contours of that group (Pascoe, 2011). What is interesting in Jamal's account is the way he is able to identify these processes and then speak back. He is able to cultivate the PRR required to resist the pitfalls of *toxic masculinity* (Kupers, 2005).

In the USA, Reggie spoke more explicitly about his efforts to distance himself from what he saw as the problematic masculine culture he was surrounded by,

> I took karate when I was younger ... I started finding other ways to release aggression, rather than going into

violence and falling into traps like that. You know, reading and writing. Writing my feelings down. I started to do things like that, that I think were better, they were better outlets for me than what I could have gone in to, which would have been very easy. But I found other outlets for me to overcome that. And then finally just simply growing up helped me just get over it once and for all.

In this account, Reggie (USA) appears to share the sentiment of Jamal's inference: the suppression of emotions has the potential to be damaging. Therefore, Reggie's aggression is not supressed but channelled in a productive way. Rather than engaging in acts of violence that might see him fall 'into traps', he takes up karate in order to 'release aggression'. Rather than suppressing his feelings (Majors & Billson, 1993), he engages them through reading and writing. This, for Reggie, sits in stark contrast to what he 'could have gone in to'. That it would have been 'very easy' for him to engage in other forms of violence, aggression and masculinity speaks to the toxicity of masculine culture. His ability to identify and reject those norms speaks to Reggie's PRR: his identity and sense of self remains intact despite the threats posed by gender norms. The reader may recall that earlier in this chapter, Reggie spoke about a masculine culture of 'not snitching', it is apparent that Reggie simultaneously adheres to and subverts this masculine peer culture.

Another informant who troubled pressures to be hypermasculine was Derrick (USA). Derrick shared Jamal and Reggie's sentiments that emotions should not be supressed,

I had a really interesting experience with masculinity and gender. So, I felt like I didn't need to be the typical male and like I need to be better than everyone and stronger and all this stuff. I didn't feel like I need to do that because I was raised by my Mum and she always taught me like yeah, emotions are okay. Like if you have emotions show them. The more you bottle them up, the worse they are gonna get, and to talk about things and you need to be yourself. If you're trying to affect somebody else, you're tryna affect this macho guy when you're just this small little guy, you're gonna need to do that ...

Earlier, accounts from Leon (UK), Theo (UK) and Will (USA) showed how masculine toughness was a form of cultural capital often cultivated in the family. In this account, Derrick shows us that counter-hegemonic forms of masculinity can be formed in the family and can also have real benefits for Black mixed-race men. We see again, a sense that emotions should be shown rather than supressed ('emotions are okay'; 'the more you bottle them up, the worse they are gonna get'). Whilst masculine toughness might encourage emotional stoicism, these men find ways to resist and subvert those pressures. Rather than trying to affect the Black monster, Derrick suggests that 'you need to be yourself'. Recall the definition of PRR, we might read the act of being one's self as a *remaining in shape*. Of course, to be 'one's self' requires a sense of double consciousness and the PRR to maintain a positive view of the self. Erik (USA) showed both of these characteristics,

> I mean at most you give somebody a black eye. You strike fear in them for maybe a week or two. But A, they're the majority. B, you're not beating the racism out of them, you're just furthering their point that you're violent and easily moved towards that action ... it doesn't solve anything; you're not gonna change somebody's way of thought.

Earlier in the chapter, I showed how fighting can have utility for Black mixed-race men. However, in his account, Erik makes clear the value in *not* fighting. Erik is aware of the ubiquitous presence of the Black monster and this impacts upon his response to experiencing inter-personal racism. If he were to respond with violence, he argues, he would only validate his interpellation as the Black monster who is 'violent'. Whilst Erik's response differs to some earlier responses, in all of the accounts we see awareness of the white gaze, and, whether through rejection or manipulation, agentic responses.

The following account from Shaun (UK) not only demonstrates this agency but shows how Black mixed-race men's decisions are situational, contextual and can change over the life course:

> When I was younger yeah, they definitely encouraged it like, to fight back ... if somebody calls you that he'd definitely encourage me to fight back ... But now that I'm older they're like you need to be careful cos like police can get involved and things like that. So, you need to be smarter about it cos then it's affecting your life and career.

As in several of the preceding accounts, Shaun highlights the role that family plays in Black mixed-race men's cultivation of PRR (Joseph-Salisbury, 2018a). For Shaun and his parents, in his early life 'to fight back' is a useful response to racism. As has been argued – for Black mixed-race men this response, perhaps the ultimate performance of Black masculine toughness – can offer protection from future racisms. As Shaun gets older, however, his guidance changes. That is, he and his parents are increasingly aware of the ways in which he might be constructed as the Black monster, and the danger such an interpellation brings about: the spectre of a racist police force means that Shaun must be 'smarter about it'. Long and Joseph-Salisbury (2018) have shown that this is a sense widely held among Black mixed-race men. Again, this awareness is demonstrative of a rejection of 'post-racial' ideology. This rejection is the springboard that allows Shaun (UK), with the support of his parents, to cultivate the PRR to resist being torn asunder.

Conclusion

This chapter has shown the complex and multiplicitous ways in which Black mixed-race men constitute and negotiate racialised masculinities. Variously, Black mixed-race men manipulate, modify and reject intersectional discourses of race, gender and sexuality. In this chapter, Black mixed-race men show they are not only aware of negative stereotypes of Black masculinity but that they are unwilling to be rendered docile by those discourses: this requires PRR.

Building on Butler's claim that masculinities are cultivated across a heterosexual matrix enabled me to show the ways in which Black mixed-race men's ability to elicit the sexual attraction of white women constitutes a source of cultural capital, which extends to homosociality and manifests as a key component in many of the men's PRR. Whilst Black men evoke 'fear and admiration', for some Black mixed-race men, some of the time, I argue, light skin or mixedness means they are less fearsome and more admirable. That is, they are scary but not too scary. Given the pervading sense that the white gaze sees Blackness as undifferentiated, this is a claim I make tentatively. The account of Trent also showed that for gay Black mixed-race men, heterosexuality interacts with race in complex and interesting ways. Whilst Blackness protected him from homophobic bullying, Trent argued, his sexuality threatened to undermine his Black authenticity. Nevertheless, like Jake

(UK), Trent engaged in processes of hybridity that saw him refuse erasure and fragmentation.

In this chapter, I showed the irony in which the spectre of the Black monster can act to endanger Black mixed-race men. As the white gazer seeks to control the Black monster, Black mixed-race men respond in a variety of ways. Some men use that stereotype as a source of protection from bullying and racism and even for homosocial popularity. Thus, even the Black monster can become part of Black mixed-race men's PRR arsenal. Oftentimes, I argued, Black mixed-race men find themselves imbricated in masculine peer cultures that encourage performances of toughness. In these cultures, that monster stereotype is a source of capital. Whilst the performance of toughness is often enough to protect Black mixed-race men, in very few cases, Black mixed-race men reported being moved to fight. This, the ultimate display of masculine toughness, was understood to warn white interlocutors against future racisms and constituted another component in some men's PRR. Offering another warning against the homogenisation of Black masculinities, some of the men's accounts suggested that light skin meant they were susceptible to being positioned as soft, effeminate and less masculine. For a few of the men, this had implications for their positionality within the Black male peer group. It is worth reiterating that although significant, this should be understood in a context in which Black peer groups are governed along multiple lines: mixedness and light skin sit alongside class (Harris & Khanna, 2010), ancestry, sexuality and others, as determinants of one's proximity to the mythical norm of Blackness.

Finally, having shown how many Black mixed-race men manipulate the stereotype of the Black monster, I show that there are many occasions in which the men reject that stereotype and engage in identity work (Khanna, 2011a) to distance themselves from that. As I show Black mixed-race men, again, to be doubly conscious and agentic, it is clear that Black mixed-race men cultivate high levels of PRR at the intersection of race and gender. In the next chapter, let us turn to see how this PRR is enacted through racial symbolism.

Chapter 3

Racial Symbolism and the Stylization of Identities: Dress, Speech, Hair and Music

Introduction

Building upon earlier theorisations of performativity, hybridity and PRR, in this chapter, I delve deeper into the minutiae of Black mixed-race men's performative identities. My understanding that identities are negotiated at the quotidian level (Tate, 2005) leads me to consider the ways in which stylization is communicative. Mercer (2004, p. 8) observes that 'meanings are encoded by stylistic choices'. Thus, these choices become sites for the 'self-crafting that takes place in the context of norms' (Butler, 2005, p. 22). In a white supremacist society, it follows that those meanings and norms are always racialised. Thus, self-crafting is always tied up with race and racialisation. In this chapter, I consider the ways in which Black mixed-race men's race and gender identities are constructed and contested through stylistic choices.

In her study of Black cultural capital, Prudence Carter (2003, 2005) finds that dress, speech, hair and music are integral to racialised identities generally and Black racialised identities particularly. In the accounts of the Black mixed-race men in this study, those same themes emerged as key sites of stylization for Black mixed-race men (also see, Carter, 2005; Warikoo, 2011). Thus, it is these forms of presentation that I interrogate in this chapter. As dress, speech, hair and music each contribute to the ways in which a person performs and negotiates race (and racial meaning), they are perhaps best thought of as racial symbols (Khanna, 2011b). In this chapter, I argue that racial symbols are material of everyday components in Black mixed-race men's PRR.

Showing Black youth to skilfully switch between what she calls 'dominant' and 'non-dominant' forms of cultural capital, Carter's work (2003, 2005) troubles the problematic assumption that cultural capital pertains only to the white middle-classes. As I show the ways in which Black mixed-race men switch between diverse and complex cultural repertoires, I bring Carter's work on cultural capital into conversation with the concept of racial symbolism. Whilst racial symbolism may enhance Black mixed-race men's cultural capital and therefore their

PRR, the racial governmentalities (Foucault, 1991) that surround each of those areas of symbolism may pose a real threat to that PRR. Before we return to the accounts of the Black mixed-race men, let me first set out specifically what I invoke through the concept of racial symbolism.

Racial Symbolism

Writing of racially minoritised groups in the USA, Herbert Gans (1979) has argued that symbolism is a fundamental way through which ethnic identities are performed and maintained. For Gans, practices like 'dressing in ethnic clothing' can be demonstrative of ethnicity (Khanna, 2011a, 2011b, p. 1049): this is *symbolic ethnicity* or *ethnic symbolism*. However, the inextricable binding of discourses of race, ethnicity and culture mean that such symbols are not only demonstrative of ethnicity but also of race. By way of example, think of the Black British embrace of the symbols of Rastafari. This symbolism is not only demonstrative of Black ethnicity but of culture and of race (Chambers, 2016): for many, to be Rasta is to be Black ethnically, culturally, racially and spiritually. To display the symbols of Rastafari is to perform one's Blackness with pride.

Drawing upon Gans (1979), Nikki Khanna (2011b) invokes *racial symbolism* to describe the ways in which 'black-white biracial adults' draw upon symbols to negotiate their identities. According to Khanna (2011b, p. 1060), having historically been interpellated as Black, her Black mixed-race participants drew upon what they perceived to be 'symbols of whiteness' in order to resist the ascription of mono-raciality and position themselves as 'biracial'.

In this chapter, I build upon the work of Gans and Khanna in the following ways. Whilst Gans' seems to only see ethnic symbols as very obvious and deliberate ethnocultural symbols that are adopted intentionally, I suggest a much wider array of symbols are imbued with racial, ethnic and cultural meanings (Pitcher, 2014). Whilst agreeing with the general thrust of Khanna's (2011b) argument – that symbols are used to negotiate racial and ethnic identities – I show that Black mixed-race men's use of racial symbolism is far more diverse and fluid than simply using symbols of whiteness to perform mixedness. I show that Black mixed-race men's double consciousness is demonstrable again, this time in the context of racial symbolism. Put another way, I show that Black mixed-race men are acutely aware of the ways in which symbols can be racialised under the white gaze. As the men reject, utilise and manipulate symbols, I show that Black mixed-race men engage in hybridity-of-the-everyday, at the quotidian level of racial symbolism. In so doing, I join Khanna (2011b) in challenging the axiom that unlike whites, Black people – in this case Black mixed-race men – have few, if any, ethnic and racial identity options (Tuan, 1998; Waters, 1990). Black mixed-race men's stylization through racial symbolism is perhaps 'best understood as an act of aesthetic agency' (Mercer, 2004, p. 8). This aesthetic agency can and does bolster Black mixed-race men's PRR. I will begin with dress, before discussing speech, hair and music in turn.

Dress: 'Oh You Suit Every Colour Clothes; You're Mixed-Race'

According to Fred Davis (1994, p. 25) dress 'comes to easily serve as a kind of visual metaphor for identity'. Just as costumes are an integral part of a theatrical performance, dress plays an integral role in the performance, negotiation and interpretation of identities (Butler, 1990; Tate, 2005). In the theatre, if one tries to perform the role of an angel whilst wearing the costume of a devil, there will be confusion, misunderstanding, perhaps even comedy. The audience will be uncertain of the character. On the other hand, if one wishes to play the role of an angel, to don a costume typically associated with angels, would be a key step towards a successful performance. Whilst in the theatre costumes can communicate the role of an actor, in the social world dress can communicate one's identity: dress is a means of 'dialogue with society' (Tulloch, 2004, p. 18). Finkelstein (1991, p. 128) makes this point,

> When we encounter a stranger as initially mysterious and inaccessible, we refer to clothing styles and physical appearance, in the absence of any other means, as a reliable sign of identity. Clothing is frequently seen as symbolic of the individuals' status and morality, whether actual or contrived.

The mention of physical appearance is important in Finkelstein's observation. That mention points to the way phenotype serves as an identity marker that takes primacy over dress, at least for those bodies marked as non-white (Waters, 1990). So, whilst Finkelstein (1991) is right to suggest that 'clothing styles' are 'symbolic' when a 'stranger' is 'inaccessible', the white gaze does not see Black mixed-race men as inaccessible. Pervasive stereotypes of Black masculinity mean that Black mixed-race men are always already known; not as themselves but as the Black monster (Yancy, 2017). This is what is captured when Yancy (2008, p. 4) reflects upon his own interpellation under the white gaze: 'over and above how my body is clothed, she "sees" a criminal, she sees a threat'.

To say that dress is a subjugate of phenotypical body markers, how-ever, is not to say that dress is insignificant in the performance of Black mixed-race men's identities. Whilst claims of 'not seeing race' abound in 'post-racial' contexts, dress continues to serve as a metaphor for the unspeakable: race. Think of the (un)popular imagined figure of the hoodie and the way that garment takes on a life of its own. The hoodie turns from garment to character: a racialised character. He is not white, he is Black. He is a young Black man. He is a young working-class Black man. He is a Black monster who must be controlled. He is Trayvon Martin. He *was* Trayvon Martin.

It is indicative of the ways in which dress is racialised that, in the aftermath of his death, commentators have wondered, 'should Martin have known better than to wear a hoodie in an affluent, white neigh-bourhood?' (Boyles, 2015, p. 6; Coates, 2015). Under the white gaze of Zimmerman, the racialised hoodie garment combined with Martin's pre-marked Black masculine body to project the phantasm of the Black monster (Yancy, 2017). Whilst dress does not supersede phenotype (Waters, 1990), dress and phenotype can and do interact to complicate the ways in which Black mixed-race men are read (Mercer, 2004). As Tulloch (2004, p. 11) has argued, there is interaction between the 'black body and how it is dressed'. In the previous chapters, I showed that Black mixed-race men are – wittingly or unwittingly – able to play-up or play-down their proximity to the Black monster: the racial symbolism of dress is a material factor that facilitates this manipulation. To be clear, my contention here is this: *Black mixed-race men are active agents who ceaselessly negotiate positionalities and racial meanings through the symbolism of dress.*

The ways in which dress is racialised, as well as the ways in which racialised subjects are conscious of this racialisation, is evident in this following account from Freitas et al.'s (1997, p. 331) research. The inter-viewee is an African American man. We join him as he reflects upon the decisions he makes in relation to dress and race,

> I am not going to dress white. Even if I could afford to dress white, I am still not going to dress white. Afro

American culture is who and what I identify with. I don't want to identify with white culture. When I do have to do it, I want to do it as little as possible, as far as jobs [are concerned] ... I am certainly not going to conform to white norms.

In this account, we see clearly the ways in which dress is understood to be racialised. For the interviewee, there is a way to 'dress white' that is mediated by racialised 'white norms'. The inextricable links between race and culture are apparent too: as to 'dress white' is to 'identify with white culture'. Through the ancillary of culture, dress-style becomes expressive and constitutive of race: racial symbolism. The interviewee does not want to identify with 'white culture' so he does not 'conform to white norms' by 'dressing white'. Pride was a key theme in preceding chapters, and we can see this again here. The interviewee is proud of his 'Afro American culture' and he demonstrates this pride through racial symbolism. To recall the language of the definitions given in the introduction, this interviewee shows his sense of identity remains intact. This is both supported by and supportive of his PRR.

There is also a clear association between race and class in the interviewee's account. To 'dress white' is something that he might not be able to afford, and thus, performing whiteness requires economic capital. The white supremacist logic underpinning this argument is clear: to be white is not to be poor, to be Black is to be poor (Collins, 2004). The hegemony of whiteness is apparent as the interviewee acknowledges that dressing white is something he will 'have to do'. In a white supremacist, capitalist and classist society, the inference is that one must 'dress white' to gain employment. Put another way, to gain employment, one must distance themselves from the Black monster stereotype through the symbolism of dress. To understand the ways in which dress is imbued with race and class meanings, and to utilise it accordingly, is a component in Black mixed-race men's PRR. Again, to reuse the language of the PRR definitions, the manipulation of one's dress is a response to 'racist and racialised difficulties' of unemployment.

This interplay between race, class and dress was prevalent for many of the men in the current research, one of whom was Carl (USA). Here Carl reflects on the interaction between phenotype and dress,

If you wear sweatpants and a tee-shirt, if you're Black, you're a hoodlum. Wear sweatpants and a tee-shirt and you're white, you're a ball player, you play sports. That's

> why you're wearing them, that or it's a lazy day for you.
> Black people, you're a hoodlum, you come from slums,
> know what I mean?

The logics of white supremacy and social class status are at the heart of Carl's reflection: clothing is imbued with racial connotations (Pitcher, 2014). White privilege means that those racialised as white can wear 'sweatpants and a tee-shirt' and be read as a sports player. Whilst if a Black person does the same, they are a 'hoodlum', perhaps even the Black monster. *I can wear sweatpants without being considered a hoodlum* could easily be added to Peggy McIntosh's (1990) seminal list of white privileges. As a respondent put it to Kaiser, Rabine, and Hall (2004, p. 50), 'white male style can be a lot more varied because I think they don't have to portray themselves in certain ways to get the respect of others'.

Lexicologically, hoodlum is a revealing choice of word: that word is synonymous with pathological representations of Black masculinity: criminality, violence and gangster culture (Davis, 2003; Lopez, 2003; Yancy, 2017). There is also perhaps a class element to hoodlum, and the intersection between race and class is reiterated as Carl suggests that, under the white gaze, a Black person wearing those clothes is understood to 'come from slums'.

Carl's double consciousness is apparent as he attests to the notion that, 'a sort of black male code permeates black culture, a code aimed at preventing black men from seeming suspicious' (Boyles, 2015, p. 6). This consciousness is set against the backdrop of the murder of hoodie wearing Trayvon Martin; a sure contributor to the aforementioned episteme of Blackness that so many Black mixed-race men demonstrate (Yancy, 2017). Carl shows us that this consciousness persists despite the obfuscating impact of the 'post-racial'. He continues to explain how this consciousness informs his dress,

> … so, like I have to, every time I'm in my discussion group
> I wear a polo, I wear my khakis or my Nike shoes, you
> know? I walk in cos that first interaction with them makes
> the world of difference. (Carl, USA)

Carl's account shows that through the racial symbolism of dress, Black mixed-race men can manipulate their proximity to the Black monster. As Carl adopts what he perhaps perceives as respectable transracial smart casual dress, Carl seeks to negotiate his racialised positionality. This is not Carl disassociating with Blackness but his attempt to show himself to be *an-other Black*: a respectable Black. Kaiser et al. (2004) have persuasively shown how the concept of respect has been at the centre of African American dress and stylization: the cultivation of respectability through the presentation of self has been a site of African American resistance. Through racial symbolism, this is a show of defiance: a performative demonstration that one's identity remains intact despite threats of erasure. Not only this, but to a certain extent, to dress respectably is to reduce one's chances of encountering racist and racialised difficulties. Perhaps this is Carl's resistance too: hybridity-of-the-everyday through racial symbolism. The ability to utilise dress to manipulate his interpellation is a component in Carl's PRR. Of course, it is possible that as Carl distances himself from the Black monster hoodie – perhaps positioning himself as a 'good Black' or exceptional Black – he in fact reinforces the phantasm (Yancy, 2017).

There is evidence to validate Carl's perception. Psychological experimental research using Black-white morph continua has shown that 'low-status attire increased the likelihood of categorization as Black' (Freeman et al., 2011; also see, McDermott & Pettijohn, 2011). This finding supports Carl's sense that dress is important and also the chapter's argument more broadly: *although somewhat secondary to phenotype, racial symbolism, enacted here through dress, impacts upon how Black mixed-race men are perceived* (Freeman, Penner, Saperstein, Scheutz, & Ambady, 2011). It is perhaps unsurprising that people purposely select different types of clothing to wear in different social contexts' (McDermott & Pettijohn, 2011, p. 65): there is certainly evidence to suggest that those choices are successful (Bardack & McAndrew, 1985; Morris, Gorham, Cohen, & Huffman, 1996). What is perhaps occluded from those popular understandings, however, is the ways in which these processes and decisions are racialised.

Reflecting on the way his image is distorted under the white gaze, Reggie (USA) also makes reference to dress as a key component in his interpellation,

> You know they see my hat backwards. They think I'm a thug and I listen to a certain type of music. So, I'm this type of person. Like I wear hats [baseball caps] all the time because I had an accident when I was little and I have stitches so I don't like to not wear hats a lot but that's why I wear hats. But like people, that's one little thing

that they always pick apart and they're like 'okay, we'll write him off. He's this type'. And I'm like, 'no, get to know me'. I'm actually a very intelligent young man. It's just I have a certain trend of fashion that I like to do for my own personal reasons.

For Reggie, wearing a 'hat backwards' sees him interpellated as 'a thug' under the white gaze ('they'). Thug is a raced and gendered term meaning 'thief' or 'swindler' (Ellis, 2011), and so it emerges from the same discourse as the 'hoodlum' in Carl's account. These are labels for the Black monster. As he invokes the white gaze, Reggie suggests that a thug listens to certain types of music. Thus, we see an association between the racial symbolism of dress and music. 'Thug' music is often invoked to describe the music of the 1990s hip-hop/'gangsta rap' scene. One need only look to the 'Thug Life' tattoo emblazoned across Tupac Shakur's chest to demonstrate this. Perhaps we can assume that Reggie believes he is associated with gangsta rap (Garber, 2015). Dress and music become wrapped up in the racial tropes of 'thug', 'gangsta' and 'hoodlum'.

It is the conspicuous presence of Reggie's Blackness, manifest through phenotype and exacerbated by his hat, that leads Reggie to conclude he may be interpellated through anti-Black stereotypes: 'he's this type'. Reggie expresses great frustration at the ways in which the white gaze threatens him with erasure. Reggie continues to explain what he sees as the penalties of being Black in a white supremacist society: 'I'm already at sort of a disadvantage in terms of like where I can go and what I can do'. This statement could certainly be extended to include 'what I can wear'. As Yancy (2008, p. 26) might put it, even before he is dressed, the white gaze reduces Reggie to a 'pre-marked Black *thing*' (original emphasis), his 'dark body occludes the presumption of innocence' (2008, p. 4). This erasure is a source of frustration for Reggie. He speaks back to this as he implores his interlocutor to look beyond the phantasm: 'no, get to know me'. Implicitly acknowledging the way in which the white gaze equates Blackness with a lack of intelligence, Reggie speaks back: he is 'actually a very intelligent young man'. As he identifies and rejects the threat of the white gaze, Reggie demonstrates the PRR that allows him to produce a positive and defiant self-conception.

Dress is not race-neutral: this is what Reggie *tells us* in his account. Double consciousness is evident in consideration of dress: this is what Reggie *shows us* in his account. Reggie's observations are certainly well founded. In specific relation to the context of schooling, Ladson Billings (2011, p. 13) argues that disciplinary challenges to the seemingly arbitrary infractions of hat wearing and pant sagging are 'especially targeted at Black boys as a method of control'. This is a reiteration of the claim I made in the previous chapter: *Under the white gaze, the Black monster must be controlled.* Carl (USA) experienced school controls in relation to race and dress, he recalled: 'if I didn't sag, as long as I didn't sag, I was fine. But the minute I sagged, then I'm just with all the other Blacks'. Carl suggests that dress allows him some flexibility in terms of how he is interpellated. If he avoids pant sagging, he is different from the Black monster. This is Carl's hybridity-of-the-everyday. It is conceivable that Carl's ability to distance himself from that stereotype has tangible benefits for his schooling: thus, this can be understood as a component in his PRR. Whether actually challenging anti-Black stereotypes or not, perhaps Carl's ability to distance himself through dress is accentuated by his mixedness or light skin. This was certainly the inference as one participant recalled being told 'oh, you suit every colour clothes; you're mixed-race'. That mixedness and/or light skin engendered greater flexibility for using racial symbolism was not a view that was widely held but is nevertheless worthy of a mention here.

An awareness that dress might serve as a tool to impact one's interpellation was evident on both sides of the Atlantic. This is not surprising given the Transatlanticity of so many forms of Black stylization and symbolism (Tulloch, 2004). In the following account, we join the conversation as Anton and I have just discussed his clothing on the day we met. Along with his long dreads, he wore a jacket that boldly displayed the flag of Rastafari:

> I think the outward performance [of Rastafari] helped me a lot, helped me in a lot of ways cos this says like yeah, I'm proud of who I am, this is where I'm from, this is my culture kind of thing.

For Anton, clothing offers an avenue for the assertion of Blackness and Black pride (Khanna & Johnson, 2010; Pitcher, 2014). Throughout the interview, Anton expressed a strong identification with Rastafari. This was evident not only through speech acts but also through the racial symbolism of his hair and clothes (Gans, 1979; Khanna, 2011b). With religious tenets prophesising a Black messiah, and political tenets that condemn Babylon and emphasise Black empowerment, for Anton, Rastafari offers a positive discourse of Blackness. Notice the recurrence of the theme of pride: Anton's sense of pride is defiant, it speaks back to the logic of white supremacy, and, in part, it does so through the racial symbolism of dress. Anton is not a victim of degradation but a proud Black Rastafarian: as it locates him racially, spatially and culturally; racial symbolism demands that he is interpellated as such. This is Anton's PRR. Anton's account reflects a long lineage of Black Britons finding pride and belonging in Rastafari. According to Chambers (2016), identification with Rastafari has been far more central to Black British experiences than it is to the experiences of their African American counterparts. Of course, that is not to say African Americans have not also found positive discourses through which to express pride in Blackness (Lamont et al., 2013). As hooks (1990, p. 217) has noted, clothing functions in black experience 'to express resistance and/or conformity'.

For some men, the failure to dress in accordance with the way in which one's body is racialised was interpreted as a transgression of the boundaries erected through racial governmentality. Jermaine (USA) recalled being placed under racial surveillance as he was asked 'oh why aren't you wearing Jordans? Why are you wearing these shoes?'. According to his interlocutor, Jermaine's Black body dictated which shoes, which racial symbols he could adopt. Once again, we see how clothes are deeply imbued with racial connotations and meaning (Mercer, 2004; Tulloch, 2004).

Dress was not only about one's relationship to the white gaze, however. Dress also acted as a key component in the negotiation of Black peer group positionalities. As I suggested in the previous chapter, the governmentality of Black peer groups can be mediated by myriad factors: skin colour, knowledge of Black history, ancestry, race consciousness and social class were among the factors highlighted. These factors enabled Black mixed-race men to challenge the axiom of dark skin equalling Black authenticity. This is perhaps extendable to dress and clothing. As Harris and Khanna (2010, p. 658) observed in their study: by wearing clothing that was perceived by others to be Black, 'some biracial respondents worked hard to signal their black identity to others'. Whilst that study went on to highlight similar pressures impacting upon mono-racial Black middle-class respondents, and other studies have shown mono-racial Black participants to face those pressures (Carter, 2003, 2005; Warikoo, 2011), the case remains that dress and clothing are deemed impactful on the ways in which racialised identities are negotiated.

Elliot – a participant in my previous research (Joseph-Salisbury, 2013) – conveyed the ways in which Black mixed-race men draw upon dress in the performance of their identities,

> I bought some stupid clothes and made a show of myself on a few occasions, just trying to fit in and going for an image, but after a certain amount of time, you actually do pick it up.

Elliot describes his conscious efforts to validate his Blackness to his Black peer group, he attempts to do so through the racial symbolism of dress. We might interpret Elliot's confession to having 'made a show' of himself 'on a few occasions' as his acknowledgement of an unsuccessful performance (Butler, 1990). As Elliot argues 'you actually do pick it up', he shows us that the ability to use racial symbolism successfully is something that is developed over time, through the practice of social interaction. Elliot's experiences are perhaps unsurprising in a context where 'Black style' is characterised by 'complexities' and 'ongoing redefinition' (Tulloch, 2004, p. 11). Whilst many Black mixed-race men's use of racial symbolism is less self-conscious, as Claire Alexander (1996) might put it, Elliot shows there is *an art to being Black*.

In the following account, Isaac (USA) speaks of wishing he had come to know his Blackness earlier in life. He extrapolates how this manifests in clothing practices,

> My clothes wouldn't coordinate with each other. Whatever I wore was what I was wearing, and now I've learned to have a sense of style [...] put that with that and then contrast it with that. Yeah, I could wear that maybe. Maybe I could talk to a couple of girls in that. There we go, perfect. I got in touch with my African American side. (Isaac, USA)

Isaac appears to draw upon stereotypes of African Americans having a 'sense of style'. In so doing, he argues it was not until he 'got in touch with' his 'African American side' that he was able to display style and choose clothes 'that coordinate with each other'. According to Isaac, Blackness is something to be learnt and the ability to utilise racial symbolism is a component in his learning to perform Blackness. This is reiterative of a respondent in Kaiser et al.'s (2004, p. 51) research who argues 'Afro-American culture is a very rich one, and it comes out in how we dress ... dressing nicely, dressing with style'. The intersections of race, gender and sexuality are apparent in Isaac's account (Kaiser et al., 2004). Once Isaac learns to dress stylishly – apparently a consequence of his being in touch with his African American side – he 'could talk to a couple of girls'. Isaac reaffirms the assertion of the previous chapter: Black mixed-race men's identities are cultivated across a heterosexual matrix. We now see how dress particularly, and racial symbolism generally, are thoroughly implicated in the cultivation of Black mixed-race men's race and gender identities. That is, *clothing practices are impacted upon by discourses of race and gender, and discourses of race and gender are impacted upon by clothing practices.* Racial symbolism enhances Isaac's ability to access the cultural capital that comes from 'getting girls'. Thus, the ability to utilise the racial symbolism of dress gives cultural capital and strengthens Isaac's PRR.

Quoted at length in the following account, Tayo demonstrates the way in which clothing becomes racialised,

> Blackness is something important, okay? It's something really valuable. Really special to me and it's something that's under fire constantly and it's something that's appropriated, culturally. It's culturally appropriated. It's profited from. It's bastardized. It's destroyed. It's under target. So, these things, you know like, these things, Blackness it's such an interesting topic because it's everywhere but it's nowhere but it has so much value but so little value at the same time in the sense that Black culture is everywhere. Black people are everywhere. Black culture is like, I don't know, for an example du rags, you know what du rags are, right? So, like, like they'll have du-rags and that's looked at as like a Black thing and then a company like Chanel will take them and like turn them into like urban tie caps. So, this like culturally significant thing that's like looked upon a certain way or like, okay you know, it's given a certain connotation because of its Blackness. It's then taken, reinvented and they put them on white models and they're acceptable.

Tayo opens up this account by articulating a positive sense of Blackness: it is something 'really important', 'special' and 'really valuable'. These assertions are antithetical to white supremacist hegemony. This is, Tayo speaking back. In a 'post-racial' context, this is a speaking back to a threat that is obfuscated and always already denied. To understand that Blackness 'is constantly under fire', to resist those threats and speak back with positive definitions of Blackness, is demonstrative of Tayo's 'post-racial' resilience.

Tayo's account demonstrates his sense that certain types of dress are metonymic for Blackness. This is the message invoked as he suggests it is 'culturally appropriated'. It is not just clothes that are appropriated, but, through clothes, Blackness itself. It is through the racial symbolism of dress that, according to Tayo, Blackness is 'bastardized [and] destroyed'. Tayo continues to highlight some of the apparent contradictions of Blackness: that Blackness is simultaneously a site of admiration and disdain. Just as Blackness is repulsive, monstrous and threatening, it is 'exotic', fascinating and desirable (Collins, 2004; Yancy, 2017). Tayo knows all of this: this is the context in which Tayo and other Black mixed-race men negotiate their identities.

To explicate his argument more fully, Tayo draws upon the racial symbol of the du-rag. The du-rag was 'looked at as a Black thing', he argues. Through its association with Black masculinity, the du-rag is a racial symbol that has been criminalised and pathologised. This is the 'certain connotation' that Tayo refers to. Tayo argues that Chanel appropriating du-rags for 'white models' makes the garment acceptable; in so doing, he highlights the apparent double standards of white supremacy (hooks, 1992). As he does so, Tayo echoes the comments made by Carl earlier in this section. Carl suggested that sweatpants would see white people interpellated as sports players, whilst Black people would be interpellated as criminal.

Tayo's reflections on cultural appropriation parallel the analysis of bell hooks (1992, pp. 21−22) when she argues,

> Within commodity culture, ethnicity becomes spice, seasoning that can liven up the dull dish that is mainstream white culture ... bringing to the surface all those "nasty" unconscious fantasies and longings about contact with the Other embedded in the secret (not so secret) deep structure of white supremacy.

On white models, packaged by Chanel, the du-rag is not a symbol of criminality but is merely a 'spice'. It is the exotic symbol that 'can liven up the dull dish' of whiteness. Again, we see here how the pre-marking of bodies interacts with racial symbolism. According to hooks, this appropriation is indicative of 'fantasies and longings' for Blackness.

The Black monster evokes admiration and fear. Engaging with Black clothing, without truly engaging with Blackness, offers the superficial satisfaction the white appetite desires. Let us now turn to consider the way in which speech might be considered a form of racial symbolism.

Speech: 'I Can Talk White and I Can Talk Black'

As with styles of dress, participants recognised that vernacular styles of speech were bound up in discourses of race (hooks, 2014). They are, racially symbolic. Moreover, as Tulloch (2004, p. 16) has observed, stylization through dress is defined in conjunction with how one speaks. Within and through the racial symbolism of speech, Black mixed-race men recognised a degree of agency. In the USA, participants felt they were able to switch between African American vernacular and 'Standard English'. Similarly, in the UK, participants spoke of an ability to switch between Black British English and 'Standard English' (Sebba & Tate, 1986). The ability and necessity of 'code-switching' has been recognised by a number of scholars (Auer, 2013; Hall, 1993; Hewitt, 1986; Sebba, 2007; Sebba & Wooton, 1998) and has been found to be particularly salient in the school context (Carter, 2005; Warikoo, 2011). In the school, this often manifests as a balancing act between interactions with peers and teachers or a movement between peer culture and official school culture (Carter, 2003; Warikoo, 2011). Jay (USA) articulates the rationale behind his code-switching,

> Obviously understanding your audience is part of communication. So, I'm not gonna go into a business aspect or maybe where I need to talk really casual when I should be talking in a professional manner ... I'm not gonna go into a class of all white people and talk as if, talk like I'm uneducated. Not that I talk uneducated around Black people but around Black people I might, I might change, I might not, instead of saying, I don't know, I might use a little bit more slang around Black people; generally, though, because I tend to pick up their slang too.

As Jay quite rightly notes, regardless of race, 'understanding your audience is part of communication'. However, as he goes on to extrapolate, in a society that is organised along racial lines, the understanding of one's audience oftentimes involves a consideration of race. Not only does Jay's account show that speech styles can be racialised, but he also shows that, through speech, intellect becomes racialised. Jay's account seems to equate Blackness with 'uneducated' speech. For Jay, whilst that speech might be appropriate for Black audiences, it is unsuitable for his white peers. Jay seems to be caught up in the logic of racist hierarchies of intellect. This logic, perpetuated through biological, psychological and cultural mythology, has been integral to the maintenance of white supremacy (Yancy, 2017). Jay appears to recognise his imbrication in these discourses and seeks to rehabilitate his positioning ('not that I talk uneducated around Black people'). However, as he continues, Jay conflates African American vernacular with slang and invokes the popular mythology that African American vernacular is just 'a badly spoken' or mistake-ridden version of Standard (white) English (Pullum, 1999, p. 40). Thoroughly critiqued by Labov (1969) and others, this is an idea that has been used to degrade and oppress Blackness and occludes a rich history of Black linguistic resilience and resistance (Anzaldua, 1987; hooks, 2014; Pullum, 1999).

Notwithstanding his imbrication in, and perpetuation of, racist discourse, Jay shows an ability to draw upon the racial symbolism of speech to negotiate his positionality among different audiences (Goffman, 1990). As Carter (2003, p. 137) would put it, Jay recognises that 'cultural capital [as expressed through speech] is context-specific and its currency varies across different social spaces'. Through double consciousness, Jay is able to adapt his performance according to Black audiences and white audiences. The ability to do so attests to the fluid self-conceptions that enable Black mixed-race men to resist fragmentation and erasure. Recall again the definition of PRR: *elasticity*. The racial symbolism of speech becomes a form of cultural capital that enables Jay to navigate his Black peer groups, as well as white classmates, and business situations. Just as in the case of clothes, we are reminded that in a white supremacist capitalist system, business becomes coded as white. The pervasiveness of white supremacy is apparent as Jay continues to reflect upon his interactions with teachers,

> Probably because when I talk to teachers I am talking to them like I was talking, I wasn't talking to them like I was talking to my friends for the most part. I may every now and then, with some of my favourite teachers I wouldn't have a problem with slipping a cuss word in there every now and then. But generally speaking I spoke in pretty

> fluent grammar and what not. Granted all my, with the
> exception of one, all my teachers were white too.

The racial connotations as they manifest in the school context are
made clear. Through language, whiteness (Standard English) is equated
with authority (teachers), academic success and formality. Conversely,
Blackness (African American Vernacular) is equated with being uneducated and illiterate, a lack of success and a lack of authority: the degradation of Black vernacular and stereotypes of low intelligence manifest
in both the UK and the USA (Andrews, 2016). Jay code-switches in
order to 'succeed' in school. As he draws upon the racial symbolism of
speech, Jay positions himself as an-other Black who is also studious and
intellectual: this is Jay's hybridity-of-the-everyday, through speech. This
hybridity enables Jay to negate the threat of racism.

Showing clearly how the racial symbolism of speech is a Transatlantic
phenomenon, Jay's (USA) account has clear parallels with those of UK
participants, particularly Leon's,

> ... you speak to people in different ways. You speak for-
> mally and informally, and its sort of like, I can go to any-
> body and speak to them the right way, you know what I
> mean? Whereas I know how to speak to upper-class peo-
> ple, I know how to speak to people in the struggle, I know
> how to speak to middle-class people, I've had experiences
> from all different aspects of Manchester and Britain,
> which I think is a positive thing, you know?

Whilst here Leon appears to talk about social class, these comments
emerge in the context of Leon reflecting on his visiting a predominantly
Black-populated area of Manchester. Perhaps then — given the discursive association between Blackness and working-class-ness — Leon uses
class as a 'post-racial' trope to talk about race. Or, perhaps Leon perpetuates the idea that Black speech styles are symbolic of lower intelligence and lower-class status (Carter, 2003). Leon resists the hegemony
of white middle-class speech styles by recognising multiple 'right' speech
styles ('I can go to anybody and speak to them the right way'). There is
great cultural capital for Leon in his ability to code-switch; it 'is a positive thing' that bolsters his PRR (Alexander, 1996; Carter, 2003). Whilst
code-switching was widely regarded as a strength by Black mixed-race
men, many of the men simultaneously critiqued the pressures they felt
to do so. Jermaine (USA) speaks back to those pressures,

I can talk white and I can talk Black. I kind of like embrace the duality of my life; like whiteness and Blackness. But it doesn't mean anything to me like. I don't see people that talk white. I see people that talk properly, like, and there's people that talk like African American vernacular language. So, I don't look at it as an indicator for intelligence by any means.

Jermaine opens up by highlighting his ability to code-switch (Alim & Smitherman, 2012; Warikoo, 2011). In doing so, he racialises speech styles and symbolises the multiplicity of his identity. It is from this multiplicity that he cultivates PRR. There is an inference that his mixedness (constituted by 'whiteness and Blackness') allows him to draw upon both ('the duality of my life'). Jermaine goes on to attempt to challenge the associations between race, vernacular and intelligence; this is his concluding remark ('I don't look at it as an indicator for intelligence'). Demonstrating his ability to recognise the workings of white supremacy, Jermaine alludes to the discursive association between whiteness and talking 'properly' (Yancy, 2017). This is something he seeks to resist ('I don't see people that talk white. I see people that talk properly') and thus he is post-racially resilient as he refuses to be made docile by discourses of white vernacular supremacy (that are obscured by the 'post-racial'). Jermaine opens up a third space as he speaks back and positions himself as an African American who speaks 'properly'. A similar but much more vociferous critique is offered by Will (USA),

... it's funny because I speak properly and people are taken aback by it, which is something I've been dealing with my whole life. I'm like 'yo, I speak proper English, like okay'. But why does proper English equate to white English? Like why are you calling me white because I speak properly? Like, I can switch it up, [changes tone] and I can get real nigga-ish on you real quick and sound like a nigga from Baltimore. But I just, I don't do that, cos like, you know if I'm speaking to somebody I'm not gonna feel comfortable talking to somebody who doesn't understand that kind of language and just like speak in that for them. So, like people who are white don't really ever hear that cos it's not the most efficient way for me to speak like that. But that's like the only thing that kind of gets me about being Black that I'm like totally not really connected to.

In Will's account, as in those accounts that precede it, we see that even as he strives for critique, he is constrained by the hegemony of white supremacy. This is made clear early on ('I speak properly') but is something Will goes on to speak back to as he asks the question 'why does proper English equate to white English?' That language is racialised (and thus perpetuates white supremacy) becomes clear when he reveals that he is called white for 'speaking properly'. In light of this challenge to his authenticity, Will seeks to position himself as Black. He draws upon Black cultural capital as he argues 'I can get real nigga-ish on you real quick' (code-switch). This is hybridity-of-the-everyday through the racial symbolism of speech. This is Will exercising his PRR.

Will clearly and deliberately enunciates nigga, a term, in stark contrast to nigger, that he understands to be a re-appropriated positive Black self-defined term (Andrews, 2014). In his reference to, and identification as, 'a nigga from Baltimore' there are perhaps class dynamics at play here too. Baltimore is an impoverished city that has come to represent poor Blackness (the mythical norm/regulatory ideal). In invoking his class status, Will reaffirms his Blackness in the face of challenge. However, Will attributes his speech choices to a level of pragmatism ('most efficient way') that again recognises the ubiquity of white supremacy (Carter, 2003; hooks, 2014). As Will notes, however, the impact of these reputed advantages is felt through the governmentality of Blackness (Tate, 2005); his speech positions him outside of the regulatory ideal and he feels a sense of disconnection. Although they identified somewhat differently, Will's brother Derrick (USA) shared this sense of marginalisation, perhaps with greater intensity,

> ... when I went to public school for two years it was predominantly Black and I think there was a rift between me and the other Black students because of the way that I speak. So, I speak in a very proper manner and they spoke with a lot more slang than I did so it made me stick out and they kind of were like, oh well, he must be rich or he must be this or that. So, it kind of created a rift where they respected me in a strange way but also didn't really wanna get to know me as well. So, I guess that is like a way that it appeared for me ... it bothered me because it takes away my identity as a person of colour.

Here it becomes clear that speech styles take on great symbolic importance in the constitution and surveillance of Black peer groups.

Due to his speaking 'in a very proper manner' Derrick is placed at the margins. His speech is associated with class ('he must be rich') and thus it again becomes apparent that the regulatory ideal of Blackness is working class (Harris & Khanna, 2010). Whilst his Blackness ensured he was 'respected in a strange way', this was always a marginal positioning that undermined his positioning 'as a person of colour' and denied the cultural capital of Black bilingualism or the Black ability to navigate different dialects. This inability to code-switch is perhaps what leads Derrick to feel greater marginalisation than his brother. Derrick's account reminds us of the definition of PRR as his inability to use racial symbolism to perform Blackness means he is left feeling as though his identity is taken away.

Even as Derrick attempts to speak back to white supremacy, like other participants in this section, his critique is constrained by language loaded with white supremacist hegemony (proper is white; slang is Black). He goes on to deconstruct this more thoroughly,

> it's really messed up because it tells Black people that you speak in a wrong way, and it takes away from their experiences of growing up in a certain environment that has its own dialect. And people really say like, you know, that's ghetto or whatever but it's really not. It's just a cultural way of speaking that is different from the Standard English way of speaking ... for me it bothered me growing up but I had to just tell people that this is the way that I speak. It's not white or Black, cos I'm obviously Black speaking this way, so it's not white.

Derrick speaks back to white supremacist discourses that 'tell Black people you speak in a wrong; he argues 'it's just a cultural way' of speaking' and need not be degraded because it differs from 'Standard English' (whiteness). It is in so doing Derrick and others demonstrate PRR – they first highlight and then challenge and reject the workings of 'post-racial' white supremacy. Again, the discursive association with class is apparent as he argues Blackness (through speech) is perceived as 'ghetto'. Finally, in order to reposition himself as Black, Derrick deconstructs the racial essentialism underpinning these ideas around speech. He refuses to be rendered docile by discourse as he asserts that, regardless of speech style, he is 'obviously Black'. This is Derrick engaging in processes of hybridity-of-the-everyday (Tate, 2005).

In the next account, Trent (UK) talks about how he and his peer group utilised the racial symbolism of Black British English within their school,

> They [friends] would never speak the way they did in school around their mums, and nor would I … language is an odd one cos the Black British thing is like, it's a brilliant thing and it's an amazing thing but I always question why I used it because it wasn't actually natural to me to use … It wasn't natural for a lot of them to use but we'd still all crack it out to try and act tough or when we felt threatened we'd just try and use some.

Trent suggests that he and his peers switch codes dependent upon social situations. Whilst they would 'never' speak in Black British vernacular 'around their mums', it has utility among their peers (Warikoo, 2011). In the previous chapter, Trent spoke of how he and his Black men peers performed toughness as protection from racist bullying. Here he shows how the racial symbolism of speech is integral to their ability to perform this toughness. That is, the men utilised Black British speech codes in order to perform racialised masculinities that offered protection from racist bullying. White 'post-racial' logic would position speech as racially neutral, as Trent shows, the racial symbolism of speech becomes an important component in Black mixed-race men's PRR.

Whilst Trent reflects on using speech to perform Black masculine toughness, in the following account, Nathan (UK) shares a quite different experience,

> I think some people just judged me straight away. Thinking I might be thuggish, maybe, or a gangsta of some sort. But I think that once they hear me speak and stuff, they might get a bit surprised or something. I know I sound quite posh when I speak.

Nathan notes that his Black body is pre-marked along lines of race and gender. Under the white gaze, he is a thug and a gangsta: he is the Black monster (Yancy, 2017). In the preceding section, Carl showed how he used the racial symbolism of dress in order to distance himself from the Black monster stereotype. In Nathan's account, we see how the symbolism of speech has similar utility. Again, racial symbolism is bound up with class, and as Nathan speaks 'quite posh', he distances himself from the Black monster stereotype. Nathan opens up a third space of hybridity in which he is an-other Black who is 'quite posh'. It is this, a disruption to their racist schema (Sullivan, 2006), that leads his interlocutors to be 'surprised'. With somewhat more explicit intent, Jermaine's (USA) account shows how this identity work transcended the Atlantic,

> I guess I just never played into the stereotypes. Never gave them a chance. You couldn't use a stereotype against me. Like you could try to as much as 'you're dumb cos you're Black, you don't speak right cos you're Black', but I spoke more proper than anyone cos I had to take classes as a kid cos I was foreign. So … I guess they couldn't use anything against me. I was just me, I wasn't the typical Black person playing into all the stereotypes and I mean I guess that's just you but I guess I was a little safer cos I didn't play in to any of those stereotypes, possibly. (Jermaine, USA)

If we recall from earlier in this section, it was Jermaine who so strongly disavowed the mythology around race, speech styles and intelligence. Here he again shows a consciousness of the anti-Black stereotypes that he faces as a Black mixed-race man. Jermaine argues that the white gaze associates Blackness with a lack of intelligence, and this is symbolised through speech. This is his double consciousness. From this double consciousness, Jermaine then engages in identity work to resist the imposition of that stereotype. However, rather than challenging the white supremacist and classist logic that underpins idea of 'right' and 'proper' speech codes, Jermaine merely distances himself from those pathologised Black speech codes. Jermaine therefore occupies the position of an *atypical Black*. Through his identification as a foreign Black, this is his hybridity-of-the-everyday. However, the consequence of Jermaine's speech act, intentional or otherwise, is perhaps to interpellate other Black people, particularly non-foreign Black people, as 'dumb': these 'other Blacks' cannot help playing into the stereotypes because 'that's just you'; they *are* the stereotype (Yancy, 2017). We see that even though he is at least partially cognizant of the processes at play, the racist logic of white supremacy permeates Jermaine's thinking. This is the ubiquity of white supremacy. What of hair as racial symbolism?

Hair: 'Everyone Wants to Touch Your Hair'

As Mercer (2000, p. 112) argues, hair is not merely a 'natural aspect of the body'. The socialisation of hair through stylization makes it a 'medium of significant statements about self and society and the codes of value that bind them, or do not'. Hair is imbued with meaning, and in a society structured along racial lines, it is no surprise that hair is attributed racial, cultural, social and political meanings (Byrd & Tharps, 2002; Erasmus, 2011; Ifekwunigwe, 1999).

Hair represents the 'most visible stigmata of blackness, second only to skin' (Mercer, 1994, p. 101) and is central to constructions of Black style (Mercer, 2004; Tulloch, 2004). It is unsurprising therefore that hair is impactful on Black mixed-race men's presentation of self. Indeed, as Suki Ali (2003, p. 81) notes, 'for those who are "racially ambiguous" [...hair] is a powerful statement of allegiance to their Blackness' (also see: Ifekwunigwe, 1999). This relates to a plethora of scholarship that has suggested that the wearing of 'Black hairstyles' significantly impacts upon the way Black mixed-race populations are interpellated (Khanna, 2011b; Khanna & Johnson, 2010; MacLin & Malpass, 2001; Noels, Leavitt, & Clément, 2010; Sims, 2016).

Anton (UK) spoke about how his hair shaped his interpellation,

> ... being the only Black kid, you get kind of put on a ped-
> estal [laughs] and everyone wants to touch your hair and
> stuff and so like, so it was really easy. I became very popu-
> lar but that also put me in a dangerous spot cos I was in
> the spotlight cos everyone sort of knew me so I could be
> ·very popular or anything could happen where I'd be really
> unpopular. That's how it was really, yeah.

In this extract, it becomes clear that Anton's hair is a constitutive part of his racial identity (Khanna, 2011a; Mercer, 1994; Sims, 2016). His hair, a race symbol, is positioned within discourses of Black exoticism (Yancy, 2008) and mixedness as exotic, fascinating and mysterious (Sundstrom, 2016). Through the symbolism of hair, we are reminded that, as bell hooks argues (2004, p. 155), Black masculinity is the 'apex of "cool"'. Thus, 'everyone wants to touch'. The agency Anton exercised in having an Afro hairstyle saw him become 'very popular' and this was viewed positively. Thus, his hairstyle manifests as a form of cultural capital that is important in Anton's negotiation of identity. Stylization of hair allows Black mixed-race men some control over the ways in which they are interpellated and is therefore a component of PRR. However, as I have argued, Blackness is always haunted by concomitant fear. It is this that leads Anton to argue his Blackness, symbolised through hair, made him hypervisible, and placed him 'in a dangerous spot'. In the preceding chapter, I suggested that the apparent dangerousness of the Black monster can actually place Black mixed-race men in danger. Anton shows these processes to occur at the micro level of racial symbolism, and the popularity accrued through Blackness is haunted by the spectre of unpopularity. It is worth noting that the intrusion of people touching ('exotic') hair was not as welcomed by others as it was by Anton. This is something I return to discuss more fully in the following chapter.

Hairstyle regulations in schools have been widely noted to restrict 'Black hairstyles' and thus disproportionately discipline Black pupils (Blyth & Milner, 1993; Carter, 2012). This in-school discipline can be seen as part of a broader attempt to discipline and constrain the Black body (Yancy, 2017) and evidently implicates Black mixed-race men. Tayo (USA) highlights what he sees as a racist double standard in schools,

> ... Black children are like in public schools they get in trouble like for their hair, their natural hair, they're told to do this and this and this, and then white people get dreadlocks and that's okay.

Tayo importantly emphasises that the hair is 'natural' here. The implication being that if Black children 'get in trouble' for wearing natural Black hair, it is in fact their Blackness for which they are in trouble (Erasmus, 2011): Blackness is troublesome. Recall that Tayo argued that dress styles were made 'acceptable' when white people wore them; this is extended to hair here as he argues that dreadlocks are deemed okay only when white people get them (hooks, 1992). Again, we are reminded that racial symbols interact with the pre-marking of racialised bodies. Tayo's account is a demonstrable rejection of the logic of the 'post-racial'.

Showing how these in-school challenges manifest on both sides of the Atlantic, Shaun's (UK) account is demonstrative of the very issues that Tayo identifies,

> I got put in isolation, they put me in isolation in middle school, a number of times for like having too short hair.

> Cos my hair was like too short, or having a pattern in my
> hair. But then like white kids would come in with pink
> hair. Rockers would come in with pink hair, blue hair, and
> spikes. Yeah, and that was acceptable.

Shaun's hairstyles were constrained as the school sought to discipline
him and take away his agency. This was a regulation of the stylization
of the Black body (Yancy, 2017) that he felt did not apply to his white
peers (Carter, 2012). Shaun's perception is supported by research from
Iwunze (2009, p. 88) who argues that 'the school sought to ban Black
boys from having patterns in their hair whilst no such regulation
applied to white boys'.

Much of what has been discussed thus far can be understood to be
consistent with the experiences of mono-racial Black men. This is unsurprising given that the majority of the men felt that white interlocutors
saw Blackness as undifferentiated. Nevertheless, it is conceivable that
stylising of hair may take on particular importance in the Black mixed-
race context (Tikly et al., 2004) as authentic Blackness is often defined
by dark skin (Tate, 2005), and the racial symbolism of hair has been
shown as one way to influence one's racial interpellation (Sims, 2016).
The reader will recall Claude (UK) from previous chapters. Claude has
very light skin and recalls often being mistaken for white. In the account
that follows, he recalls an experience with school regulations that per-
tained specifically (and explicitly) to his light skin,

> I had like really high hair, I had like a flat top, I looked
> like Kid 'N Play and erm, there was a friend of mine who
> had the exact same haircut but he was, his skin colour was
> really dark, but we had the same haircut right. I was
> stopped and I was told that my haircut was inappropriate
> as he walked by me, and I said what about him, he's got
> the same haircut and she said 'yeah I know but you can't
> really tell can you?'

Here Claude argues that his light skin precludes his ability to wear a
'flat top', a hairstyle associated with Blackness (Alexander, 2003).
Seemingly neutral school policies on hairstyles become racialised as
Claude's 'really' dark-skinned peer is allowed to wear the haircut that
Claude is prohibited from. It appears that it is in fact a perceived
contradiction between Claude's light skin (white) and his racially symbolic hairstyle (Black) that is considered 'inappropriate'. Again, we are

reminded of the ways in which symbolism/stylizations interact with the pre-marking of racialised bodies. Whilst the school's racial schema may permit his darker skinned Black peer to perform Blackness through the racial symbolism of an apparently Black hairstyle, Claude's positioning outside of typical Blackness means he is not permitted. Under the white gaze, he is quite literally not Black enough. For his apparent racial transgression, Claude is subject to the discipline and normalisation of the school; the borders of racial boundaries are surveilled to prevent Claude from transgressing racial norms. Claude's experiences suggest that white supremacy is predicated on narrow and essentialised ideas of race generally, Blackness particularly. Much like dress and speech then, hair is racialised and stylised. Whilst hair can and does allow Black mixed-race men to negotiate their positionalities, the white supremacist desire to control the Black body means this agency is often curtailed. Music is another racial symbol through which Black mixed-race men perform and negotiate their identities.

Music: 'When I Bond with Black People Musically; Its Innate'

Music manifests as a form of racial symbolism. As Tulloch (2004, p. 18) puts it, 'music shapes all aspects of black life as a soundtrack to its identity'. Music shapes collective identities and individual identities. Through music, one can identify racially. A sense that music is imbued with racial meaning is evident as Isaac (USA) argues,

> There are Black aspects of me and there are white aspects of me. Do I love my English bands and my Australian AC/DC? Course I do. Do I love my American rap music? Absolutely. So, I don't really see myself as this much white, this much Black. I see myself as human.

To elicit this response, Isaac was asked a general question about his sense of identity. That he answered in such a way attests to how central the racial symbolism of music can be to racial identities (Carter, 2003; Tulloch, 2004; Warikoo, 2011). Music appears to serve as a 'post-racial' metonym for race as music tastes are not mere preferences but are important aspects of Isaac's identity. These aspects are racialised as Black and white. Whilst English and Australian bands symbolise whiteness, American rap symbolises Blackness. Through the symbolism of music, Isaac engages in a bricolage-like assemblage of identity: this is his speaking back to essentialised discourses in order to assert the multiplicity of his identity. For Isaac, his diverse music tastes symbolise an unwillingness to be bound by racial boundaries. As he speaks back against racial expectations that threaten to fragment his identity, this account is demonstrative of Isaac's PRR. The centrality of music to understandings of race and identity emerged again for Isaac as he recalled discussing the car radio with a white friend,

> I was like dude, I've listened to this white music like Green Day, Foo Fighters, stuff like that, I listen to, you know, I'm gonna put on a little rap. He's like 'ah, dude, really?' and I'm like 'dude, can I just listen to something that I enjoy'. I didn't call him out on it cos I really value his friendship but I was like dude, can I just be me? I like rap. (Isaac, USA)

Again, Isaac makes clear that, for him, music is deeply racialised. His white friend listens to 'white music', whilst, in contrast, Isaac likes 'rap'. Through the racial symbolism of music, Isaac is able to distance himself from whiteness (Green Day, Foo Fighters) and identify with Blackness (rap). For Isaac, listening to rap music – which is coded as Black – allows him to be himself. Thus, we see how race, symbolised by music, goes to the core of Isaac's sense of self. Whilst sharing the commonalities that come with 'friendship', Isaac is different from his white friend. As Isaac vies to take control of the car radio, he affirms his identity through the symbolism of music.

Music was central to the constitution of identities in the UK too. The racial symbolism of music is central to the cultivation of collective Black identities (Tulloch, 2004), and Paul Gilroy (1993) has argued that the influence of African American artists has been central to the cultivation of a Black Atlantic identity (also see, Warikoo, 2011), it is no surprise therefore that music is central to the ways in which Black mixed-race men in the UK make sense of their identities. Discussing why he identifies with Black peers, Leon (UK) made reference to music,

> When you've got nothing in common with somebody musically, it's sort of like they're a different person to you, do you know what I mean? It's sort of like the whole life-style is different, I don't know if that's weird to say, but that's how it felt to me.

Leon's account shows just how central music is to his conception of identity. Music is symbolic. If somebody does not share the same music preferences, Leon argues, they are a 'different person'. We see how, for Leon and his peers, the racial symbolism of shared music is a factor in the cultivation of a common Black identity (Carter, 2003; Tulloch, 2004; Warikoo, 2011). Simultaneously, through music, there is a dis-identification with white peers and whiteness generally. Perhaps music becomes a 'post-racial' stand-in for race, or, perhaps, contrary to 'post-racial' mythology, we see that music cannot become deracinated. Leon was not alone in emphasising the centrality of music. This was a view prevalent among participants in the UK and the USA, particularly in the following account from Reece (UK),

> I feel like, sometimes, when I bond with Black people musically, I'm like it's innate, it's inherent. Not to say that, for a long time when you're a kid, the Black kid that listened to rock was a bit weird. He was a bit of an Oreo or a bounty, whatever you wanna call him. And at a period in my life, I would agree, know what I mean? Because there was a perception of what I thought Black was. Do you know what I mean?

In the first instance, musical tastes are essentialised by Reece as he argues Black musical tastes are 'innate' and 'inherent'. He goes on to demonstrate how the racial symbolism of music preferences become a marker of Black authenticity and a form of Black cultural capital that is used to surveil the boundaries of Blackness (Alexander, 1996; Carter, 2003; Tate, 2005; Warikoo, 2011). The governmentality of Blackness means that the 'Black kid that listened to rock' is pathologised as 'weird' or as an 'Oreo'; he is an inauthentic Black (Carter, 2005). Reece talks reflexively as he attempts to deconstruct the racial essentialism underpinning these ideas. By recognising his holding of a narrow definition of authentic Blackness (Harris & Khanna, 2010; Tate, 2005), as a thing of the past, Reece positions himself away from this conception. The adoption of a more expansive definition of Blackness bolsters Reece's PRR, or his *elasticity*, to occupy a Black identification. Returning to Isaac's (USA) account offers an example of how authentic Blackness is asserted through music,

> ... you find more white kids where I grew up that are listening to new rap, which is like your Little Wayne's and

your Wale's … and for me, my rap base isn't common. Like I listen to a lot of older stuff like Run DMC, Wu Tang Clan. I listen to a lot of Black artists that a lot of people have not heard of. A lot of people are like, yeah, I listen to big Shaun, and Kendrick, and Jay Z and J. Cole. And I'm like, I want you to go and look up, his name is Big L, Harlem born rapper from New York. Sold guns, drugs, grew up in that environment. Without him; no Jay Z. He was the guy that I would say found Jay Z and when he started to collaborate with Jay Z that's when Jay Z started to hone his skills.

In this account, Isaac draws upon the racial symbolism of music styles to assert his own Black authenticity to me, the interviewer. This is achieved through several moves. In the first instance, Isaac situates new rap as something that 'more white kids' are listening to. It is commercialised and common. Indeed, commodification and subsequent popularity is commonly seen as 'depleting its authenticity and reducing its value' (Pitcher, 2014, p. 37). Isaac positions himself away from this depleting authenticity as he affirms that his 'rap base isn't common'. He displays his Black cultural capital as he demonstrates his niche knowledge of 'Big L'. Isaac goes on to assert Big L's credentials for a claim to Black authenticity when he asserts that he is 'Harlem born' (a place famous for Black culture), and in selling guns and drugs, lives up to the stereotype of Black masculine criminality. In the final cementing of Big L's (and vicariously Isaac's) Black authenticity, Isaac reveals that Big L 'found Jay Z'. This positions Isaac as someone with great knowledge who is ahead of what is popular (Carter, 2005; Song, 2003; Warikoo, 2011). It was noted in Chapter 1 that Isaac's light skin often meant he was marginalised through the governmentality of Blackness; this display of Black Cultural Capital might be read as Isaac's speaking back and reconfiguring what defines Blackness (Carter, 2005). Thus, Isaac draws upon music knowledge as a form of cultural capital that enhances his PRR to withstand risks of identity erasure (or threats to his position). This identity work is notably similar to that of Claude in Chapter 2: there I showed how Claude drew upon his knowledge of African history in order to validate his Blackness.

Whilst Isaac shows how the racial symbolism of music might have utility in the performance of Black mixed-race men's identities, there was also a sense that music was used as a way to surveil behaviours for race appropriateness. As Devron (USA) tell us,

I'm a Political Science major so I'm really interested in politics. I listen to a lot of music. And when I start talking about politics, or like shit going on with Washington or something like that, I've heard 'you're so white', like 'what are you doing?', or if I listen to Kendrick Lamar, or A$AP Rocky or something like that, and I'm with friends, they're just like 'you're not Black', like 'stop dancing, turn that down. Stop singing along'. I've heard that so often.

Devron's reflections offer a stark reminder that racial identities are not 'simply the enunciation/practices of volitional subjects' (Youdell, 2000, p. 33) but are discursively constructed and negotiated between people (Pettersson, 2013). Thus, there is a policing of Devron's interest in politics (coded as white) as this is considered a betrayal of his pigment (Murray, Neal-Barnett, Demmings, & Stadulis, 2012). Similarly, his engagement with African American rap music is policed as he is told 'you're not Black'. Music becomes about a struggle over authenticity in a society dichotomised by Black and white. This positions Devron in a struggle against racial governmentalities, in which he is threatened by identity erasure and fragmentation. As Devron (USA) continues to explain,

I think that has to do so much with the fact that I'm in that bit of limbo. I'm not Black but I'm not white. So, when I do something that's considered Black, it's like 'stop, you're not Black' but when I do something that's considered white, it's like, I don't know. There is no like set place for me to be in. There is no group for me to fully fit in to. And that was just, it got so frustrating by the end of high school that it just, it kind of sent me over the edge.

Devron shows a great sense of frustration as Black/white dichotomised discursive practices threaten to render his performances outside of racial norms. Devron attributes this to his mixedness; being 'not Black' and 'not white'. Devron's exasperation is expressive of his sense that discourse acts to restrict and erase his identity as a Black mixed-race man; 'there is no set place'. So, whilst Devron asserted elsewhere that 'I am who I am but I have a darker skin tone' his inability to perform a hybrid identity that is recognisable and not subject to the regulation of racial governmentalities is a real threat to his PRR and therefore cause of distress. Whilst participants were able to draw upon a range of discourses and racial symbols to constitute hybrid identities, Devron was not alone in highlighting this ongoing struggle. As Reece (UK) argued, 'there wasn't a perception of, there's no mixed-race model as a kid. There's no-one to go, he's who you're trying to be' (see Rockquemore & Laszloffy, 2005). Reece's comments here might easily be read as his expression that his performance of mixedness is discursively unrecognisable. For Reece, this was not necessarily problematic: He argued he was proud to be identified as a Black man *or* a mixed-race man. However, for Jamal (UK), this was a source of contention,

> I think they would call me a coconut because I don't conform to a stereotype that they expect, this bothers me, because to me to be Black means nothing more than the colour of your skin and the blood running through your veins. Speech, clothes, walk, hair, grades ... have nothing to do with it.

Being called a coconut – an injurious term for somebody who is raced as Black but 'acts white' – is a consequence of Jamal's performances being deemed race-inappropriate and thus his subjection to regulation. There is an apparent disjuncture between the pre-marking of his body and the racial symbolism – 'speech, clothes, walk, hair, grades' – he draws upon. This regulation is something that bothers Jamal and something he speaks back to. Jamal challenges his interlocutor's belief stylizations and tastes that have something to do with race. In so doing, he repositions himself as Black by drawing upon the biological essentialism of 'blood' and 'skin'. This speaking back is demonstrative of Jamal's PRR as it enables him to resist fragmentation. Black mixed-race men's identities then are constituted through a bricolage-like process, in part through racial symbolism that seeks to open up a third space for hybrid identities.

Conclusion

Building upon the preceding chapters on the naming and articulating of Black mixed-race men's identities, the current chapter has demonstrated how processes of hybridity occur at the level of the everyday for Black mixed-race men, through *racial symbolism*. As the Black mixed-race men in this study are acutely aware, seemingly race-neutral symbols are in fact deeply imbued with racial meaning. These racial meanings are fluid and always subject to negotiation but are nevertheless subject to the regulation of processes of racial governmentality. Thus, racial boundaries are surveilled as the circulation of racial norms dictate what constitutes race-appropriate behaviour and use of racial symbolism.

In the discussion of dress, I argued that Blackness can restrict clothing choices as certain clothes accentuate the white gaze's construction of the Black monster. Simultaneously however, clothing provides an opportunity for Black mixed-race men to perform their Blackness with pride. The display of Black pride represents a speaking back to white supremacist ideology that degrades Blackness and is a theme recurrent from the preceding chapters.

The consideration of speech-style highlighted the pervasive impact of white supremacy as Black mixed-race men showed their clear imbrication in normative assumptions about the apparent superiority or normality of white speech styles. Nevertheless, Black mixed-race men were reflexive and resisted racial governmentalities. The ability to draw upon different speech styles was seen as a great strength and a key symbolic component of PRR. In some cases, this was seen as a particular result of mixedness.

In the section on hair, I demonstrated how, for Black mixed-race men, hair can constitute an important form of cultural capital that is integral to the negotiation of racialised positionalities. Significantly, however, it was noted that forms of cultural capital differ within and between contexts; thus, whilst one hairstyle might bring about popularity in the peer culture, it might be more problematic in terms of, for instance, official school culture. Whilst hair certainly has the potential to bolster PRR, it is subject to tight regulation and control.

The fourth section on music styles showed that music is oftentimes central to the way in which Black mixed-race men understand their identities and positionalities. Moreover, the cultural capital that music endowed was utilised in the negotiation of positionalities and identities. Much like speech, hair and dress styles, music styles offered a 'post-racial' trope for discussions about race.

Whilst the chapter again reminds us that identities are discursively constrained, it is also apparent that, partly through racial symbolism, Black mixed-race men draw upon a range of discourses to constitute hybrid identities. The ability to do so, as Black mixed-race men see beyond 'post-racial' mythology to understand and manipulate the racialisation of dress, speech, hair and music, is essential to the 'post-racial' resilience that enables Black mixed-race men to resist fragmentation and erasure and to minimise the threat of racialised and racist difficulties.

That the four forms of symbolism discussed in this chapter are significant for a group largely descendent from the enslaved and colonised should not be surprising. Slave masters often deprived the enslaved of their clothes, separated slaves who shared a language, shaved and cut their slaves hair and prohibited music and singing. From this oppression came subversive styles of dress, clandestine speech codes, a lineage of resistance and protest songs (most notably negro spirituals), and attempts to affirm Black pride through hair (Kaiser et al., 2004). These are acts of elasticity or springing back into shape. As bell hooks has argued, 'the ways we imagine ourselves, our representation of the self as black folks, have been so important because of oppression and domination' (hooks, 1990, p. 217). This chapter shows that resistance endures through the symbolic practices of Black mixed-race men. In the next chapter, I consider how Black mixed-race men identify, engage with, and resist a particularly pernicious form of racist difficulty: experiences of racial microaggressions.

Chapter 4

Black Mixed-Race Men and PRR in the Face of Racial Microaggressions

Introduction

In each of the preceding chapters, I considered the ways that Black mixed-race men cultivate 'post-racial' resilience and negotiate identities through hybridity-of-the-everyday. In Chapter 1, I argued that Black mixed-race men draw upon multiple discourses in the bricolage-like assemblage of complex and fluid identities. In so doing, Black mixed-race men refuse to be rendered docile by discourse but *speak back* and continually refashion their identities. Chapter 2 built on this as I showed how the intersection of gender shapes the racialised identities of Black mixed-race men and how masculinity is performed and negotiated. Following this, in Chapter 3 I demonstrated the way that Black mixed-race men stylise these hybridised identities through their everyday utilisation of racial symbolism. Building upon the work set out in each of these chapters, the current chapter seeks to explore how these hybridised identities are negotiated in the face of everyday racisms. As I will argue, these everyday racisms pose a very real threat to the 'post-racial' resilience of Black mixed-race men. In a sense then, whilst racial microaggressions may be read as an underlying theme in each of the preceding chapters, this chapter brings PRR into much sharper focus. In the introduction, I formulated two definitions of PRR that I have worked with throughout. These definitions are bare restated here:

1. *The capacity to withstand and/or recover quickly from racist and racialised difficulties that are denied: toughness against the invisible.*
2. *The ability of one's sense of self to remain in, or spring back into shape, amidst threats that are deniable: elasticity.*

The racial microaggression is ubiquitous in each of these definitions. In the first, the microaggressions is a manifestation of those deniable 'racist and racialized difficulties' that — through the cultivation of PRR — Black mixed-race men 'recover quickly from'. To use the second definition, racial microaggressions are that from which PRR enables 'one's sense of identity' to spring back into shape. So, what precisely is a microaggression and how can it advance our understandings of Black mixed-race men's PRR?

First theorised by the African American psychiatrist Chester Pierce (1969, 1974, 1980, 1988), the concept of the racial microaggression allows for the capturing and exploration of the more 'subtle, everyday forms of racism' that Black mixed-race men experience and remain resilient against (Johnson & Joseph-Salisbury, 2017; Pérez Huber & Solórzano, 2015, p. 297; Pierce, 1969, 1980, 1988; Profit, Mino, & Pierce, 2000; Sue, 2010). As I have contended, in 'post-racial' contexts, whilst being denied (Bonilla-Silva, 2006), racism continues to permeate the lives of Black mixed-race men. In this sense, the concept of racial microaggressions offers an analytical response to the *changing face of racism* (Fleras, 2016; Sue, 2010) and thus 'allow[s] us to "see" those tangible ways racism emerges in everyday interactions' (Pérez Huber & Solórzano, 2015, p. 302). The preceding sections have emphasised the ways in which racial identities are always intersectional. Describing them as 'layered assaults', Pérez Huber and Solórzano (2015, p. 298) show this to be evident in consideration of microaggressions. Most notably to the focus of this book, we see this at the intersection of race and gender. These 'layered assaults' are verbal and non-verbal assaults and, according to Derald Wing Sue (2010) and others (Sue et al., 2007), are often enacted unconsciously. However, framing racism as unconscious absolves the perpetrator(s) of responsibility (Tate & Page, 2018), in turn maintaining the conditions of what Bonilla-Silva (2006) describes as *racism without racists*. In essence, framing racism as unconscious – as beyond the perpetrator's control – is little more than a 'post-racial' alibi for racism (Tate & Page, 2018). Charles Mills' work on 'white ignorance' has challenged the dominant framing of ignorance as a form of passivity, instead, he argues that ignorance is 'active, dynamic' and is 'propagated at the highest levels' (Mills, 2007, p. 13). Thus, it is through *epistemologies of ignorance* that the conditions of 'post-racial' white supremacy are maintained.

Pierce (1969, p. 303) understands microaggressions to be a form of 'systemic, everyday racism'. The emphasis on the systemic here is important: microaggressions emerge as a consequence – a surface level, interpersonal, manifestation – of the macroaggressions: 'post-racial' white supremacy. In turn, it is the circulation of those microaggressions that act to reinforce those very conditions of 'post-racial' white supremacy (Pérez Huber & Solórzano, 2015). In isolation, a microaggression can seem relatively innocuous: this engenders a certain degree of deniability.

In a sense, it is the deniability of significance — the 'post-racial' severing of the links to systemic racism and other microaggressions — that acts to make 'discriminatory acts more oppressive than ever' (Bell, 1993, p. 6). Nevertheless, whilst deniable and somewhat difficult to identify, microaggressions pose a cumulative threat to racially minoritised people, including Black mixed-race men. In this chapter, I show that, through PRR, Black mixed-race men are able to identify and respond to racial microaggressions.

Of course, as the Black mixed-race men in this study made clear, microaggressions take on many forms. Without wanting to downplay the significance of other forms of microaggressions, particularly those that are enacted through institutions — the curricular (Joseph-Salisbury, 2018b; Joseph-Salisbury & Andrews, 2017) or low-teacher expectations (Joseph-Salisbury, 2016b) — in this chapter, in keeping with the book's focus on the quotidian, I focus specifically on those microaggressions that occur at the interpersonal quotidian level through interactions with peers, teachers and strangers. In the sections that follow, I first consider Black mixed-race men's ability to reject the 'post-racial' and identify the threat of racial microaggressions. I then show how Black mixed-race men view racial microaggressions as an inevitable factor in their lives. Having laid this groundwork, I turn to focus directly on experiences of microaggressions, in turn, as they manifest in forms of *microassaults, microinsults* and *microinvalidations* (Sue, 2010).

Black Mixed-Race Men Identifying and Understanding Racial Microaggressions

In previous chapters, I suggested that a fundamental component of Black mixed-race men's PRR manifested in the racial literacy that enables an understanding of the ways in which 'post-racial' white supremacy shapes lived experiences. Oftentimes this involves an acute sense of double consciousness and a refusal to be duped by racism's apparent demise. The ability to pinpoint microaggressions is an important component in this racial literacy and thus Black mixed-race men's PRR. The discursive framework for understanding microaggressions remains an emergent one (Fleras, 2016), nevertheless, Black mixed-race men find a range of ways to articulate their lived experiences. Reece (UK) demonstrates this,

> … it's not damaging, it's not something that I'll look back and go rah, I've had some broken years since that but it is,

just that's a bit odd. And when you look back it's the odd
stuff, and like I say the weird vibe stuff that is often the
kind of, somewhere there might have been a racial issue
there.

Reece's awareness of the everyday enactment of subtle and micro
forms of racism – the ways in which racism operates in 'unseen'
ways – is captured in his account. In absence of a developed microaggressions discourse (Fleras, 2016), Reece refers to 'weird vibe' and
'odd' stuff as he grapples with the apparent intangibility of 'post-
racial' racisms. This is Reece's racial literacy as he 'struggle to identify
racism's invisible touch' (Tate, 2016, p. 68). Reece notes that these
incidents are not so damaging as to lead to 'some broken years', but,
as he looks back, Reece is able to recognise a pattern in the accumulation of these 'weird vibe' instances. It is this accumulation that poses
a threat and leads Reece to conclude that there 'might have been a
racial issue'.

The use of 'might' is revealing here, as it perhaps reflects the intangibility of microaggressions (Sue et al., 2007). The reasoning goes that
one must be cautious in calling out the microaggression because this
intangibility renders it always possible that one is wrong. However,
George Yancy (2017) argues that the ability to recognise racial microaggressions is part of an episteme of Blackness that is cultivated overtime,
individually, collectively and intergenerationally. The microaggression
need not always be experienced directly. In fact, the perspectives of a
number of the men in the study were shaped by an awareness of the
maltreatment of other Black and Black mixed-race men (Pérez Huber &
Solórzano, 2015). An episteme of Blackness is born out of a recognition
of recurrent patterns; this is evident in Reece's account. Whilst he
hedges his assertion with 'might', he is explicit in noting the racist
undertones of these encounters. In so doing, Reece shows the 'firm
theoretical grasp of racism' that Pierce (1988, p. 33) argues is necessary
'in order to dilute its crippling effects'.

As the interview continued, Reece further demonstrated his racial literacy: 'racism isn't just saying nigger. That's the language of it. Racism
is a system of oppression', he argued. In this remark Reece shows
his sense of the connections between interpersonal and structural
racisms, or, micro and macroaggressions, and his cognizance of the less
tangible forms of racism. As racism shifts to increasingly micro forms,
racial literacy as displayed by Reece, allows Black mixed-race men to

cultivate the PRR needed to withstand the threat posed by racial microaggressions.

In a similar vein to the aforementioned analysis from Chester Pierce, Derrick Bell (1993, p. 12) argues that,

> African Americans must confront and conquer the other-wise deadening reality of our permanent subordinate status. Only in this way can we prevent ourselves being dragged down by society's racial hostility.

It is confrontation with the reality of racism and racial microaggressions that Reece engages in: a task undoubtedly complicated by the 'post-racial' turn. For Bell, it is this that enables Reece to resist 'being dragged down by society's racial hostility'. Trent (UK) shares the sense of importance Bell (1993) places on recognising racisms,

> I think racial consciousness is important because, for like lots of reasons but it will probably explain a lot of the things that happened, that you don't want to accept. Like it can be the case that shit happens to you and if you're not racially conscious you can build up stories as to why that shit is happening to you and making it about like personal you, when it's like obviously the system of oppression.

There are clear parallels between Trent's comments, Derrick Bell's analysis above and Reece's comments before that. What Trent refers to as racial consciousness is perhaps the confrontation and conquering that Bell describes or the firm theoretical grasp that Pierce refers (1988) to. This, in essence, is *racial literacy*. According to Trent, it is precisely this that enables Black mixed-race men to resist the internalisation of racist messages and identify the root cause of why 'shit is happening to you'; that is, a white supremacist 'system of oppression'. This observation requires a rejection of 'post-racial' ideology. As Trent continues, he touches upon the challenges posed by this 'post-racial' obfuscation,

> I think we could obviously be here all day talking about little, no, not little, but incidences where we have had racism … there was probably loads every week … we wanna always label it as something that is subtle … that happens but is all really, really micro. So, we never really actually discuss it and talk about it.

'Post-racial' logic encourages us to see these incidences in isolation, and as relatively insignificant. Trent challenges this as he emphasises the frequency of these occurrences: it would take 'all day' to relay each incident. He refuses the dominant framing of microaggressions as 'little' and seems to share Pierce's (1974, p. 520) assertion that microaggressions are 'only micro in name'. The 'post-racial' threatens to strip the racially minoritised of the language to discuss and critique racial processes (Goldberg, 2015). Anton (UK) conveys his sense of this challenge as he argues that, 'when we cry out racism, white society says they've just got a chip on their shoulder'. This is certainly a challenge that Black mixed-race men face, but, as Trent reframes microaggressions as something significant, he opens up a space to identify and talk about issues that, obscured by the 'post-racial', are too often left unspoken. This is Trent's PRR; PRR informed by the inevitability and normalisation of racism.

As Trent implicates me as the interviewer, he conveys his sense that these instances are not only cumulative in his own experiences but also in the experiences of other Black mixed-race men. This is an invocation of an episteme of Blackness (Yancy, 2017). That Trent *knows* I will face these experiences is indicative of their ubiquity and inevitability. In both the UK and the USA, this sense of inevitability was shared by the Black mixed-race men in the study.

The Inevitability of Racial Microaggressions: 'Your Blackness Is Constantly Gonna Be under Attack'

The men's sense that racism was a normalised everyday experience is akin to the experiences of the Black men in Rhamie's (2007) study (also see Gillborn, 2003) and reflects a CRT epistemology that insists on understanding racism as normal and ubiquitous (Bell, 1993; Gillborn, 2008; Delgado & Stefancic, 2012). As I have suggested, for Critical Race Theorists, these instances are not only underpinned by, but act to normalise and perpetuate, white supremacy (Pérez Huber & Solórzano, 2015).

For Black mixed-race men, inevitability becomes inescapability. Racial microaggressions are inescapable because white supremacy is inescapable. As Tayo (USA) puts it, 'your Blackness is constantly gonna be under attack': the nature of white supremacy means that there is always need for Black mixed-race men's PRR. It is in this sense, the 'thick skin' discussed in Chapter 3 − a component of some Black mixed-race men's PRR – re-emerges as a theme in the context of racial microaggressions. The apparent value in this thick skin is captured by Jermaine (USA) as he boasts, 'I just feel like I'm emotionally strong my whole life'. In a similar vein, Calvin (USA) reasoned that 'people are gonna say stupid things really so it's just better to not get torn up about something'. This account demonstrates at least two things. First, it reiterates my suggestion that the inevitability of microaggressions renders PRR a necessity. Second, as Calvin frames those microaggressions as 'stupid', his agency to *speak back* to whiteness is apparent. This rhetorical move enables Calvin to resist his negative interpellation, retain his sense of 'self-worth and identity', and avoids potential 'feelings of humiliation, isolation and self-hatred' (Delgado, 1982, p. 137).

Acknowledging the pernicious presence of race was not only evident on the individual level for Black mixed-race men but also at the familial level (Joseph-Salisbury, 2018a). In her research with Black mixed-race families, Heather Dalmage (2000, p. 116) suggests it best that 'families did not ignore race but addressed race issues regularly'. This sentiment rang true among the participants in the current research and facilitated the cultivation of an 'awareness of a shared tradition of resilience in the context of continued discrimination which helps individuals to make sense of their experience' (Lamont et al., 2013, p. 144). Luke (UK) talks about being prepared for experiencing racial microaggressions,

> They told me all the words so like, nigger, coon, Black bastard, or whatever; stuff like that. It kind of got to a point where I didn't really care what it meant.

As Luke conveys, being aware of pejorative words and their meaning allowed him to reach a position of PRR where very little threat was posed to his identity as he 'didn't really care what it meant'. Luke's comments support the findings of Morley and Street (2014, p. 53) who argued that 'where families were affirmative and prepared to face these occurrences with their child, helping to develop their resilience, the insults and injuries are not reported as having had as serious or lasting effect' (also see, Brown & Tylka, 2010; Caughy, O'Campo, Randolph, & Nickerson, 2002).

Whilst the sense of inevitability is starkly apparent among Black mixed-race men, there remained a sense that the ability to withstand the pressures of everyday racism is not something that should be required and is certainly not a requisite for the possessors of white privilege.

This is an important point. Whilst referring earlier to his own individual resilience to racial microaggressions, Jermaine (USA) went on to note, 'personally I dealt with it well but I understand how others don't'. The pernicious and insidious threat of racial microaggressions was acutely felt by Black mixed-race men like Anton (UK),

> Man, its left an imprint in my brain where like, I can't help but see race now like ... it's just become one of them things and I think that's a shame cos even though I'm more aware, it does make me see myself as different from others ... My identity got really affected cos before I'd have no issue in like mixing with white people and thinking I'm in the group and now like I'm with white people but then I see myself as different so then I've always got that sort of separateness within me, from the rest of the group, and it's a shame, but, yes. (Anton, UK)

Whilst in earlier accounts race consciousness was deemed integral to a person's ability to cope with microaggressions, for Anton his acute awareness of race is understood to have had negative effects. The cumulative impact of, what Pierce (1969, p. 303) describes as, 'subtle blows [that] are delivered incessantly' takes a toll on Anton as he can't help but see race; *the 'post-racial' is nothing more than a myth for those living with the effects of racial stratification.* Through his sense of double consciousness, Anton is made acutely aware of himself as 'the other' (Yancy, 2017). As the white gaze seeps into Anton's consciousness, his identity is irrevocably affected. He experiences feelings of isolation and alienation from whites as he is ever aware of his Blackness (Du Bois, 1994). Anton continues,

> It had a huge impact on my life, cos one, it gave me a lot of anger and it's still within me that anger. I sense it every now and then, when I see injustices. But it also drove me to actually research my own culture and history and so from a very young age I was already studying African history and on the educational aspect of course African history isn't really taught in school and so like I was able to look into that due to that drive of being, of being called nigger and this and that and getting into fights. So, I think it influenced me a lot, definitely.

Here it becomes clear that experiences of racial microaggressions do not always have solely negative effects, but many Black mixed-race men like Anton develop a sense of PRR that enables them to turn the embedded threat into a positive outcome. In Anton's instance, he is able to use the initial anger to inspire his studying and engagement with African history.

Having described some of the characteristics of racial microaggressions, and explored in a general sense how they can and do impact upon the lives of Black mixed-race men, I will now explore Black mixed-race men's experiences of specific microaggressions. Derald Wing Sue and his colleagues have argued that racial microaggressions can be understood to take on three forms; microassaults, microinsults and microinvalidations (Sue et al., 2007; Sue, Capodilupo, & Holder, 2008; Sue, 2010). Microassaults are conscious and deliberate, most obviously manifesting in racial epithets and racist jokes. Microinsults are often unconsciously communicated through stereotyping, insensitivity and rudeness and subtly convey a 'hidden insulting message' (Sue, 2010, p. 31). Microinvalidations are those racial microaggressions that threaten to 'exclude, negate, or nullify' the lived experiences of the racially minoritised (Sue, 2010, p. 37). Whilst there is oftentimes considerable overlap between the three forms, as I consider how they impact upon the lives of Black mixed-race men, I consider each in turn.

Microassaults

Whilst they are often subtle, microassaults can also be blatant. Characterised by the purposeful communication of white supremacist ideology, and the intent to degrade or harm, microassaults are the most explicit of the three forms of microaggressions. As such, they are the form most akin to 'old fashioned' racisms (Sue, 2010), exemplified by, but not limited to, racist name-calling and racist jokes. Conceivably, their more explicit nature makes microassaults the form of microaggression that Black mixed-race men are most prepared to deal with.

In a 'post-racial' era where few would admit to being racist (Bonilla-Silva, 2006, 2015), microassaults only become permissible under certain circumstances. Sue (2010) identifies three such circumstances: where the perpetrator has a sense of safety, a sense of anonymity or a loss of control. It is possible, however, that the 'post-racial' turn renders all racist expressions safe. As Goldberg (2015, p. 72) observes,

> Living in a postracial state seems to have entailed the pos-
> sibility of subjects expressing themselves in ways as bla-
> tantly and explicitly racist as they choose with little risk of
> being called on it.

The Black mixed-race men in this study recalled a range of microassaults: racist epithets being shouted out of car windows, being chased
by racist gangs, being offered the worst seating at a local bar, being
refused admission to the local swimming pool, refusal as a hotel guest,
and the parents of a white girl prohibiting a prospective date. Whilst
recollections I could discuss here are near endless, I will focus on a few
that best reflect the range and nature of the microassaults that the men
recalled.

In one of the most obvious and explicit experiences of a microaggressive assault, Alex (UK) recalls an incident that was both physical and
verbal,

> One boy, he was older than me, can't remember why he
> did this, but like he must have grabbed me up against the
> wall and said something like, 'I'll squeeze the Black shit
> out of your eyes and make you white'.

In noting that he 'can't remember why' his interlocutor assaulted
him, Alex implies that there must have been a reason. 'Post-racial' logic
presupposes that in revealing the aggressor to be a racist, an explicit
microaggressive act must be a consequence of a loss of control (Sue,
2010). Indeed, according to Sue (2010, p. 30), 'many people who pri-
vately hold notions of minority inferiority will only display their biased
attitudes when they lose control'. However, perhaps a loss of control
becomes a 'post-racial' alibi for racism that enables the aggressor to
distance themselves from their racist actions. As Alex's interlocutor
threatens to 'squeeze the Black shit out of his eyes' he attributes the
reason for Alex having aggravated him to his Blackness. If Alex was not
contaminated by 'Black shit' he would not have caused such a volatile
response. If Alex could simply be 'made white' he would know how to
behave so as not to aggravate his aggressor, or so the reasoning goes.
Blackness is enough to cause a 'loss of control'. In this instance, the
aggressor draws not only on discourses of anti-Blackness to degrade
Alex's identity, but he also reproduces and perpetuates longstanding
anti-miscegenation discourse that renders the Black mixed-race child an
infected, unnatural and contaminated problem (Alibhai-Brown, 2001;

Tizard & Phoenix, 2002; see for early examples of this discourse see, Long, 1772; Thicknesse, 1788). Underpinning the messages embedded in the microaggressions of Alex's aggressor is the ideology of the macroaggression: white supremacy. Whilst there is evidence to suggest that Black mixed-race men experience racial microaggressions similar to those experienced by their mono-racial Black peers (Herman, 2004; Tutwiler, 2016), this account suggests that in some instances racial microaggressions can take on particular forms for Black mixed-race men (Nishimura, 1998). As Johnston and Nadal (2010, p. 126) argue,

> multiracial people may be targets of "traditional" racial microaggressions ... in addition to multiracial microaggressions, which are daily verbal, behavioral, or environmental indignities, whether intentional or unintentional, enacted by monoracial persons that communicate hostile, derogatory, or negative slights toward multiracial individuals or groups.

Whilst the majority of microaggressions were predicated on notions of Blackness, the current study certainly contains further evidence to support this analysis.

As the following account from Devron (USA) shows, the perpetuation of anti-miscegenation discourse was apparent in both the UK and the USA,

> I don't know how we got on topic but we got on the topic of my race and that I was biracial. He asked which one of my parents was white and which was Black, and I told him. I told him my Dad was Black and my Mum was white.

Devron's recollection is one of an intrusive stranger. Despite being a relative stranger, Devron's interlocutor deems Devron's race an open area of discussion. As such, he proceeds to ask a question about the race of Devron's parents. The normalisation of whiteness means that such a question would never be asked of a white person (Dyer, 1997). Thus, this intrusion is a microaggression that acts to 'other' Devron. Whilst this interaction might be best identifiable as a microinvalidation, it acted as a precursor for a more explicit microassault. As Devron continues,

> And his, I mean he's an idiot, just cos he says stupid stuff. I mean he's a smart kid. Like I don't know, he likes to push people's buttons and the first thing that came out of his mouth when I said that was 'so your Dad raped your Mum, right? And she had a baby'. And like at this point, I didn't know who this kid was. I wasn't friends with him.

Devron's interlocutor draws upon pervasive racist myths of the Black man as a predatory rapist and the white women as innocent and vulnerable (Yancy, 2017). The inference is this: *it is only through rape that a Black/white relationship can be intelligible. It is only through rape that Devron's racial identity is intelligible. It is only through rape that Devron is intelligible.* Devron refuses to be rendered docile by his interlocutor's microassault: he does not simply become the illegitimate progeny his aggressor interpellates. Instead, Devron positions his interlocutor as 'an idiot' and his comments as 'stupid stuff'. This is Devron speaking back and springing back into shape. Whilst Delgado (1982) suggests that pathological internalisation might be a realisable consequence of such an encounter (see Joseph-Salisbury, forthcoming-b), Devron demonstrates the PRR to reject the embedded message. Recalling Sue's (2010) three conditions that can give rise to microaggressions – anonymity, safety, or loss of control – it seems that neither anonymity of a loss of control are evident in this account. Thus, perhaps owing to his whiteness, Devron's interlocutor feels a sense of safety that creates the conditions for the microaggression. That this sense of safety is felt in the school environment attests to the inaction of schools in combatting racism. Indeed, participants in the study were near unanimous in the perception that school responses to racial microaggressions rarely matched the seriousness they attributed to it.

Sporting activity emerged as another context in which racial microaggressions appeared to be particularly safe. As Trent (UK) suggested, 'you've got the school rules that are against racism and then suddenly they disappear on the football court'. Again, demonstrating the Transatlanticity of Black mixed-race men's experiences, Erik (USA) offers an account that demonstrates this,

> sometimes when we played other schools that were like predominantly white in football, American football [laughs], like you'd hear them call us like 'nigger' or 'spick', on the field and then like as soon as we told the refs they'd be like 'nah, nah, nah, just play on, play on'.

It is clear that in the context of 'football', and perhaps being in a predominantly white team, the use of racial epithets is deemed safe by Erik's aggressors. For Erik, this is compounded as the referee is unwilling to listen to protestations and urges Erik to 'play on'. Erik continues to consider the sports field as a specific environment,

> I think the rationale behind that is just, you know they're trying to evoke a reaction to set you off your game so the best thing you can do to stay focused is to not react … if they say something that provokes you to like move to violence or something, that's more visible and you'll get called out on it. So, it's like, the prime environment to bring in racist slurs I guess.

As well as the sport field being deemed a safe environment for racial microaggressions, it is also possible that the competitiveness of sport engenders a loss of control in the aggressor: the desire to win overrides the desire to hide a person's racist sentiments.[1] Nevertheless, the aggressor, according to Erik, is acutely aware of the power of racism as this is something that is drawn upon to 'evoke a reaction to set you off your game'. Erik finds his PRR to this threat in his ability to identify the motivations of his aggressors and to consider what the best response will be. Racialised power becomes apparent in Erik's account. The seeming innocuousness of the racial epithet means it is somewhat less 'visible' than any potential reaction from Erik; this is the 'post-racial' at work. Whilst many of the men in the current study considered violence to be a commensurate response to experiencing racism, Erik is aware that he, and not his aggressor, would be reprimanded. It is this — as it operates through white supremacist discourses of Black violence and white innocence — that makes the racial microaggression so powerful, and this that makes the sports field a 'prime environment' for their enactment. Erik went on to note, however, that 'even on the football field like, it was rarely very blatant'. Oftentimes microaggressions were much subtler than the one described here. Thus, for Erik, there 'was this constant thought … I'm always on my toes around him cos I know

---

[1]In March 2016, England International Rugby player Joe Marler was found to have called a Welsh player 'Gypsy boy' during a game. On their decision to take no disciplinary action, Six Nation's Rugby invoked this notion of a loss of control as they issued a statement explaining that the microassault was said 'in the heat of the moment' (BBC Sport, 2016).

he might say something that's not right. So, like, I feel like that even that's without football'. As Chester Pierce (1969, 1980, 1988) and others' (Pérez Huber & Solórzano, 2015; Sue, 2010; Sue et al., 2007, 2008) work suggests, the ability to be aware of and identify racial microaggressions is imperative to Black mixed-race men's PRR.

Racial microassaults were not always communicated verbally, nor were they always directed specifically at the individual. Indeed, racial microaggressions that were non-verbal, and somewhat indirect, were treated with the same sense of seriousness. Erik spoke about written microassaults in his school bathroom,

> ... you'd get like just some instances like people painted like 'White Pride', or 'The South Will Rise' was often written in the bathrooms. Like I don't think you even know what the fuck that means [laughs] while you're writing 'The South Will Rise' in the bathroom.

Again, the repetition and reiteration of these microaggressive acts is made apparent as Erik recalls these messages were '*often* written'. The two messages contain a (very small) degree of attributable ambiguity that often characterises microaggressions. Although 'White Pride' and 'The South Will Rise' are white supremacist and white separatist messages that have been popular mottos of groups like the Ku Klux Klan, advocates often suggest the messages are about State rights or celebrating Southern heritage rather than anti-Black racism (Dobratz & Shanks-Meile, 2000). In 'post-racial' times, this is somewhat unsurprising (Bonilla-Silva, 2006). Not only does the aggressor derive a sense of safety from this apparent ambiguity but also from their anonymity (Sue, 2010). In his consideration of these racial microaggressions, Erik again demonstrates his PRR as he is not only able to identify the racism but he also delegitimises the message through ridicule. In his suggestion that the author doesn't 'even know what the fuck that means' Erik places himself in a position of knowledge over his unintelligent (white) aggressor who is not even aware of the history of the racist discourse they perpetuate. Erik's knowledge of racism enhances his PRR to withstand the threat of racial microaggressions (Pierce, 1988). From Erik's experiences on the football field, to his experiences visiting the school bathroom, a picture of the ubiquity of racial microaggressions starts to develop. As Erik conveyed earlier, beyond those described, there are a multitude of subtler racial microaggressions at play, and thus in a typical day, Erik must remain resilient against these incessant blows (Pierce, 1974, 1988).

Having earlier recalled an incident in which his interlocutor suggested he was the progeny of interracial rape, Devron (USA), like Erik (USA) continues to demonstrate some of the relentlessness of racial microassaults. In this instance, in the form of anti-Black jokes,

> ... it became such commonplace that it was just normal for me to hear. Obviously, it got later in high school where it was just so annoying, cos I'd heard it so much. Erm, without any malicious intent behind their words, like I never felt demoralized by it, that they were making these jokes but at the same time, more than anything it was just annoying. Really, it was just persistent. I don't know, it just got to the point where I wouldn't laugh. I wouldn't respond. They just said what they said and I was like 'yeah, okay, whatever'. Shrugged it off and kept going about my business.

Devron conveys how the incessant repetition of these microaggressive assaults means they become normalised (Dumas, 2014). Such repetition not only acts to normalise the jokes but also normalises and perpetuates the macroaggression of white supremacy (Bell, 1993; Pérez Huber & Solórzano, 2015). Chester Pierce (1969, p. 303) argues that, by their very nature and power, a microaggressive act can be 'considered of itself to be relatively innocuous'. It is perhaps this that Devron conveys as he notes the lack of 'malicious intent'. However, the cumulative threat is considerable as 'later in school' Devron found these jokes increasingly 'annoying' and 'wouldn't respond'. Implicit in Devron's assertion that he 'never felt demoralized' by these jokes is the possibility that, had he not the PRR, he could become demoralised. With anonymity and loss of control being easily discountable, it is apparent that it must be a sense of safety from repercussions that enables Devron's interlocutors to continue making anti-Black jokes. This safety is perhaps part of the ambiguous nature of jokes but perhaps more troublingly is again a consequence of a white supremacist school that creates a safe environment for the perpetuation of racist views. A further point of interest is in Devron's responses to these microassaults. Sue (2010, p. 55) argues that 'the most frequent reaction to microaggressions seems to be doing nothing'. Whilst Devron's decision to 'shrug it off and keep going' would perhaps fit into Sue's analysis, it would be a great understatement of

Devron's agency specifically, and Black mixed-race men's agency generally, not to recognise his 'keeping going about my businesses' as a defiant act demonstrative of Black mixed-race men's PRR. Zak (UK) shares this sense of defiance,

> It wasn't serious racism, it was banter, like having a laugh but cos I'm the person I am, I don't take it to heart. I say things back and all that. Know what I mean? But there's been a few times when it's been proper serious. When they've like meant it. Like yeah. Hurt my feelings. But, just get on with life. (Zak, UK)

What Zak describes is an incredible degree of PRR. In the first instance, he argues that the racism is 'banter', and he is thus able to 'say things back'. He reflects the 'tough skin' or masculine toughness discussed in Chapter 3 as he does not 'take it to heart'. The persistent threat is made apparent, however, as he notes occasions where it had 'been proper serious'. Whilst acknowledging that such instances did hurt his feelings, he nevertheless acts defiantly as he, like Devron, 'just gets on with life'. Microassaults were often experienced somewhat indirectly as Black mixed-race men would be present to hear racially denigrating jokes (Jackson, 2009) as they were not seen to be part of the denigrated race (Johnston & Nadal, 2010). As Carl (USA) recalls, 'cos I was seen as mixed, people felt okay to say things to me'. It might also be recalled from the second chapter that Brendon's (USA) light skin tone meant that he was often privy to 'awful Black jokes' but felt unable to challenge them. At this point, the microaggression also acts as a microinvalidation as Brendon and Carl's claim to a Black identity is invalidated. However, before considering microinvalidations more fully, let us consider how microinsults manifest in the lives of Black mixed-race men.

Microinsults

According to Sue et al. (2007, p. 278), microinsults are often unintentional 'behavioral/verbal remarks or comments that convey rudeness, insensitivity and demean a person's racial heritage or identity'. Often manifesting in the transmission of stereotypes, microinsults act to unintentionally, as Sue (2010) puts it, perpetuate racist and white supremacist messages. As I have suggested, drawing upon white ignorance, as theorised by Charles Mills (2007), it is possible, and indeed necessary, to trouble the notion of unintentionality. Indeed, Mills' talks of epistemologies of ignorance that are knowing. That is, white epistemologies of ignorance are based on the normalisation of whiteness, white historical amnesia and the denial of white privilege. What appears to be unintentionality or ignorance then is in fact a consequence of the 'post-racial' normalisation of racism and a white social epistemology that fails to recognise the humanity of racially minoritised people generally and Black mixed-race men specifically. To argue that racial microaggressions are unintentional, as Sue (2010) does, takes away the responsibility from whites for facing up to the realities of racism and white supremacy (Mills, 2007). Indeed, it is upon the very illusion of unintentionality, of not seeing, that the maintenance of white supremacy depends.

In the previous chapter, a number of participants recalled being told that they 'speak well' when they spoke in what they argued were typically white vernacular forms. On the surface, this may appear to be an individual compliment. However, the embedded message acts to perpetuate ideologies of white supremacy. If to 'speak properly' is to speak in 'Standard English', to speak in African American vernacular is to *speak improperly*. As Derrick (USA) argues as he decodes this embedded message, 'it's really messed up because it tells Black people that you speak in a wrong way'. Again, some specific examples will be useful to more fully extrapolate how microinsults manifest in the lived experiences of Black mixed-race men.

Microinsults in the form of stereotypes manifest in constructions of Black men as deviant or criminal. In the following account, Reece (UK) describes an incident that occurred whilst he was attending a house party,

> someone came across this packed basement, it was a decent size, big house and came over to me and said 'I heard you're selling coke' and nothing, I was like, in the instance I was like 'well no I don't' and the person obviously looked like they might have had something already so they were kind of like 'but I heard that you', 'no I don't mate sorry'. But it is just this perception of, this perception of Black people, solely Black people sell drugs.

In emphasising the size of the 'packed basement' Reece is keen to emphasise the number of people at the party and thus implies that the reason he was approached is the gendered racist assumptions of his interlocutor. These assumptions of the white-gaze pre-mark Reece's body as the criminal Black man: the drug dealer (hooks, 2004; Yancy, 2017). Much like in the previous chapter where participants spoke of white people crossing the road in fear, the embedded message is not only that all Black men are the same but that all Black men are criminals (Sue et al., 2007): this is a discourse that helps to maintain white supremacy. However, through his ability to identify and unpick the racist assumption (Pierce, 1974), Reece is able to speak back and highlight the fallacies in his interlocutor's gaze; he refuses to be locked-in by this gaze. This is his PRR as he resists the pathologisation and opens up a third space of hybridity in interaction. He is *not* the embodiment of the racist perception of Black people (Yancy, 2008) but something else, something more. Through Reece's resistance, it is the interlocutor who is problematised, not Reece's identity as a Black mixed-race man.

Again, showing how the phenomenological experiences of Black mixed-race men have a degree of Transatlanticity (Caballero, 2004), Devron (USA) describes an occasion in which he, like Reece, is pre-marked,

> ... the biggest instance of racism or profiling that I experienced didn't even come at my high school. It was at my girlfriend's prom. She's white, and she went to a high school in the suburbs that was, like, overwhelmingly white. I was at her prom where there were probably five hundred or so kids there, everybody is wearing their tuxes and their vests and everything. And I got up to go to the bathroom and a girl at a table flagged me down and mistook me for a waiter and asked me to get her waiter. And at the time I didn't think much of it. And some people, my Mum, my Girlfriend, they don't insist, but they kind of question the fact that it was racially motivated. Whether it be subconscious or conscious, but I, until this day, I'll attest to the fact that she thought I was a waiter because I was Black.

By noting this instance as 'the biggest', Devron implies that there are a number of smaller racial microaggressions that go perhaps undiscussed: this is the veritable tip of the iceberg. Like Reece, Devron places importance upon the location (suburbs) and the overwhelming whiteness of those present; the implication here is that microaggressions are contextually contingent. In the previous chapter, I argued that dress-style is always racialised. This is made evident again here as whilst his white peers in 'tuxes' are assumed to be prom attendees, Devron as a Black mixed-race man is assumed to be a waiter: he is a *body out of place* (Puwar, 2004). Thus, he is interpellated through a white gaze that limits the parameters of what Blackness can be (Yancy, 2017). This is not an uncommon occurrence. In 2016, in the UK, Black female MP Dawn Butler was mistaken for a cleaner (BBC News, 2016), Black scientists are regularly mistaken for cleaners (Williams, Phillips, & Hall, 2014), and like Black grime artist Stormzy, Black academic Henry Louis Gates was accused of breaking into his own home and arrested (Joseph-Salisbury, 2017c). In this instance, Devron's white mother and white girlfriend remain unsure about the racist underpinnings of the assumption, and in the first instance Devron is too. This uncertainty, the struggle to recognise the racist underpinnings, may not only be a consequence of 'post-racial' mystification (Goldberg, 2015) but also reflective of the stunning nature of racial microaggressions (Pierce, 1980). Upon reflection, however, Devron is in no doubt. As a Black mixed-race man, his 'judgement is fundamentally a social epistemological one, one that is rendered reasonable within the context of a shared history of Black people noting, critically discussing, suffering and sharing' (Yancy, 2008, p. 7). Indeed, Devron goes on to recall relaying the incident to his Black father, '[I] told my Dad, he was like "you know why she thought that, right?" and I was like, yeah I guess I do'. Devron and his Dad share a knowing that comes from their shared experiences of Blackness (Yancy, 2017). This is in contrast to the *not knowing of whiteness* that characterises the (white) episteme of Devron's mother and girlfriend (Gillborn, 2005; Rollock, 2012). Again, Devron's ability to identify and deconstruct this racial microaggression means he is resilient to its pernicious affects (Pérez Huber & Solórzano, 2015; Pierce, 1969). Devron continues,

> I said, I don't work here and walked away. And as I said that I heard her entire table was just like 'you did not just do that', they were all screaming at her. She came up and apologized afterwards. My Girlfriend's best friend like brought her over and was like 'this was the kid that you thought was your waiter', and she was like, she was about to cry. She was like 'I'm sorry, I wasn't wearing my glasses'. I don't know what that has to do, I didn't know

what that had to do with anything. Obviously, I wasn't
mad at her at all but she came up with a pretty crumby
excuse to explain for it.

As Devron and Reece's account here attests, racial microinsults are
not always perceived to be conscious or intentional. Indeed, this deniability is something of their essence and power (Pérez Huber &
Solórzano, 2015). Devron notes that he 'wasn't mad at her at all'.
This is perhaps because Devron understands this is just an everyday
articulation of white supremacist ideology in which his interlocutor is
imbricated (Pérez Huber & Solórzano, 2015). Nevertheless, he is
unsatisfied by her explanation as it does not reflect what he knows to
be a racist assumption. In essence, Devron is dissatisfied by the ways
in which his interlocutor is unable and unwilling to look beyond epistemologies of ignorance. Through his interactions, Devron refuses to
be interpellated as the archetypal *Black man who is a service worker*
(Sue, 2010) and opens up a third space for new identifications.

As in the cases of Devron and Reece, the spectre of anti-Black stereotypes was felt by Jake (UK). However, in Jake's account, this was experienced somewhat differently,

For a long time, when people highlighted the fact that I
wasn't like a typical Black person, that I'd take pride in
that. Like, I was somewhat aware of the Black stereotypes, and I was then thus aware that I'd managed to
break free of these in order to completely fit in with my
peers. Obviously, I recognize that such thinking is not at
all ideal or solving the problem, but I do think that's how
I felt if I were to really have considered my thoughts at
the time.

For Jake, his imbrication in discourses of white supremacy means he
is not only aware of negative Black stereotypes but that he seeks to distance himself from them. In the first instance, he takes pride in his
hybrid performance as different from the *pathological Black monster
same* (Tate, 2005; Yancy, 2017). This performance had value for Jake as
it allowed him to 'fit in' with his white peers. However, as he reflexively
conveys, this engenders some regret. As Jake recognises, his performance does not necessarily act to challenge or destabilise the Black
monster of the white gaze. His comments are somewhat reminiscent of
the ponderings of George Yancy (2008, p. 17):

I wonder to what extent other Black men, under similar circumstances, have felt a certain rush of joy to announce, 'I am not your typical Black male. I am better. In fact, if you look closely you will see that I'm not really Black' and in doing so reinforce the prevailing racist imaginary while attempting to 'other' one's self.

Like Yancy, Jake reflexively identifies the microinsult embedded in his interpellation as an *atypical Black man*. The message is one of Black inferiority. In Jake's interpellation as different from this, the inferiority of Blackness is reinforced (Fanon, 2008; Jones, 2004; Yancy, 2017). The recognition of such is what leads Jake to argue his thoughts of the time were 'not at all ideal'. What Jake longs for then is a jettisoning of the pathological Black of the white imaginary; this would enable him to be intelligent and non-deviant whilst not being considered exceptional. The subtlety of microinsults is made apparent in Jake's account; it is only looking back that he is able to identify the 'insulting metacommunication' (Sue, 2010, p. 35).

Another subtle and somewhat ambiguous microinsult is relayed, as Theo (UK) talks about the experiences of his older brother in school,

> there was one mixed race girl in his year and he was the mixed-race boy and everyone came up to him and was like 'oh you and her should go out, you and her should go out' and I was just like 'why are they saying that to you?' but obviously we've clocked on now, years later. We still know the girl, we've clocked on now years later, why they've said it, cos it just makes sense that, well you're a mixed-race girl, mixed-race boy, you know stuff like that. So, we found that quite weird.

What Theo describes is a process of racial 'othering' through which his brother and the mixed-race girl in question are rendered hyper-visible and *different*. Vicariously, as a Black mixed-race man and as a brother, Theo is also interpellated as conspicuously different from the white peer group of the school. Given their apparent racial difference, it is assumed that as 'a mixed-race girl' and a 'mixed-race boy' the two should 'go out'. In this, a sense of 'us' and 'them' is articulated as the Black mixed-race students are homogenised as 'them' − outsiders. There is also a clear evocation of miscegenation discourse as the assumption is that one should 'go out' with someone of the same race;

this 'just makes sense'. Moreover, normalised heterosexuality is evident as it is assumed that as a Black mixed-race man Theo's brother should pursue someone of the 'opposite' sex. The subtlety of the microaggressions at play are made apparent as Theo notes that it was not until years later that they realised the racist underpinnings of the interactions. Indeed, whilst race is enacted by Theo's 'post-racial' peers, it is not named. Nevertheless, the racial othering is resisted as it is positioned as 'weird' and thus refuses the normalisation of racial segregation. The hypervisibility and othering, evident in Theo's account, also became apparent in accounts of microinsults concerning Black mixed-race men's hair: so frequent were these accounts, that they are worthy of their own subsection.

'Does This Look Like a Petting Zoo to You?'

Black people's hair manifest as a common site of racial microinsults (Paludi, 2013; Paludi & Coates, 2011; Sue et al., 2008). The pervasiveness of this microaggression is reflected in the 2014 satirical film *Dear White People* (Simien, 2014a). With the tagline of 'a satire about being a Black face in white space', the film includes the popular line, 'Dear white people, please stop touching my hair. Does this look like a petting zoo to you?' The film also uses the image of a white hand intruding into a Black male student's hair as a movie poster. The cover of Justin Simien's (2014b) book of the same name shows a white hand similarly touching the hair of a Black woman. That this is a skit that the satirists utilise conveys the commonplaceness of such microaggressive acts. Indeed, the vast majority of Black mixed-race men in the current study reported microaggressions of this kind being a part of their school lives. This is conveyed in the UK by Max,

> That was a gimmick; they was always putting pencils in my hair, all sorts of crap like that. Trying to do that. Yeah, 'aw, I just wanna touch your hair man'. Oh yeah, it was never really negative, but yeah.

As Max argues, the individual microaggressions were 'never really negative' but were significant enough for him to recall them and for him to describe them as 'all sorts of crap'. The frequency of the repetition of microinsults is made apparent as 'all sorts of crap' was 'always' happening. Trent (UK) recalls similar experiences,

> You know everyone touched it. Everyone would put stuff in it or I would be the kid with the afro, or they'd do pictures with them touching it but it was like this novelty like 'ha ha ha' [mock laugh], Trent you've got your afro like it's so cool but also like, it was you know boundaries weren't there.

The parallels between Max and Trent's accounts are uncanny. Just as Max describes his hair as a 'gimmick', Trent describes his as a 'novelty'. Both experience the intrusion of touching as they are 'implicitly being exoticized or treated like an object' (Paludi & Coates, 2011, p. 216); a contemporary manifestation of a fascination with the Black body that has deep white supremacist roots (Yancy, 2008) and takes on particular forms for Black mixed-race men (Johnston & Nadal, 2010; Root, 1990). Similarly, the intrusion Trent identifies as his interlocutors 'do pictures' is reminiscent of a long history of the Black body as property (Alexandre, 2012; Yancy, 2008) in which postcards of the lynching of Black bodies became a huge industry (Apel, 2004; Mowatt, 2008), and Black bodies were displayed as spectacles and exhibited to feed the fascination of whites (Qureshi, 2004; Sharpley-Whiting, 1999; Van Thompson, 2004). This is the long racist history that 'post-racial' logic seeks to deny (Goldberg, 2015). That 'the boundaries weren't there' shows how systemic white supremacy is continually re-enacted through racisms of the everyday (Pérez Huber & Solórzano, 2015). In his account, Trent challenges the idea that he is 'the kid with the afro'. By challenging the perceptions of his interlocutor, Trent draws upon his sense of double consciousness as he engages in a process of *hybridity in talk* in which he positions himself as something different from (something more than) that 'kid with the afro'.

Jake (UK) shared the experiences of intrusion as he recalls being irritated by 'stuff like everyone feeling they have the right to touch my hair constantly (which has been so common in life that I no longer mind)'. Jake makes apparent that, through repetition, these everyday racisms become normalised. He continues to extrapolate his experiences more fully,

> it only really started in secondary school and at first I wasn't keen on the fact that I'd become so well-known

throughout the whole school because of my hair (mainly
because people in older years were obviously pretty scary)
so I'd refuse to tell such people my actual name to retain
some form of anonymity and just because it was annoying
to be constantly approached or asked silly questions about
it, but it's continued to the extent that I'm very much used
to being the centre of attention nowadays and attention is
something that I very much enjoy too, so I'd say in the
long run it's actually done wonders for my self-confidence.

Jake conveys his unease with his sudden hypervisibility as his Black
mixed-race male body, through the metonym of hair, becomes a conspicuous presence in the school. This is a positioning he seeks to resist
through refusing to tell people his name: this is his response to mitigate
racial and racialised difficulties. The routineness of the microaggressions
is made apparent as he is 'constantly approached'. However, in positioning the questions as 'silly', he speaks back to his conspicuousness
and seeks to delegitimise the intrusion of his interlocutors. In so doing,
Jake opens up a third space of identification in which he positions himself as different from the mythical and pathological image constructed
by the white gaze. Jake's agency is apparent as he notes that his positionality is negotiated through interaction with his interlocutors. In the
first instance, Jake describes resisting his positioning as exotic and fascinating but more latterly this becomes something that Jake begins to
'enjoy' and use for his own ends as a source of cultural capital. Indeed,
by not providing his name, Jake is perhaps also adding to the fascination as well as resisting it. The development of PRR to microaggressions
is therefore a process.

Like Jake, Luke (UK) talks about his experience of microaggressions
of hair and demonstrates how his resilience is cultivated over time,

I did get quite a bit of abuse for my hair … 'you've got
worms in your hair' and all that … at this moment I was
probably about six or seven. So, I did take it on board but
I kind of grew out of that. So [laughs], so I think you'd be
a bit of an idiot if you told me that now, to be honest.

Luke recalls being racially othered through his hair; as his hair style
falls outside of white hair norms, his twists are injuriously interpellated
as 'worms'. This is something that, in the first instance, Luke takes 'on
board' as the insult 'injures the dignity and self-regard of the person to

whom it is addressed' (Delgado, 1982, pp. 135–136). However, as he gets older, Luke develops the PRR that means he is able to avoid that internalisation (Joseph-Salisbury, forthcoming-b). Luke is able to disrupt power dynamics by laughing and position his interlocutor as 'a bit of an idiot'. This is Luke's elasticity.

Showing again that microaggressions can be experienced less directly, Trent (UK) recalls his mother's visiting his school and how this led to him experiencing microaggressions as hair once more becomes the trope of racism,

> You know my mum would come up to the school some-times in like a head-wrap, or like when she had her natural hair out and like I could see people staring or someone would make comments ... she came in with an afro and I remember everyone talking about it but not in the way that I wanted them to talk about it at the time, like kind of it became this spectacle.

The 'staring' and 'commenting' position Trent's mum's Blackness (embodied in her hair and dress), and therefore Trent, as conspicuous. As Trent argues, this was unwanted negative attention. Not only did Trent's mum become the subject of 'everyone talking' but this was nega-tive; Trent's mum was discussed 'not in the way' he wanted her to be. There is a power dynamic at play here as Trent is unable to control or influence the 'talking'. Trent's mum becomes something of a 'spectacle'; through racial microaggressions, Blackness becomes a 'spectacle'. In this account, we are reminded that microaggressions need not always be experienced directly (Sue et al., 2007). Microaggressions did not always manifest in the kind of hypervisibility evident in Trent's account but also through invisibility and erasure. This brings us to microinvalidations.

Microinvalidations

According to Sue (2010, p. 37), microinvalidations 'may potentially rep-resent the most damaging of the three microaggressions because they directly and insidiously deny the racial, gender, or sexual-orientation reality of these groups'. This is a microaggression predicated on 'post-racial' logic. For Black mixed-race men, the threat of the erasure of complex and hybrid identities is ubiquitous. In Chapter 2, I demon-strated just some of the ways in which Black mixed-race men refuse fragmentation and constitute complex identities. In that chapter, the accounts of Claude and Brendon were particularly striking as they grappled with microinvalidations; Claude recalled being told 'you're not mixed-race' and Brendon expressed frustration that he 'couldn't even be Black'. The frustrations of Claude and Brendon are clear examples of the pernicious threat of incessant microinvalidations (Pierce, 1974; Sue et al., 2008). Similarly, the accounts in which participants refused to be interpellated as mono-racially Black demonstrated their resistance to the microinvalidations of their Blackness as Black mixed-race young men (Johnston & Nadal, 2010). The everyday hybridity demonstrated in Chapter 2 represents Black mixed-race men's response to the threat of microinvalidation. Recollections of *'what are you?'* and *'where are you from?'* interrogations are an oft-cited experience for mixed-race people (Caballero, 2004; Gaskins, 1999) and such questions act as a microinvalidation,

> Although these inquiries may seem innocuous, hearing them on a regular basis is something that monoracial persons may not experience, which may result in a unique type of stress for multiracial people. (Johnston & Nadal, 2010, p. 138)

The metacommunication in such questions is one of racial ambiguity, of being rendered outside of the Black/white racial dichotomy. A collective and pertinent example can be found in the multiracial movement's fight for mixed-race categories to be included in the census (Farley, 2004; Hochschild & Powell, 2008; Morning, 2005; 2012; Perlmann & Waters, 2002). A manifestation of white supremacy through the *de facto* and *de jure* one-drop rule and the census erasure of mixedness in the UK and USA acts as a microinvalidation for those who see their racial identities as mixed. This is enacted at the everyday level when Black mixed-race men deal with mono-racial demographic forms (Johnston & Nadal, 2010; Townsend et al., 2009). Notwithstanding limitations with current census enumeration, the activism that made it possible to be enumerated as mixed-race offers an example of collective resistance to a normalised microinvalidation at the institutional level – the activists involved demonstrated the PRR that allowed them to refuse to be bound by mono-racial categories. However, despite changes to the census, Townsend et al. (2009) found that school forms such as the 'SAT questionnaire' continue to offer only mono-racial options. It is clear that Black mixed-race men constantly grapple with the threat of microinvalidations on a range of official forms. The agitation for changes to racial categories represents a collective engagement with processes of hybridity; a *yoking together* of existent categories to create new identifications. Let us now consider more closely examples of some specific examples of the microinvalidations that Black mixed-race men face.

Jake (UK) expressed his frustrations at the threat posed by a microinvalidation he was faced with on a semi-regular basis,

> ... people not being able to understand that I'm not adopted despite being told; it seems that some people in the Southwest find it rather difficult to comprehend interracial relationships.

The enactment of the everyday racism that Jake highlights threatens to delegitimise his identity; it is beyond the comprehension of his interlocutors (Johnston & Nadal, 2010). Despite an ever-increasing number of interracial unions, mixedness is still apparently lacking the requisite citationality to normalise Jake's presence (Dalmage, 2000). This is the same lack of citationality that earlier enabled Devron's interlocutor to interpellate him as the progeny of interracial rape. In this instance, Jake's family is made intelligible through the discourse of interracial adoption (Patel, 2009). Indeed, in a society still dominated by biracialised (or, Black/white dichotomised) discourse (Ifekwunigwe, 1999), the presence of a white mother and her biological Black mixed-race son is apparently inconceivable. This is the microinvalidation, or the erasure of not only Jake's parent's relationship but also of Jake's Black mixed-race identity. However, by placing his interlocutor's inability to understand his identity as the problem, rather than his own identity, Jake resists this message. In so doing, Jake refuses to be fragmented and resists identity erasure through microinvalidation. It is in his ability to recognise the microinvalidation that Jake develops the PRR needed to resist identity erasure. Despite 'post-racial' logic suggesting that racial boundaries are no longer significant, the unwillingness and inability to comprehend the Black mixed-race family was a recurrent theme in the research. Theo (UK) recalls a similar experience. Referring to his Mum, he recollects,

> we are all her kids but still every now and again she gets people going, the other day she had a text from someone going you know 'are they yours?' and it's like fuck

me ... It's cringe. It's really awkward, really awkward. Erm, but we dealt with that. That was when we were younger mainly. I've not had it for years but if I'm walking through town with her, some people, they wouldn't look at us as Mum and Son. Some people would just be like, I don't know, friends or Aunty. But you know, that's just, I guess that's just education.

Theo begins by affirming that he and his siblings are their Mother's children. This is his response to, and rejection of, the microinvalidation. Despite his knowledge of such, the intrusion of strangers as they stare and ask questions seeks to question not only his and his Mother's relationship but his identity as a Black mixed-race man; he cannot be her son and thus he cannot be Black mixed-race. Based upon the apparent inconceivability of Black mixed-race men with white parents, this everyday microaggression engenders a process of erasure (Dalmage, 2000). However, rather than accepting this erasure, Theo identifies the microinvalidation and thus the problem as that of his interlocutors who need educating. This is Theo's elasticity: PRR.

Reece (UK) remembered his experience of a microaggression of this kind whilst he had been attending a training course arranged by his school,

... we were invited to kind of like an awards evening ... my Mum couldn't come, so I brought my Dad and my Dad is white. So, I was introducing him to all the people that I'd been working with ... one of the women was like 'oh is this your teacher?', because at that point she had no idea that I was mixed-race. She just sees me as Black and I was like no it's my Dad. She was, there was no malice in it or anything ... she was completely embarrassed; really embarrassed.

As in each of the accounts above, Reece's interlocutor is unable or unwilling to recognise the Black mixed-race family and thus Reece's identity as a Black mixed-race man. As she asks whether Reece's white father is his teacher, she interpellates Reece as a Black man who could not possibly have a white father. His mixedness undergoes a process of erasure and he is reminded that, for the white gaze, Blackness is monolithic. Reece is not bound by this, however. Despite his teacher not knowing, he remains mixed-race: his identity remains intact. As Reece notes, and as appears to be the case with many racial microaggressions, 'there was no malice' (Pérez Huber & Solórzano, 2015). Not only this, but Reece's tutor was 'really embarrassed' as she became conscious of her microaggression. As Reece knows, she is merely the vehicle through which a macroaggression is articulated at the level of the everyday (Pérez Huber & Solórzano, 2015). Perhaps what is needed, on his teacher's part, is a desire and effort to move beyond her epistemology of ignorance.

Leon (UK) recalls an incident in which an interaction with a teacher produces a microinvalidation,

> I was in science one time, I was writing, I wrote a word with an '*i*' in it, just the letter '*i*' not capital, just a normal '*i*'. She went mental at me, she said '*in this country we put dots over our i's*', but I never, I never thought anything of that at the time until I told my mum [laughs] like nobody told me, it didn't sink into my head, I didn't for a minute assume that she was being racist until I went home and spoke to my Mum about it but that is racist, you know what I mean? That is really racist. Like, '*in this country*', you know really exaggerated it, '*in this country*'.

The subtlety of this microinvalidation is apparent as Leon recalls that he 'didn't for a minute assume it was racist'. However, after discussing the incident with his Mum, Leon comes to recognise that this interaction 'is really racist'. Earlier in this chapter, Trent spoke about the need to develop 'race consciousness' because otherwise 'you can build up stories as to why that shit is happening to you and making it about like personal you'. Leon's account is a case in point of this assertion. Had Leon not become aware of the racist underpinnings of this interaction, not been able to see through 'post-racial' obfuscation, he may have assumed that his misspelling was such a considerable transgression of school expectations that it should elicit a response like this. He might have internalised messages of his own individual lack of ability and therefore not been able to overcome racial and racist difficulties (Bell, 1993; Delgado, 1982; Joseph-Salisbury, forthcoming-b; Stockdill & Danico, 2012). However, after discussions with his Mum, Leon is able to identify the root cause as racism. The metacommunication embedded in the microinvalidation here is, according to Sue (2010, p. 37), that of 'alien in one's own land'; 'this theme involves being perceived as a perpetual foreigner or being an alien in one's own country'.

The teacher attributes Leon's misspelling to his apparent foreignness and in doing so produces a microinvalidation that threatens erasure of Leon's identity as a Black mixed-race *British* man (Ifekwunigwe, 1999). Another example of this discourse was recalled in the UK by Theo:

> I remember I was probably thirteen, fourteen and some guy was stood in front of the door and I was like 'scuse me, watch out the way please mate, you know? I need to get past, or 'scuse me mate or whatever. And he was like 'I'm not your mate you Black cunt get back to your own country' and I was like 'who the fuck are you talking to?' and he grabbed me up against the wall and he was like 'yeah you Black this, you Black that, fuck off back to your own country', strangling me.

Whilst this account includes recollection of a physical assault that moves way beyond the definition of a microaggressive act, the verbal assault is a reminder of the old adage that *there ain't no Black in the Union Jack* (Gilroy, 2013). This microinvalidation acts to *other* Theo and seeks to position him as an outsider, or foreigner. Both Leon and Theo, in discussing the absurdity of these events, open up a third space in interaction in which they are able to reposition themselves as Black mixed-race men *who are also British*. They are not the foreigner the white gaze attempts to interpellate. They are post-racially resilient to threats of erasure.

Sue (2010, p. 37) highlights being 'alien in one's own land' as something that 'Asian Americans and Latino Americans [in America] are most likely to experience', this research finds that this is extendable to Blackness in Britain generally (Gilroy, 2013) and Black mixed-race men in Britain specifically (Joseph-Salisbury, 2016b). That this is a particularly British phenomenon is perhaps attributable to the relatively recent rise of the Black presence in Britain (at least in the popular imagination), and the comparatively much longer substantial Black presence in the USA (Sue, 2010). Simultaneously however, it is apparent in the current research that, with respect to their mixedness, Black/white dichotomised thinking renders Black mixed-race men and their families everywhere alien; this is the metacommunication in the archetypal 'where are you from?' (Mahtani, 2001, 2002a, 2002b; Root, 1990).

Another common microinvalidation manifests in the inability and unwillingness of white people to see and acknowledge racial inequality. As I noted in the introductory chapter, this came to the fore recently when Bill Clinton remarked that 'we're all mixed-race'. As I have argued elsewhere, 'to deny race – to state blithely that "we are all mixed race" and therefore seen as and treated as equals – is to be complicit in the maintenance of the racial hierarchies that operate at all levels of US society' (Joseph-Salisbury, 2016a). Colourblind ideology is increasingly pervasive in 'post-racial' times (Bonilla-Silva, 2006; Goldberg, 2015) and this is a frustration reflected by Black mixed-race men in the current research. Tayo (USA) conveys this,

> White people need to understand so much and they don't. I often find myself saying white people just don't get it and they don't. And it's like, they're like in a world where they're not really meant to get it and it's like they don't want to get it and like they don't understand what they have to get like [laughs]. It's like hard for white people ... White people like they look at discrimination as like individual. Or like something that happens like on instances instead of like a system ... it's like half white people's fault, half not, cos like they don't really know. It's like hard to teach somebody about privilege that they grew up with.

The microinvalidation of colourblind thinking manifests in the denial of the racial inequalities that permeates society. This preclusion engenders an erasure or an invalidation of the lived experiences of Black mixed-race men (Bonilla-Silva, 2006). This is what leads Tayo to reason 'white people just don't get it'. However, Leon also notes the subtlety of microaggressions as he acknowledges that it is 'hard for white people' to recognise the privileges bestowed upon them by systemic white supremacy (Gillborn, 2005; Leonardo, 2004; McIntosh, 1990; Rollock, 2012). As Nicola Rollock (2012, p. 70) notes, somewhat echoing Tayo, '[w]hiteness tends to benefit and advantage whites in ways that they seldom see or care to acknowledge'. The 'post-racial' mist is perhaps thicker for those who are not living with the pernicious effects of the racial (Goldberg, 2015). In this sense Tayo argues, it is 'half white people's fault, half not'. Just because the workings of white supremacy are subtle and increasingly invisible, it does not mean that white people cannot make a concerted effort to become conscious of systemic white supremacy (Mills, 2007). Tayo's argument might be taken as a call for white people to destabilise the normalisation of whiteness and to recognise the long history of structural discrimination that shapes the present (Mills, 2007). He continues to talk about a prominent example of microinvalidation,

> White people love to make things about them. Like when we see Black lives matter and they say all lives matter and it's like, we're not saying that all lives don't matter but all lives aren't under fire. It's like we're talking about Black lives.

As Tayo suggests, the 'all lives matter' slogan acts as a microinvalidation that, through epistemologies of white ignorance (Mills, 2007), acts to erase or invalidate the racial inequalities that shape the lived experiences of racially minoritised people; indeed, it is this that 'Black lives matter' slogan seeks to capture (Joseph-Salisbury, 2016c). Charles Mills (2007, p. 19) argues that '[o]ne learns to see through identifying white blindness and avoiding the pitfalls of putting on the spectacles for one's own vision'. It is perhaps this ability that Tayo's account aptly demonstrates. This is Tayo's racial literacy that sees through the 'post-racial' and bolsters his PRR.

Conclusion

This chapter has argued that as a theoretical concept, racial microaggressions respond to the increasing subtlety and invisibility of contemporary forms of racism. In a 'post-racial' epoch in which few recognise racism as a problem, and fewer still would admit to being a racist, this is a necessary development for Critical Race theorists and for Black mixed-race men. The racial microaggressions set out in this chapter are in no way exhaustive. Indeed, to capture the multifarious racial microaggressions, Black mixed-race men encounter in their daily lives would be an impossibility. There are several accounts in preceding chapters that may well be identified as racial microaggressions and, although beyond the scope of this book, the microaggressions presented by curricular erasure (Joseph-Salisbury, 2018b), low teacher expectations (Joseph-Salisbury, 2016a), and the white supremacist school environment are worthy of consideration. That said, what I do in this chapter is begin to demonstrate just some of the ways racial microaggressions are enacted at the interpersonal level of the everyday.

As has been argued, microaggressions are often subtle and are normalised through repetition. As the microaggressions become normalised, so too do the metacommunications of white supremacist ideology. It is the subtlety that makes microaggressions not only difficult to identify but difficult to challenge. However, it has been shown that Black mixed-race men are adept in their ability to do so. Indeed, a sense of the inevitability of racial microaggressions means that the ability to identify them is essential to the cultivation of the PRR that enables Black mixed-race men to withstand the embedded pernicious and degrading messages. Not only do Black mixed-race men resist these messages but they frequently *speak back* as they refuse to be rendered docile. The chapter explored three forms of racial microaggressions; microassaults, microinsults and microinvalidations.

Microassaults take on the form most comparable to old-fashioned racisms. However, in this 'post-racial' epoch, they are distinguishable because of the limited circumstances in which they occur. The aggressor must have a sense of anonymity, safety, or a loss of control. The use of racial epithets and racist jokes were recalled by a number of Black mixed-race men. It was argued that the school can, and often does, offer a site of the requisite safety for racial microassaults.

Microinsults are somewhat subtler and are engendered by epistemologies of white ignorance. Microinsults often manifests in the imposition of racist stereotypes; *the criminal* and *the service worker* were just two examples Black mixed-race men were able to recall. Racial othering and exoticising was also found to be prevalent, particularly surrounding Black mixed-race men's hair. Despite the apparent subtlety of microinsults, Black mixed-race men appeared to be adept in decoding and resisting the metacommunications.

The third form explored were microinvalidations. It has been argued that microinvalidations represent the most insidious and threatening form of racial microaggressions, not least due to their subtlety. The chapter argued that microinvalidations are a particularly pernicious threat for Black mixed-race men who, given the persistence of the imagined Black/white racial dichotomy, constantly resist the erasure and fragmentation of their mixed identities. The denial of systemic racism and white privilege was another source of microinvalidation that threatened to erase the lived experiences of Black mixed-race men. Again, Black mixed-race men demonstrated an adeptness in their ability to resist and speak back to these invalidations. In so doing, Black mixed-race men remained resilient against ubiquitous threats to their hybridised identities. To be clear, PRR takes on two clear forms. In the first instance, it is the ability to see through the 'post-racial' mist. This allows Black mixed-race men to understand racial microaggressions and to refuse their pernicious effects. In the second instance, it is, in response to racial microaggressions, the engagement in processes of hybridity that reflect a multiplicitous and fluid sense of self. Building upon this chapter, and those preceding, in the following chapter, I consider the way that Black mixed-race men form and negotiate peer groups.

Chapter 5

Black Mixed-Race Men, Friendships, Peer Groups and Black Regulatory Ideals

Introduction

Building upon each of the preceding chapters, and focusing specifically on the context of the school, in this chapter I consider how Black mixed-race men's racial identification influences and is influenced by friendships and peer groups. The importance of peer groups and friendships in the lives of adolescents has been widely noted (McGill, Way, & Hughes, 2012). As Sandra Winn Tutwiler (2016, p. 136) argues in her work on *mixed race youth and schooling*, peers are 'instrumental in the socialization process'. This assertion is consistent with an argument underpinning this book: *identifications are perpetually constituted and reconstituted through interactions with the social world; through (responses to) racial microaggressions and through friendships and peer groups* (Alexander, 1996). Not only are peer groups essential to the fashioning of identities (Mac an Ghaill, 1988) but participation in peer groups is influenced by a pre-existent sense of one's identity (McGill et al., 2012). As will be demonstrated, peer groups are a source of social and cultural capital and can serve a range of purposes for racially minoritised men generally (Carter, 2012; Mac an Ghaill, 1988; Sewell, 1997; Warikoo, 2011) and Black mixed-race men particularly (Khanna, 2011b; Quillian & Redd, 2009; Tutwiler, 2016).

Unsurprisingly given the various forms of segregation that persist in the USA (Dunsmuir, 2013; McPherson, Smith-Lovin, & Cook, 2001; Rivkin, 1994), and to a lesser extent in the UK (Burgess & Wilson, 2005; Phillips, 2007), school peer groups are often racially homogenous with racial boundaries, sometimes understood to be defined explicitly by race (Clark & Ayers, 1992; Doyle & Kao, 2007; Feagin & Van Ausdale, 2001; Quillian & Redd, 2009) and often more implicitly through the kind of racial symbolism I discussed in Chapter 4 (Carter, 2003, 2005, 2012; Khanna, 2011b; Tutwiler, 2016; Warikoo, 2011). Whether explicitly or implicitly, *symbolic boundaries* are made salient (Lamont & Molnár, 2002). (The racial microaggressions explored in the preceding chapter act, in some way, to maintain and strengthen these racialised boundaries.[1])

That peer groups are often structured along racial lines raises interesting questions for the experiences of Black mixed-race men, particularly given the apparent absence of a mixed-race group (Tutwiler, 2016). Whilst such groups may well arise as mixed populations grow, and the beginnings of this has been found in other research (Sims, 2014), like Tutwiler, in the current research I similarly found little evidence of mixed-race peer groups. In this chapter, I argue that the perceptions and engagement of Black mixed-race men with friendships and peer groups are as multifarious, diverse and complex as are their identities. Black mixed-race men show an ability to understand and utilise peer groups to enhance their PRR, whilst simultaneously drawing upon PRR in order to negotiate their own positionalities within peer groups. Ultimately, what is painted is a complex picture in which Black mixed-race men draw upon a range of discursive practices in their interactions with peers.

In the next section, I consider Black mixed-race men and their Black men peer groups. In that section, I pay attention to the processes of racial governmentality that mediate those peer groups. I then turn to consider how Black mixed-race men develop friendships with white peers, before considering how some Black mixed-race men seek to respond to and move beyond the apparent constraints of the Black/white racial dichotomy. Throughout each section, I argue that Black mixed-race men utilise PRR in order to develop friendships. In the chapter's conclusion, I return to explicate this argument.

'Birds of a Feather Flock Together': Black Men, Friendships and Peer Groups

> I'm not gonna say its coincidental that you gravitate towards someone that's like you, it's natural that you're gonna find someone who has the same skin colour, same background, racial makeup, same kind of interests that you do, and you're gonna gravitate towards them. (Isaac, USA)

---

[1]Recall in the previous chapter the cumulative burden of racial microaggressions led Anton (UK) to regretfully note, 'I've always got that sort of separateness within me'.

Given the suggestion in previous chapters that Black mixed-race men see Blackness as central to the constitution of their identities, it is unsurprising that many of the Black mixed-race men in this study formed close friendships and peer groups with Black men peers (Brunsma & Rockquemore, 2001; Tikly et al., 2004; Tizard & Phoenix, 2002). As captured by Isaac's comments above, there was a strong sense of commonality and shared experiences for Black mixed-race men on both sides of the Atlantic. Whilst Warikoo's (2011) findings of greater peer group segregation in the USA than the UK may have some validity, for many of the men in this study, racial segregation did play a considerable role in UK peer group formations too. For instance, having grown up in a predominantly white area, Leon (UK) describes his conscious efforts to form friendships with 'Black boys',

> Being in a group of white people, I didn't feel like we all had the same things in common, you know? So, I'd say when I went into year ten, probably about [age] fifteen, something like that, that's when I started to go out in different areas … so yeah when I got into year ten I started going around in the areas and I did feel like I had more in common with the boys there … there are a lot more similarities with me and Black kids, I just don't know why. It's just one of them, it feels more natural, and I'm not being racist.

Leon's sense of a lack of commonality with white peers leads him to actively seek interactions with Black boys from a different area. Here, he argues, he finds he has 'more in common' and 'a lot more similarities'. This act can be considered part of Leon's PRR as he seeks a peer group where he feels more 'natural'. Similar notions are echoed by Zak (UK) who argues that 'there is certain stuff you can say to Black kids'. For Leon, there is a sense that race is somewhat 'natural' and so Leon reifies race generally, and his own racialised identity specifically. However, noticing that he might have implied a racial preference for friends, like the Black men in Alexander's (1996) research, he is quick to assert he is 'not being racist'. Despite Leon's acute awareness of the way race shapes experiences, 'post-racial' logic means that, in talking about race, he feels the need to assert that he is not being racist (Bonilla-Silva, 2015). In this vein, Leon continues to describe the relationships with white peers that led him to seek new friendships,

> It felt to me that they didn't understand what I was about,
> you know what I mean? They didn't really understand,
> sort of like segregation, but they were not trying to aim
> anything at me, sort of like I'm a red dot and they're all
> blue dots, you know what I mean? I just felt out of place,
> I don't feel like anybody was doing it on purpose.

Again, here Leon shows such wariness in talking about race that he uses a somewhat cumbersome metaphor as he substitutes white and Black people for blue and red dots. Rather than an isolated Black mixed-race man, he is an isolated red dot. So, whilst race is somewhat taboo in Leon's 'post-racial' linguistic repertoire, it remains nevertheless present in his lived experiences and friendship making. Goldberg (2015) argues that 'post-racial' conditions attempt to strip the racially minoritised of the language to identify and critique racial processes. Leon's metaphor is his resistance to the work of the 'post-racial'. Leon again naturalises racial differences as despite feeling out of place, he notes that this segregation was not intentional. His sense of commonality is further extoled as he continues, 'in the Black areas, with the Black kids … you feel like you're in a community when you're with the same people, the same as you' (Leon, UK). It is apparent that Leon's mixedness does not constitute a barrier to his sense of sameness (Mahtani, 2014).

Demonstrating the Transatlanticity of experiences like Leon's, Erik (USA) shares those sentiments as he recalls, 'when it came to lunch time I'd always sit with my Black friends and like we had our own table and stuff'. In an attempt to explain this, Erik continues,

> I feel like you can rationalize it by saying like you are of
> the same interests. So, like obviously you'll hang out cos
> like you're from one type of culture … so course you're
> gonna hang out with people who share that type of cul-
> ture. Who like laugh at the same things you laugh at, who
> like do the same things, I don't know. Birds of a feather
> flock together. If you have the same interests you're gonna
> hang out.

As in Leon's case, and Isaac's (at the opening of this section), Erik argues there is an inevitability about his engagement with his Black peers. Erik draws upon a sense of shared culture; culture being inextricably bound up with race (Alexander, 1996; Tate, 2005), to demonstrate his sense of racial homophily; 'birds of a feather flock together' seems to capture the sentiments of both Leon and Erik. These homophilic tendencies are unsurprising; Plato (1968, p. 837) observed that 'similarity begets friendship' and Aristotle (1934, p. 1371) noted that people 'love those who are like themselves'. In societies stratified along racial lines, Leon and Erik's perspectives are no surprise (McPherson et al., 2001). For them, interests seem to be mediated by culture and this shapes peer groups. To be in a peer group with shared interests means Black mixed-race men are better able to express their interests and thus to have one's sense of identity validated: To be in a Black peer group can strengthen one's PRR.

What is apparent in both Leon and Erik's accounts is that they understand their identities as Black. This is not to say that their mixedness is rejected or forgotten (indeed elsewhere both have noted their mixedness) but that it is not salient in this moment and not in any way counterintuitive to performative Blackness. This speaks to the contextuality, fluidity and perpetual hybridity of the identities of Black mixed-race men; as Black mixed-race men are always agentic in the development of friendships (Khanna, 2011a; Tutwiler, 2016). This fluidity was captured too by Alex (UK),

> I kind of click with Black people a bit easier in a social setting. Maybe interests too, like the music that I like, and all that stuff … I'd say Black males have probably influenced maybe the way I speak a bit, the way I act a little bit, but then maybe that's cos I kinda see myself as a Black male sometimes as well.

For Alex and other Black mixed-race men, it was not only race that influenced peer groups but also gender: race is always gendered, and gender is always raced. This was explicitly evident in Leon's account too. Alex understands his commonality with Black men through racial symbolism; shared interests in music 'and all that stuff'. The stylization of speech and other actions act to shape the sense of commonality (Tutwiler, 2016) through racial symbolism (Khanna, 2011b); the individual and group identities are symbiotically constituted. Alex captures the dialectical nature of this in his account. It is not simply the case that Black mixed-race men perform to fit into the group but that their sense of their identity helps to constitute the parameters and identity of the group. Put another way, it is not just that Alex seeks to self-consciously mimic his Black men peers but his sense of himself as a Black man shapes his performance; he is inextricably imbricated in discourses of Blackness.

The fluidity of identities is captured again as Alex notes that it is 'sometimes' that he sees himself as a Black man. Perhaps then, it is the development of what Minelle Mahtani (2014, p. 207) terms 'strategic sameness' that Leon, Erik and Alex are able to cultivate. The identity work (Khanna & Johnson, 2010) of cultivating strategic sameness acts to enhance Black mixed-race men's 'post-racial' resilience as the men are able to perform and validate their identities: this was evident in a number of accounts. Take Will (USA) for instance, in the following account, he describes his positionality in his Black peer group,

> They knew that I was a mix of stuff, um, but like they didn't give a shit. Like we were all just the Black kids. Cos Vee was African which is a whole other thing in America. Like you might as well be mixed if you're African, that's how it is here. Kevin was just Black. And Linton was from the islands so, and then there was RJ who was our white friend in the group. So, we were all different. Like I was just the mixed up Black kid. Linton was the Caribbean Black kid. Vee was the African Black kid. Kevin was the actual Black kid and then RJ was the white kid [laughs]. So, my group was just kind of like every kind of Black kid and a white kid. Which is actually kind of cool.

As Will (USA) argues that 'we were all just the Black kids', he invokes a sense of strategic sameness that shapes the collective identity of his peer group (Mahtani, 2014). As he goes on to demonstrate, however, and as Audre Lorde (2003, p. 2) puts it, this does not mean 'a shedding of our differences, nor the pathetic pretense that these differences do not exist'. Will engages in a dialectical movement between sameness and difference as he at once recognises a collective identity and his individual identification.

In describing his peers, Will positions 'mono-racial' African American Blackness as the authentic ('actual') form, the regulatory ideal, against which others are judged. However, in so doing, he also makes clear that conceptions of racial purity (or mono-raciality) do not form the only marker of racial authenticity in the governmentality of Blackness (Harris & Khanna, 2010; Tate, 2005). As he argues, to be Black African is comparable to being Black mixed; that is, it deviates from the regulatory ideal. Similarly, being 'from the islands' is a marker of difference from the Black same. This difference is not problematic as those identities are still considered part of the Black same; they are each a 'kind of Black kid'. The definitions deployed by Will and his peers are so fluid that the group even includes 'a white kid'. Thus, racial boundaries are often defined by racialised interests (in the pursuit of PRR) rather than an illusory subscription to biological differences (Warikoo, 2011). This really refutes the claims from scholars like Melissa Herman (2004) that rejection from Black peer groups is inevitable for Black mixed-race youth. It is perhaps because studies on mixedness are often based on predominantly women samples – and have focused on the intersection of race and gender for Black mixed-race women (Rockquemore & Laszloffy, 2005) whilst ignoring Black mixed-race men – that Herman is able to make claims such as this. In this regard, the accounts of Black mixed-race men in this research suggest that relationalities to Black peer groups take on particular forms for Black mixed-race men who are, as a consequence of their masculinity, more likely to gain acceptance (Sims and Joseph-Salisbury, forthcoming). Thus, the findings of this study present a long overdue challenge to gendered generalisations in Critical Mixed Race Studies.

Again showing Transatlantic parallels, In the UK, Trent recalls strategically drawing upon conceptions of the Black same in his participation in the Black masculine peer group:

> I was one of four Black people in my year, you're not gonna stop trying to wonder what Blackness you are. You're just gonna club together, otherwise I'd be separating myself even more, you know. So, I didn't really think about it then.

With clear parallels to Will's account, Trent here demonstrates the importance of conceptions of the Black same (Mahtani, 2014). As Alexander (1996, p. 32) has argued, 'the potency of the idea of the 'black community', for both black people and wider society, depends on its perception as a unified and largely separate entity'; this is what Trent invokes. In this instance, difference is necessarily minimised in order to maintain the performance of the Black same and thus, the potency to which Alexander refers, enhances the PRR of Trent and his peer group (Khanna, 2011b; Tate, 2005; Stubblefield, 2005). It is noteworthy that this excerpt comes in the context of Trent talking about his ancestral heritage being African American as opposed to the African Caribbean heritage of his peers. Again, the parameters of authentic Blackness are defined and redefined along various lines, of which mixedness is just one (Harris & Khanna, 2010; Tate, 2005).

For Trent and his peers, the performance of the Black same is necessary to combat feelings of isolation and threats of racial microaggressions from white peers. If Trent were not to perform the Black same, he would be further isolated in an already isolating environment. In this sense then, the Black masculine peer group becomes highly functional for Black mixed-race men like Trent (Alexander, 1996; Mac an Ghaill, 1988). It was often in these groups that the masculine toughness, discussed in Chapter 3, was cultivated and performed. As Trent and others conveyed in that chapter, Black mixed-race men were able to cultivate masculine tough group identities for protection, to attract girls and for popularity with other men. Thus, acceptance in the Black peer group is a particularly gendered phenomenon that, in comparison to existing research (Herman, 2004; Rockquemore & Laszloffy, 2005), appears to be far easier for Black mixed-race men (Sims and Joseph-Salisbury, forthcoming). Trent's comments here are not surprising; research suggests that it is in groups that boys become masculine (Connell, 1989, 1996; Pascoe, 2011; Woody, 2002). It is therefore often in groups that Black and Black mixed-race men perform toughness (Majors & Billson, 1993) and demonstrate 'power and control' (Alexander, 1996). In a hostile environment, the Black masculine peer group functions to bolster Trent's PRR (Mac an Ghaill, 1988).

A similar sentiment is conveyed by Reece (UK) who discusses a sense of Black men's support in combatting the threat of racial microassaults,

> If you made a racist comment ... I would have told my Black friends. My Black friends are bigger than me. Now you've got a really, really big problem.

The sheer presence of Black peers acts as a source of Black cultural capital that responds to the ubiquitous threat of racial microassaults. The Black masculine peer group was seen as a threat and thus seemed to amplify the sense of the threatening and deviant Black man (Hall et al., 2013).

Drawing upon a sense of double consciousness, it is perhaps this discourse of the threatening Black man that Reece and Trent manipulate to enhance their PRR. Alex demonstrates this as he considers his Black masculine peer group through the white gaze,

... when we're in a group as well. When we're in a group, that's when I noticed that people are a lot more like, like scared of us. (Alex, UK)

According to Alex and others, toughness becomes accentuated in the Black men's peer group. For Alex, the Black masculine peer group offers a source of PRR in the face of racist harassment from white peers, teachers and the police. He continues,

It was like we were living in a different world from even like the Asian boys, or like the white boys. So yeah, this was specifically a Black boy thing, and a mixed-race boy thing, that we felt like we had to protect ourselves, every-where we go.

From Alex's comments, the way that race and gender intersect to create specific and unique experiences begins to become clear. The sense of a need to protect one's self 'everywhere we go' is specifically felt by Black and Black mixed-race men who reject 'post-racial' logic as they develop an important understanding of their lived experiences and of the racist and racialised difficulties they may encounter. As a consequence of gendered racism, Black mixed-race men (know that they) are particularly vulnerable to violence, murder and police harassment (Harrell, 2007; hooks, 2004). Of the Black men peer group in her ethnographic study, Alexander (1996, p. 141) notes that 'what was of significance was the social function of the group'.

The potential fear of racists that Alex conveys as a potential reason for Black peer group formation is conveyed too by Reece (UK),

If I'm walking down the street and I see a group of Black lads or a group of white lads just walking in the direction of me – they're walking that way anyway – I'm more worried about, worried is loose but, more worried about the group of white kids than the Black, because there's a really weird sense of knowledge that if any trouble happens with the Black kids, it's not cos I'm Black, or not cos I'm mixed-race, just because that's the person that they probably are. I feel like if some kind of trouble kicked off with white lads, I'd definitely consider, was there some kind of racial charge behind it?

Reece shows an awareness of pervasive white racism and how a sense of double consciousness impacts upon his interactions with the social world. If he were to encounter trouble with a group of white lads, he reasons this could be attributable to anti-Black racism. Reece makes clear how the spectre of racism is always in some part constitutive of Black mixed-race men's identities (Alexander, 1996; Mac an Ghaill, 1994a; Yancy, 2017). Like Reece, Tayo (USA) conveys his acute sense of difference from white peers. This is constitutive of his Black identity,

> I went from like a diverse group of people to being like the only Black kid, right? So, it was, it was like, it made my Blackness important to me because I was Black. I was one of the only Black kids. So, Blackness became something really important to me. So, when I first came in the school I didn't make any friends for half a year cos I just didn't wanna be there and I was really like stand offish … I'm in this environment, I don't know anybody, like, there's no Black people here [laughs]. I mean even now that's kind of like a frustrating or intimidating environment to be in just because there's nobody to relate to.

Tayo's sense of his Black identity becomes much stronger in the presence of that which he is not: white. Much like Leon (UK) who earlier discussed how an alienating school environment led him to seek out Black friends, Tayo (USA) feels a sense of isolation because 'there's no Black people'. Racial difference is made real by Tayo as he feels like *a body out of place* in a 'frustrating or intimidating environment'. That he suggests he has 'nobody to relate to' shows just how impactful racial homophily can be on the formations of friendship groups (McPherson et al., 2001). This is perhaps what leads to Brendon's (USA) description of his friendship with an African American peer,

> I guess my friend, there's not like a whole bunch of African Americans here and it was easier for me to be really accepting and us to develop a relationship.

In Chapter 2, Brendon spoke of his frustrations at not being able to 'just be Black'. However, it appears that Brendon too is able to deploy a sense of 'strategic sameness' in his friendship (Mahtani, 2014). Their shared racial difference means they are able to be 'accepting', presumably in contrast to the lack of acceptance from predominantly white peers and with the absence of a 'whole bunch of African Americans'. Strategic sameness is something that is deployed contextually by Black mixed-race men. As Brendon went on to argue, 'I feel like it is easier some places than others'. Black mixed-race men then are able to engage in identity work 'to highlight, downplay, or conceal particular racial identities with others' (Khanna, 2011a, p. 80). Whilst strategic sameness was indeed useful for many of the participants in the current study, the Black masculine peer group was also a site for processes of racial governmentality.

Black Mixed-Race Men and the Governmentality of the Black Peer Group

As I have argued in previous chapters, a key marker of 'authentic' Blackness is dark skin (Harris & Khanna, 2010). Thus, this marker is significant in the establishment of boundaries to the Black peer group (Harris & Khanna, 2010; Tate, 2005). So much so that researchers like Herman (2004) have suggested rejection from the peer group is somewhat inevitable. Whilst the findings of the current research refute this apparent inevitability (also see Sims and Joseph-Salisbury, forthcoming), there is some acknowledgement of the surveillance of Black mixed-race men in Black men peer groups. Indeed, Max (UK) recalls having had particularly difficult times with his Black men peers,

> They were proper hating me for being light skinned. Don't know why. Never did nothing to them; never said nothing to them. But I was fucking 'lighty'. They'd always try and give me grief but it didn't quite work, one tried to push me once and it didn't end well.

Whilst this experience is striking and noteworthy, it was somewhat atypical (Harris & Khanna, 2010). Although apparently not in Max's case ('it didn't quite work'), the pressures of the Black masculine peer group can, for some, lead to what some researchers describe as 'over-compensatory' performances (Root, 2003; Tikly et al., 2004; Tutwiler, 2016). Demonstrating this belief, Alex (UK) argued that 'a lot of mixed-race boys that are surrounded by Black males sometimes do overcompensate'. He continues to consider his own relationship with Black men,

> I don't always try hard to fit in with Black males or what-
> ever but I just feel like I need to prove myself in certain
> ways before I'm accepted and before they can like take me
> as myself. I know like, a lot of my friends are Black males,
> but I remember like, just some of their attitudes when they
> first met me, was kinda like oh I'm not really tryna mess
> with this guy over here. I think sometimes maybe it was
> the way I was dressed. Maybe my jeans were a little bit
> too tight or something like that.

Alex notes his sense of a need to validate his Blackness in order to
gain acceptance from his Black peers. His positionality is something
to be negotiated as he must 'prove' himself 'in certain ways' in order to
resist his marginalisation. However, as Alex clearly conveys, this is not
solely about his mixedness; there are a multiplicity of factors at play in
the racial governmentality of the Black peer group (Harris & Khanna,
2010; Tate, 2005). Whilst Alex does highlight mixedness, it might also
be something to do with the way he dressed: that his 'jeans were a little
bit too tight'. The importance of racial symbolism discussed in
Chapter 4 is reiterated here. Alex (UK) continues to discuss how he
negotiated his positionality,

> But then, yeah, like just after having like a few words with
> me and just seeing that like, I'm down to earth, I under-
> stand, like we go through the same kind of issues, we do
> see life the same way, after that I noticed that they did
> ease up a lot around me and accepted me innit.

After 'having a few words' with Black peers, Alex was able to subvert
the trope of racial purity as an exclusionary practice of Blackness (Tate,
2005). He is able to display commonality through shared issues and a
shared understanding: an episteme of Blackness (Yancy, 2008). Thus,
Alex speaks back to narrowly defined conceptions of Blackness and
engages in discursive practices to reposition himself away from the
margins (Khanna, 2011b; Tate, 2005). Rather than acting in an 'over
compensatory' fashion then, perhaps Alex is merely speaking back to
the governmentality of the Black peer group. As Alex exercises his
PRR, he is not only repositioning himself but redefining the borders of
Blackness. The reader might recall that, in Chapter 2, Claude (UK)
spoke of drawing upon his knowledge of African history to disrupt and
speak back to skin as *the* marker of Blackness. This is what Tate (2005,

p. 153) describes as a 'disruption of the regime of truth in which skin colour does not signify outsiderness'. Black mixed-race men, as Alex demonstrates, engage in hybridisation at the level of the everyday as they draw upon competing discourses in order to define and redefine not only themselves but the contours of race. As has been argued, the ability to do so is integral to the PRR of Black mixed-race men. Reflecting upon how his performances have changed over time, Alex goes on,

> I never really tried too hard. Maybe when I was younger I would have tried a bit harder but now obviously being a bit more comfortable being in my own skin, having better self-esteem and things like that.

Alex talks about his engagement in a certain amount of identity work when he was younger (Khanna, 2011a, 2011b), as he engaged in the negotiation of positionalities within the Black peer group. As he gets older, however, Alex no longer feels the need to engage in such conscious performances. He is 'comfortable' with his identity as a Black mixed-race man. This is consistent with the argument made earlier that PRR is something that is developed over time and through experience.

In the following account, Reece (UK) sheds some light on the dynamics that he suggests can be at play in relationships with Black peers,

> … it's often you can have the more problematic kind of occurrences in instances with Black people, you know, and it's more based off the back of that, and not rightly or wrongly, but the kind of resentment that a lot of Black people tend to have towards, you know the long-lasting effects of racism, whereas they go well you know, you being mixed-race you've kind of got a good deal where society might like you a little more. And I feel like they can resent you, not everybody but people can resent that so it's like yeah, you're Black when it suits us but any moment that kind of sets that alight, we'll quickly remind you.

Here, Reece echoes findings of Harris and Khanna (2010) as they, like he, argue that perceptions of mixed-race and light-skin privileges during enslavement created a sense of resentment from darker-skinned slaves (Williamson, 1980). According to Reece, this has 'long lasting effects', that means his positionality in the Black community is always marked by precariousness. He is always subject to being reminded of his marginal status. In highlighting these 'long lasting effects', Reece rejects the 'post-racial' in order to understand his positionality in the racial order; this is an important component of his PRR. Whilst the 'internal politics of colorism may still ripple below' (Russell, Wilson, & Hall, 1992, p. 35) the majority of participants generally 'felt accepted and embraced by other blacks' (Harris & Khanna, 2010, p. 651; Khanna, 2010; Sims and Joseph-Salisbury, forthcoming). This is unsurprising given the legacy of the one-drop rule, shared experiences of racial discrimination, and shared ancestral heritage (Harris & Khanna, 2010; Stubblefield, 2005).

It should be noted that mixedness was just one of a multiplicity of factors that defined the borders of Blackness. This was demonstrated in Chapter 3 as Trent (UK) spoke about his experiences at the intersection of Blackness and homosexuality. In the following account, he elaborates on how he feels his sexuality rendered him outside of the Black man same,

> But with the [Black] guys, it was a weird relationship.
> I knew that I wasn't like them. I knew that there was
> something different about me that was meaning that I
> couldn't talk completely to them, and then obviously with
> hindsight that was my sexuality.

Recall earlier (and in Chapter 3) Trent noted that the Black peer group served a protective function in the face of a hostile white school environment (Alexander, 1996). Here, however, he also notes an apparent lack of internal cohesion. This is perhaps not surprising: as Alexander (1996, p. 142) notes of the Black masculine peer group in her study, 'when this external stimulation was not present, the group became much looser and more internally divided and competitive'. Despite his inability to 'talk completely' to other members, the functionality of the peer group remains intact as the group still seeks to elicit and control the external responses. However, as Trent goes on to demonstrate, once he is outed as gay his positionality within the peer group is placed under threat and he is ultimately rendered an outsider,

> Unfortunately, you do lose the Black clique that you're
> friends with at that time. I mean I'm friends with them

again now but obviously, there was like five of us in the year like I said so having a gay Black dude in there is really not gonna help that.

Trent's account here demonstrates the complexity and multiplicity of identity constitution. Whilst elsewhere he had spoken about feeling different because of his African American heritage, he now highlights his sexuality as reason for his rendering outside of the Black peer group. It appears that for Trent, both of these factors are more centrally constitutive of authentic Blackness (and the parameters of the Black peer group) than mixedness. In this instance, Trent (UK) is threatened with the prospect of being the aforementioned marginal mixed-race man as his sexuality sees him rendered outside of Blackness, and his race sees him rendered outside of whiteness. However, this is, of course, a positionality that Trent persistently negotiates. As Trent is rendered outside of authentic Blackness, recall too that Will (USA) likened being the 'mixed up Black kid' to being 'the African Black kid'. As the following account from Anton (UK) attests, the borders of the Black peer group should be seen as fluid, malleable, and demarcated by a range of intersecting factors. This is demonstrated by Anton (UK),

I was never called a mixed-race this or a hybrid that or something. The only time I've had like, a different kind of racism is when I've met Africans who either refuse to, like they'll call me white or something like that or I've had an experience where they were saying like, cos we're Jamaican, or cos I'm of Jamaican heritage that Jamaicans aren't Black at all and we're sons of slaves and we're definitely not Black. But then again, I discussed with him and we got through it kind of thing and he said sorry.

In Anton's experiences then, Black ancestral heritage is a far more influential determinant of authentic Blackness than mixedness. Whilst his mixedness is never mentioned, African peers pathologise his Jamaican heritage as being outside of the parameters of authentic Blackness. This is perhaps due to a popular perception that all Jamaicans are mixed-race due to enslavement. It is apparent then that conceptions of racial purity are about far more than proximity to whiteness through a white parent. According to Anton's interlocutors, 'Jamaicans aren't Black at all'. A further injurious degradation is offered as Anton's interlocutors draw upon pernicious discourses of African Black authenticity and superiority (see, Mwakikagile, 2007) in order to interpellate Jamaicans as 'not Black' and the 'sons of slaves'. It should be noted that drawing upon ancestral heritage to undermine others' claims to Black authenticity was seen to be multidirectional and not just about those with African heritage degrading those with Caribbean heritage[2]. Anton's account offers a reminder that Black mixed-race men's identities are 'never singular but multiply constructed across different, often intersecting and antagonistic, discourses, practices and positions' (Hall, 1996, p. 17). Moreover, however, it is apparent that this multiplicity is brought into play in the governmentality of Blackness. Anton is able to resist the erasure of his Blackness as he remains resilient to this racial degradation. He is able to engage his aggressor in a discussion and elicit an apology from him.

Born in Cameroon but having spent most of his life in the USA, Erik (USA) spoke about his experiences with Black African American peers,

> ... people knew I was African. Like born in Africa but like because I don't sound African I feel like it was a lot easier to fit in with the group. So, I actually like, I don't know how people perceive me cos I know I'm a very confusing person.

As Erik suggests it is because he does not 'sound African' that he is able to 'fit in', the implication is that if he were to 'sound African' he may be marginalised by his Black peers. Thus, African American Blackness emerges as the regulatory ideal. It is perhaps the multiplicity of his identity that Erik seeks to capture as he describes himself as a 'confusing person'. This is not indicative of a pathological sense of self but a realisation that others may struggle to comprehend the complexities of a hybridised identity that draws upon a multiplicity of discourses in its bricolage-like constitution. It also nods to the importance of speech as racial symbolism. As an African American, Reggie

---

[2] ... with boys being boys and just cussing each other, like sometimes we would bring up race or whatever, especially between Africans and Jamaicans, like we always used to get at each other. (Alex, UK)

shows the multi-directionality of these encounters as various actors vie to claim authenticity,

> The racism that I experienced the most in like my elementary middle school years was from Africans. Like there was a time in middle school when the African males and like regular Black males were at war like for no reason and like I never understood that but because I was like on the fence and I had a bunch of different races within me, it was just like what am I supposed to be like. Am I supposed to be angry? Am I supposed to be that? (Reggie, USA)

Notice here that Reggie positions African American men as the 'regular Black males' against which other Black men are judged (Waters, 1999). The apparent heterogeneity of Blackness, whether strategic or otherwise, expressed in earlier accounts is destabilised by Reggie's account in which nationality sees variously positioned Black boys as at 'war' for 'no reason'. Despite his racialised interpellation as African American, Reggie still notes his identity as multiplicitous. It is constituted by 'a bunch of races'. As he makes this affirmation, Reggie displays his PRR as he refuses to be fragmented. Nevertheless, Reggie's apparently unique positioning means he is unsure how 'to be' a Black mixed-race man.

What becomes clear in Reggie's account (and the other accounts in this section) is that although for some, at times, Black peer groups are functional and important, they should in no way be romanticised. Functioning as a 'site of surveillance, normalization and control' (Tate, 2005, p. 153), Black mixed-race men's relationships with Black men are varied, complex, and sometimes fractious. Borders to the peer group are not only marked by dark skin but also by consciousness, culture, interests, ancestral heritage, sexuality and more. Indeed, in their comparative study of Black mixed-race and Black middle-class individuals, Harris and Khanna (2010, p. 639) 'find evidence of greater tolerance for the [Black] community's racial diversity than its class diversity'. Thus, although mixedness and light skin may sometimes serve as a site for exclusionary practices, this is in no way categorical as has been suggested (see, for instance, Herman, 2004). In their hybridisation, Black mixed-race men, to varying levels of success, draw upon a range of discursive practices in order to reconstitute themselves as insiders and speak back to a 'Black politics of skin' (Tate, 2005).

Friendships with White Peers

Whilst racial homophily often ensured that Black mixed-race men formed friendships and peer groups with Black men, this was not their only source of friendship. Indeed, friendships were highly varied not only between participants but for each individual Black mixed-race man. Earlier in this section Erik (USA) remarked that 'birds of a feather flock together', whilst having noted his imbrication in racial homophily, he goes on to deconstruct this,

> At the same time, I also feel like a lot of Black people don't feel like they have common interests with white people and that preconceived notion kind of makes you cut yourself off from white people, more than usual. Cos it's not like we're aliens. It's not like we don't have anything in common. So, I don't know why we just like ostracize yourself from that group entirely. But it's just a mentality, I feel like.

Here Erik identifies racial homophily as the 'mentality' shaping friendship groups but goes on to challenge the validity of race as a determinant factor in friendship choices. It is a 'preconceived notion' that leads to self-ostracisation based on the sameness of Black men and the difference of white men. However, as Erik notes 'it's not like we're aliens'. The perpetual experience of racial microaggressions discussed in the last chapter might, however, play a role in shaping this perception of difference (Yancy, 2008). For some, like Jermaine (USA), the specific (mono-racial) form microaggressions can take on for Black mixed-race men (see, Johnston & Nadal, 2010) meant that his friendships were shaped by discourses of Black/white mono-raciality. As he recalls,

> Black people make jokes about me being white, and white people make jokes about me being Black. So, it's like weird, I guess. I have white friends but, just you know, minor stuff; the common microaggressions for a light-skinned kid.

It becomes apparent here that Jermaine's interpellation occurs through a Black/white dichotomised paradigm in which only Blackness and whiteness are intelligible (Johnston & Nadal, 2010). Thus, his mixedness becomes a subject of attention. As such, Jermaine is subjected to jokes about his Blackness from his white peers and jokes about his whiteness from his Black peers. In each context, the totality of his identity undergoes a process of fragmentation and erasure. It is worth noting that, generally, microaggressions from Black peers were understood to be somewhat less serious. As Jermaine (USA) argued, these microaggressions were 'more as a joke ... I don't think it was meant to be fully offensive ... but it's definitely still classed as discrimination'. Perhaps it is the absence of white supremacist systemic power that means the microaggressions from Blacks are treated as somewhat less serious. Perhaps, it is, as Jermaine suggests, a sense of the way in which these microaggressions are delivered. However, the cumulative burden of these microaggressions creates an experience unlikely to be faced by Jermaine's mono-racial peers (Johnston & Nadal, 2010). It begins to become clear here how racial microaggressions (as discussed in the preceding chapter) are inextricably bound up with the processes of friendship and peer group formations.

Whilst friendships with Black peers were largely understood to be somewhat homophilic in nature, friendships with white peers were rationalised in slightly different terms. These friendships were not understood through Black mixed-race men viewing themselves as white, or sharing racial heritage with white peers, but based upon more instrumental factors. Contrary to what one may assume, the spectre of racism and the presence of racial borders were as perceptible to the Black mixed-race men who formed friendships with white peers as they were to those who formed friendships with Black peers. Carl (USA) conveys this,

> I think people are racist completely out of ignorance. Everyone creates boundaries completely out of ignorance. So, whenever I grew up with them, and I was one of the smartest kids in my class always, I was always the top kid in my class, so they would see me and be like 'this Black kid is like completely smarter than me, he's been around us so long he's okay, he's one of us'.

As with the majority of participants, Carl recognises racial 'boundaries' but seeks to destabilise their meaning as he argues they are created 'completely out of ignorance'. As I suggested in the last chapter, Mills (2007) encourages us to understand white ignorance as a social epistemology that refuses to recognise a long history of structural racism. In so doing, he argues, white ignorance maintains white privilege and white supremacy. We see that even when participating in the white peer group Carl remains 'this Black kid'; his friendship does not engender the erasure of his Blackness (Modica, 2015). He might be 'one of us', but he's still 'this Black kid'. Although he remains the Black kid, it is Carl's academic success – a stereotypical marker of whiteness – that gains him acceptance. Thus, 'intelligence' becomes the form of cultural capital, the strategic sameness, Carl seeks to display as he subverts 'boundaries'. Carl here positions himself as *an-other Black*. As he is 'the top kid' in the class, he is an exception to the unintelligent Black norm (Yancy, 2017) and this allows him to navigate racist and racialised difficulties.

Carl goes on to argue that it is not just his intelligence that allows him to engage with the white peer group but also his apparent familial proximity to whiteness,

> I grew up with them, then they had to come in and it was the fact that I wasn't full Black, that I was part white and I lived with my white mom and my white family and my mum remarried to a white guy and they had a kid, my half-sister but she's full white.

For Carl, his mixedness, and his living with his white mother, her white husband, and his white sister, positioned him as a more acceptable Black; he 'wasn't full Black'. In this sense, Carl experiences a certain amount of 'white' privilege through his mixedness. However, this privilege and partial whiteness is always probationary[3] and subject to retraction (Bonilla-Silva, 2004, 2002; Leonardo, 2004, 2009). He continues to consider how his Blackness may have been made salient and pathologised in any instance that he refused conformity,

> Whatever you're being taught, you sit down and you listen to it. But I was always that defiant one and now thinking back on it I don't know if other kids in the class were like 'oh, the Black kid is speaking out again'. Or like the kids that I don't know that much, or, here was just like 'oh this Black kid causing trouble in the class'.

---

[3]Jake (UK) described being positioned through a '"you're basically white" exception'. The word basically embodies the temporality and partiality of this positionality.

Through Carl's double consciousness, he considers how his performances in these instances were subject to being read through discourses of pathological Blackness; the Black man as the trouble causer: The Black monster. It is because he is a 'Black kid' that he 'is speaking out' and 'causing trouble', so the reasoning goes. Of course, any white peers who caused trouble would not have this attributed to their race. Carl's participation in the white peer group then was always characterised by its precariousness. Understanding this, through double consciousness, is an important component in Carl's **PRR**.

The theme of academic intelligence, as it intersected with streaming in the schools (Carter, 2012; Gillborn, 2008), was evident in a number of the accounts of those who reported forming peer groups with white peers. Devron (USA) conveys this,

> I'd say predominantly, for the most part, most of my close friends were white and I always say that's a direct manifestation of the academic environment I was in; just because like I said, I was in the honours programme. That was, I'd say, like 90% white kids. So, that's just who I was around, and who I felt as though I was most similar to, just because I had the most experiences with them.

Whilst many Black mixed-race men drew upon race as a marker of sameness in order to form peer groups with Black men, in his account Devron draws upon a shared 'academic environment' to develop a sense of similarity. Given the racialised streaming of peer groups, Devron is a racialised exception in the 'honours programme' (Gillborn, 2008). He therefore has to draw upon academic experiences as the primary marker of sameness in order to cultivate friendships and avoid racist and racialised difficulties: the ability to cultivate strategic sameness is an important component in Black mixed-race men's **RPR**. A similar experience was recalled by Derrick (USA),

> I was in an advanced math and science programme there, which was like the pocket of white students at the school. So, I was friends with them because like I could relate to them in my classes. Because by the time I was a sophomore, almost all of my classes were with them so I didn't really interact with the other people so it was mostly white students once again. But I didn't like them. They were super elitist and were better than everybody else and I'm like, you go to the same school.

Due to racialised streaming, academic success meant that Derrick was, like Devron, submerged in a 'pocket of white students'. This is the primary reason for his friendships as proximity determines who he interacts with. It is through the shared experience of advanced classes that Derrick is able to 'relate' to his white peers. Despite developing friendships, Derrick ultimately concludes that he 'didn't like' his white peers who he considers to hold a sense of superiority over the students outside of the advanced programmes. Nevertheless, to avoid racist and racialised difficulties in his classes, Derrick draws upon strategic sameness; this is Derrick's PRR.

In the UK, Trent (UK) having earlier described the importance of his Black peer group spoke about his cultivation of friendships with white peers due to racial streaming within the school,

> I was in the top sets and the other Black lads were in the lower sets, so my friends were mixed. Cos obviously I had the friends that I had to make in class that were predominantly, well, everybody was predominantly white. So, they were like more white.

Much like his USA counterparts then, Trent's academic success meant that he was isolated from 'Black lads'. Note that Trent regards his friendships with white peers as pragmatic; these are friendships he 'had to make' rather than friendships he wanted to make. Nevertheless, it appears that Trent is able to move between racial groups as racial homophily shapes his relationships with Black boys, and a shared academic environment shapes his relationship with white peers (Warikoo, 2011). As he shows the fluidity of his identity, and his ability to draw upon multiple forms of strategic sameness, this is Trent's PRR. Friendships with white peers were not only a consequence of academic environment; to varying degrees, the majority of the informants resisted the imposition of race as a determinant factor in friendship formations.

Moving beyond Racially Prescribed Boundaries: 'We Were Friends with Anyone'

Despite 'post-racial' logic, participants generally acknowledged the way that race continues to be a factor in the formation of friendships and peer groups (Clark & Ayers, 1992; Doyle & Kao, 2007; Modica, 2015; Quillian & Redd, 2009; Warikoo, 2011). As Warikoo (2011) has suggested, this appeared to be somewhat more apparent among the Black mixed-race men who had been to school in the USA. Nevertheless, a certain degree of segregation was also apparent in the UK. In both contexts, however, acknowledgement of racialised borders did not necessarily mean acceptance, and many Black mixed-race men 'deconstructed traditional racial boundaries and allowed free passage to friends of different racial backgrounds' (Modica, 2015, p. 23). Carl (USA) demonstrates this point,

> Whenever you went and ate lunch those were who they ate lunch with. The Blacks ate lunch with the Blacks, the whites ate lunch with the whites, but I was with the whites. I would go to the Black table; I would go to the Asian table and say wassup. I'd go to my Bosnian friends and talk to them. Know what I mean? I was able to move around.

Recall that earlier Carl reported his primary friendships were with white peers. However, despite noting the archetypal lunch-time racial segregation (Tatum, 2003), he now describes his ability to move between these racially segregated peer groups. For Carl, this is a *skill* or an *ability (perhaps a component in his PRR)*; something he, unlike (monoracial) others, 'was *able* to' do. Carl goes on to attribute this to his (mixed) racial identity,

> ... being half Black, here in America, I can talk to any race. To like, my Bosnian friend, I have a sense of understanding. Since I have that Black in me; I have that sense of being a minority. I have that sense of being pushed back against a corner, know what I mean? So, I'm able to fit into all the conversations in some type of way.

For Carl, his mixedness acts as a source of cultural capital that positions him as racially liminal[4], and thus he engages in the identity work that enables him to move between racial borders (Doyle & Kao, 2007; Quillian & Redd, 2009). As Tutwiler (2016, p. 137) suggests of

---

[4]Nicola Rollock (2012) challenges the assumption that liminal positions are inherently advantageous and argues that there is oscillation between liminality as advantageous and liminality as disadvantageous.

mixed-race youth, 'the compatibility they perceive between the different aspects of their racial identity allows them to skilfully negotiate differently raced homogenous mono-racial contexts, as well as heterogeneous diverse contexts' (also see, Bunning et al., 2009). Carl shares a minoritised position in the context of white supremacy, and this, he argues, gives him a shared positionality that he is able to draw upon in forming friendships. In seeking to move beyond racialised borders, Carl engages in processes of everyday hybridisation (Tate, 2005) that allow him to find and draw upon commonalities with different groups (Khanna, 2011b; Quillian & Redd, 2009; Tutwiler, 2016) and engage with social networks omnivorously (Warikoo, 2011). He is, as Tutwiler (2016, p. 142) notes, of many mixed-race youth, 'skilled at frame-switching': this is a component in Carl's PRR.

Whilst Carl's attribution of liminality to his mixedness is indeed valid, it should be noted that research from Warikoo (2011) finds that this ability to move between racially segregated peer groups is evident among mono-racial students in her study, and this is understood to be the 'morally correct' way to engage with peers. Like Carl, Isaac (USA) identified racial segregation but spoke of his ability to move beyond racial boundaries,

> I witnessed a lot of segregation, where oftentimes the Black kids wouldn't have white friends but the Black kids would hang out with the other Black kids, white kids with white kids, err, and everybody else with everybody else. Like everybody had their own kind of clique, that they would be friends with. And for me, I tried to be friends with everybody. I didn't look at someone as different, I'm like yeah, they're Black, but you know, I'm Black. And I'm like yeah, they're Asian, I'm not Asian, so what. Like some of my best friends are people who are in no way shape or form like me. Like I've got a friend of mine who is a South Korean that I met in like seventh grade. I never thought I'd be friends with him six, seven, eight years later, but I'm still great friends with him. There's a kid that I know whose mixed Laos and Thai. I remember I met him at kindergarten, I never thought I'd be friends with him fifteen years later, still friends with him.

Here Isaac destabilises the importance placed upon racial boundaries as he develops friendships with 'people who are in no way like' him.

It is apparent that this is a conscious move on Isaac's part as he initially 'never thought' he'd be friends with his peers who have different racial identities. Rather than not recognising race, Isaac speaks back to and deconstructs racial boundaries (Modica, 2015; Warikoo, 2011).

In the UK, Theo too felt his mixedness offered him a uniquely liminal position within the school. Here he recalls a specific incident he argues encapsulates this,

> ... there was this real big divide between like the Asians and the [...] white people and then I was in the middle, cos I was friends with a lot of the Asian lads and I was friends with a lot of the white lads. Literally, physically one time there was, in the diner, there was loads of white lads stood there, loads of Asian lads stood there, and I'm physically stood in the middle of them like, 'Shut the fuck up, leave it. Shut the fuck up, leave it'.

Theo not only recognises himself as liminal between racial groups but he positions himself as the mediator who, given his friendships and understandings with 'the Asians' and 'the white people', is able to act as arbiter in an attempt to quell racial tensions. Theo's recollection of this account in which he is 'physically stood in the middle' might be seen to encapsulate Theo's sense of his positioning within the school. It should be noted that this for Theo seems to be a position of liminality rather than marginality; that is, he is not isolated outside of each group but is 'friends with a lot of' both groups. Reggie (USA) too shared Carl's (USA) and Theo's (UK) sense of liminality,

> Like there are definitely, there were definitely times when it was like alright Black kids eat with Black kids, white kids, white kids. But me myself, like I ate with everyone. I knew a little bit of everyone. Like I was from the rough side of town, I knew some of the rougher guys. I knew some of the people from the nice side of town. I knew people who had just flown in from other countries, lived here for like fifteen years.

Reggie, much like Carl, saw himself as having the ability to move beyond the borders of racial groups. For Reggie, this was not only about race but also about class; he knew people from the 'rough' and the 'nice' side of town. He also was able to make friends with new migrants. He refuses to be bound by the borders of racially segregated peer groups. This, for Reggie, is something to be celebrated. In her comparative study of peer cultures in London and New York schools, Warikoo (2011, p. 133) found that though segregation persisted, students were also 'flexible enough in their identities' to move beyond these boundaries when desirable or necessary. The accounts here support these findings as many of the men who reported being part of predominantly Black or white peer groups, elsewhere in their interviews, also reported an ability to move beyond racially prescribed boundaries. This is evident in Trent's accounts earlier as he notes his presence in a Black masculine peer group as well as his friendships with white peers.

Recall Alex (UK) too who earlier spoke of his friendships with Black men, here he elaborates on his omnivorous engagement with friendships,

> Me and my best friend, a big Black guy, we just used to roam around the playground, and go from clique to clique, I don't know, cos we were friends with anyone really.

Now, much like his US counterparts, Alex recalls his ability to move 'from clique to clique' and be 'friends with anyone'. Whilst it is perhaps noteworthy that his best friend is Black and a man, he is able to move beyond race as a defining feature of his friendships. For Brendon (USA), the ability to engage with social networks omnivorously was something of a skill,

> I had to like switch sometimes so like I had like a group of friends, we all hung out together and they usually were like, the white people hung out with the white people I guess and then I had a group of friends who were all mixed and we all hung out together and then I had people who were like, they was like multiple. So, I sat at lunch with somebody who was Black and Jewish, and somebody who was, somewhere South Asian. And so those were like my friends that I was with every day. And then it was weird having to go into these circles. I had to like change my behaviour in order to feel like I fit in.

Brendon notes his engagement in *identity work* (Khanna, 2011a, 2011b) as he has to 'switch' his performance as he moves between social groups. The ability to adapt his behaviour and thus selectively utilise and display a repertoire of forms of cultural capital positions Brendon as *socially omnivorous* (Carter, 2003; Khanna, 2011a; Tutwiler, 2016; Warikoo, 2011). This adaptability was a necessity for Brendon to 'fit in' with a range of peers (Carter, 2003, 2005) and manifests as a component of his PRR. However, it is noteworthy that Brendon has to 'go into these circles'. His position in each group is perhaps always temporal and conditional; he is a visitor. When asked how he adapted his behaviour, Brendon continued,

> Oh, I don't know. I felt like a lot of times, I don't know. It's just kind of a weird thing, like I felt like I could like do certain things. I don't even know. I just, I don't know. It's like subtle too. Like the way you talk about stuff. Um, I don't know. Just kind of like, I don't know how to describe it. It's just like we do those little things.

The apparent subtlety and intangibility of the markers of racial groups shows how Brendon is ceaselessly bound up in the discursive practices that define racial boundaries. Consistent with Chapter 4 of this book, and work elsewhere (Carter, 2003, 2005), he here mentions 'the way you talk' as a form of cultural capital marking the boundaries of various groups. During his interview, Brendon also showed me a range of handshakes that manifested as another way in which group boundaries were maintained (Carter, 2003).

It was generally accepted among participants that racial boundaries became much more apparent as they got older. This is consistent with findings from Máirtín Mac an Ghaill (1988a, 1994a, 1994b) who argues that race and peer groups become more pronounced in the latter years of compulsory schooling. Whilst Alex spoke earlier about his ability to move beyond racial boundaries, he now reflects on the changes as he got older,

> I don't even know if it was explicitly a racial thing but maybe underlying there were some things that drove people apart as they got a bit older. I remember just like there being a few incidents of people saying like racist stuff, and then people falling out over that, but yeah, it's kind of childish.

Alex's inability to categorically attribute divisions to 'explicitly a racial thing' is consistent with the last chapter's theorisation of microaggressions as subtle and intangible. However, he does go on to pinpoint 'people saying racist stuff' as the reason for fall outs and divisions. Racial microaggressions, and the ubiquitous *threat* of racial microaggressions, therefore play a restrictive role in the shaping of Black mixed-race men's friendships.

Some of the Black mixed-race men in the study felt that their awareness of racism and their racially minoritised positionality encouraged them to reject racial boundaries. For Shaun (UK), it was his experiences of being stereotyped that made him resist the pressures of racial homophily and develop friendships across racial lines,

> Mixed-race, Black, white, everything. Yeah, yeah, Asian like, yea … I've always tried to keep an open mind-set, definitely, always. Don't like to get stereotypes, so definitely.

Shaun, as a Black mixed-race man, does not like to 'get stereotypes'. He therefore places importance upon his own 'open mind-set' and this is reflected in his friendships. As in each of the accounts, it is not that race is unimportant or unseen, but that Shaun makes a conscious decision not to be bound by race. Whilst for the most part the majority of participants – including those who placed great importance on the Black peer group – viewed their ability to make friends positively, there were others who felt a certain sense of marginality and isolation.

As the following account from Tyrone (USA) demonstrates, even under circumstances or apparent marginality, these Black mixed-race men were active agents in their responses to this marginalisation,

> Pretty much everyone was a different ethnicity in my group, so I guess that was a sign that I didn't really think that people had to hang out just because they came from the same background … I feel like my group was kind of like kids who couldn't really, like back in middle school couldn't find the exact place they wanted to be in. Or they felt like they didn't fit in whatever group they were in before. So, once we all got to high school we just kind of like came together, I don't know. That's just how I see it.

Here Tyrone notes the ethnic and racial diversity of his peer group. This, he argues, demonstrates his resistance to the pervasive idea that 'people had to hang out just because they came from the same background'. However, as Tyrone goes on, it becomes apparent that his racially diverse peer group is perhaps formed in response to shared experiences of marginalisation. Rather than being isolated and marginalised, Tyrone and his peers invert potentially negative experiences of outsider-ness and create a third space for a hybridised peer group defined by shared outsider-ness. Exclusion becomes inclusion as racial meanings are redefined. Bradley (USA) also spoke of forming minoritised peer groups across racial lines (Quillian & Redd, 2009). He reflects on this here,

> I guess I connected to more, were the ones of minority. I had a Saudi friend, I had a Spanish friend and we'd get to the point where we'd go to each other's houses. And it was mostly with those cultures that you'd have a grounded family background. You know what I mean? But I still had white friends as well. Their family was just as grounded. Some cultures are just like that.

Here Bradley finds connections with racially and ethnically minoritised peers through conceptions of cultural similarities. It becomes apparent then that the semiotics of racial sameness and difference are malleable and subjectively negotiated. As Bradley notes, he also 'had white friends' that he identified as sharing the cultural similarities of 'a grounded family background'.

Recall that earlier Brendon (USA) described his socially omnivorous nature as he skilfully frame switched to move between different groups (Tutwiler, 2016). In contrast, here Brendon talks about his lack of a sense of belonging,

> The only place that I felt like I really belonged was like, I wrestled and I feel like that was the one place I could feel like totally comfortable. I mean we're all going for the same thing; we're all trying to reach the same goal. We're all trying to help each other, it wasn't like race; you were just a wrestler.

It appears then that Brendon experiences both liminality *and* marginality. Whilst he is able to move between groups, he also has a sense of outsider-ness and a lack of belonging. In Chapter 2, it may be recalled that, due to his light skin, Brendon spoke about his frustrations as peers oftentimes failed or refused to recognise his Blackness. Brendon is not merely a victim of racial segregation but actively seeks to rework the definitions and boundaries of peer groups. In the absence of racial sameness, he finds sameness and camaraderie in wrestling; 'it wasn't like race; you were just a wrestler'. This is Brendon's resisting and speaking back to the discursive practices that make race a segregating factor in the school. Again, the particular intersection of gender is apparent here as men have far more access to sporting activities and thus situations in which sporting identities might take precedence over race.

Feelings of isolation in the school were also responded to proactively through engagements outside of the school. In the context of her decision to send him to a predominantly white school, Trent (UK) talks about his Mother's decision to send him to a theatre group,

> ... it was predominantly Black kids doing theatre. Erm, and that was like an amazing thing cos it meant that once a week, subconsciously I was surrounded by Black people. And then when I became conscious obviously it was even better but like at the time I was making theatre and got into theatre but I was also around loads of Black kids.

Worried about Trent's experiences of marginalisation and isolation in the school, Trent's mother took the decision to take Trent to a space in which he was 'surrounded by Black people'. For Trent, this had great value in reducing his feelings of alienation. As he goes on to reflect,

> ... it was the fact that the parents, I had mums that looked like my mum, cos my mum is dark skinned and I had mums that looked like my mum, I had people talking about things that I was talking about. I had people eating stuff, the same lunch as me, or you know, making the same jokes, or worried about the same thing. Like, it was just always different kind of, and it made me want to learn more as well cos I didn't have to worry about other things about my identity.

Here Trent notes his mother's resistance to Trent's potential racial isolation in his predominantly white school, and for Trent this parental intervention is of great importance (Joseph-Salisbury, 2018a). In the previous chapter, Trent spoke about his experiences of racial microinsults as other students stared at and spoke about his Mother and her hair. Now, however, in this environment, he is no longer marginal because there are other mums that look like his Mum. His lack of marginalisation manifested through cultural tropes such as food and shared jokes and the feeling of insider status meant that he wanted 'to learn more'. Trent's mum bolsters his PRR as she places him in an environment where he finds validation for his identity. Much like Trent, Theo recalls his experience of playing for a racially diverse football team that was in stark contrast to his experience at a predominantly white school,

> I just loved being with this group of lads, cos it was again multicultural. There was Black lads, Asian lads, Sikh lads, white lads and there was, it was just amazing to be in that.

Through Trent's attendance at his theatre group, and Theo's participation in a sports team, he saw as 'multicultural', each were able to resist feelings of isolation (*racist and racialised difficulties*) in predominantly white schools.

Conclusion

Building upon the preceding chapters, in this chapter I have explored the way that Black mixed-race men form friendships and groups with their peers. The picture that develops is one of great diversity and fluidity between participants, at the level of the individual Black mixed-race men.

I first argued that homophily dictates that many Black mixed-race men form peer groups with their Black male peers. This is unsurprising given that Chapter 2 found Blackness to be a central component of Black mixed-race men's identities. Conceptions of sameness were not solely understood explicitly through race but through racial tropes of interests, music and culture. The governmentality of the Black peer group meant that notions of sameness and difference were ceaselessly negotiated and renegotiated as different aspects were made more or less salient through displays of *strategic sameness*. The ability to engage in these displays was demonstrative of Black mixed-race men's PRR. Whilst previous research had suggested that mixedness engendered a marginal status among Black peers, in the current research I find that status positioning within Black peer groups is negotiated through a multiplicity of factors with mixedness being just one such factor. Whilst internal heterogeneity was recognised, for some the strategic sameness of the Black peer group acted as a source of PRR as the peer group inverted and manipulated stereotypes of 'Black gangs' for their own ends. It is in the Black peer group that toughness often becomes most pronounced.

Black mixed-race men were in no way bound by the pressures of racial homophily. A number of participants noted forming friendships predominantly with white peers. This was often (although not always) a consequence of academic environments in which academic success would see Black mixed-race men in school classes with predominantly white students. In such instances, many of the men were able to draw upon shared academic interests to cultivate friendships. These friendships did not necessarily render race insignificant but repositioned the men as different from the *unintelligent Black same*; they became an exceptional Black whose position in the white peer group remained probationary.

Whilst all of the men recognised racial segregation to be apparent in schools, they all, at times, reported being able to move between these segregated groups. For some, this was seen as a specific consequence of their mixedness. In this sense, the men were liminally positioned and in some instances even acted as racial arbiter. In moving between these groups, the Black mixed-race men engaged in identity work and drew upon a repertoire of currencies to 'fit in'.

Other participants reported a more marginal position in the school, one of isolation in which they struggled to fit into the predefined racial groups. However, these men were active agents in renegotiating their positionalities; some drew upon shared racially minoritised status, another drew upon his status as a wrestler, and another formed a peer group based upon shared experiences of marginalisation. Marginalisation was resisted and subverted. Some of the men who attended predominantly white schools (and their parents) even sought to engage in out-of-school activities that would enable them to engage with Black peers: this was of great value.

At the beginning of this chapter, I posited that various popular discourses of mixedness would position Black mixed-race men as part of the Black peer group; able to move beyond the racialised boundaries of peer groups; a 'post-racial' beacon of hope, and destined to be marginal. The chapter offers evidence to support each of these stances but argues that Black mixed-race men are active agents who constantly negotiate and renegotiate racial meanings.

It is in the acute ability to recognise the work of race, and how this work shapes their own positionalities, that Black mixed-race men begin to demonstrate 'post-racial' resilience in their friendship practices. Black mixed-race men hold fluid and multiplicitous definitions of self. This fluidity manifests as a form of PRR that engenders the ability to engage in processes of hybridity and resist identity fragmentation. As such, Black mixed-race men are able to engage in identity work and manipulate and modify conceptions of sameness and difference in order to engage with peer groups, whether that is in negotiating positionalities within Black peer groups or engaging with friendships omnivorously. It is not only the individual identities that are shown to be fluid and multiplicitous but also the collective peer group identities as Black mixed-race men constantly define and redefine meanings. In the concluding chapter that follows, 'post-racial' resilience – the concept underpinning the current chapter and the entirety of this book – is extrapolated more fully.

Conclusion: A Critical (Mixed) Race Theory of 'Post-Racial' Resilience (PRR)

Introduction: PRR, Hybridity, Performativity and 'Post-Racial' Double Consciousness

As I suggested in the book's introduction, this project has been shaped by my ongoing attempts to make sense of my lived experiences as a Black mixed-race man. Taking these musings as a starting point, I spoke to other Black mixed-race men about their experiences and perspectives, in the hope that, by identifying commonalities, I would be better able to understand what it means to be a Black mixed-race man in contemporary society. Perhaps my most fundamental aim in this book has been to provide a counter-narrative to the negative stereotypes that surround discourses on Blackness and mixedness. As I have done so, I sought to develop a Critical (Mixed) Race Theory of 'post-racial' resilience (PRR) based on Transatlantic data drawn from Black mixed-race men. Based upon my reading of the men's accounts, 'post-racial' theory and literature on social resilience, I offered the following definitions for PRR:

1. *The capacity to withstand and/or recover quickly from racist and racialised difficulties that are denied: toughness against the invisible.*
2. *The ability of one's sense of self to remain in or spring back into shape, amidst threats that are deniable: elasticity.*

The formulation of these definitions enabled me to show that Black mixed-race men are not agency-less victims of marginalisation and fragmentation but active and agentic in the negotiation of their lived experiences generally, and identities particularly. Manifest in the definitions, and in the analysis throughout each chapter, is a sense that there is something against which Black mixed-race men must remain resilient.

White supremacy provides the structural foundations for the racial conditions that necessitate PRR. Structural white supremacy produces pervasive discourses of anti-Blackness that, as each chapter has shown, threaten to shape Black mixed-race men's lives in profound ways. Whether it's the microaggressions discussed in Chapter 4, the ideologies that determine how racial symbols are constructed in Chapter 3, or the anti-Blackness that is manifest throughout, white supremacy is the governing force in both UK and US societies. As I have shown throughout, and particularly in Chapters 3, 4 and 5, we should make no mistake about the connections between the quotidian and the structural.

Particularly as it impacts upon mixedness, white supremacy is characterised by the dichotomisation of Black and white. That is, the idea that our racial order is polarised by Blackness and whiteness. Such logic threatens the erasure of anyone that does not fall neatly within these poles and thus has considerable implications for mixed-race populations. This dichotomy is not neutral, of course, but is predicated on the supremacy of whiteness and the degradation of Blackness. Thus, when Black mixed-race men are interpellated as Black, they are threatened with processes of erasure that reduce them to a monolithic, homogenous and pathological stereotype (Rankine, 2015); what George Yancy (2017) calls the Black monster. We might think of Black/white dichotomised white supremacy as the conditions in which Black mixed-race men exercise PRR, but there is more to these racial conditions.

The 'post-racial' hegemony that has gripped both the UK and the USA means that Black/white dichotomised white supremacy takes on a particular character. Put another way, the 'post-racial' poses a particular threat to the resilience of Black mixed-race men. As manifest in the definition of PRR, the 'post-racial' brings forth the *denial* and apparent *invisibility* of racism: it threatens to be all compounding through the erasure of white supremacy, the erasure of the Black/white racial dichotomy, and, ultimately, the erasure of itself (Goldberg, 2015). These are the conditions in which Black mixed-race men cultivate PRR. In each of the book's chapters, I have further developed the picture of how Black mixed-race men cultivate PRR. I have suggested that PRR occurs in two substantive and distinguishable stages.

First, Black mixed-race men demonstrate the ability to see through and beyond the hegemonic myth of 'post-raciality'. This is the foundational component of PRR. This is what makes PRR both a continuation of and characteristically different from those forms of resilience that have historically defined so much of Black and Black mixed-race experiences. To be clear, this book has shown that, contemporarily, Black mixed-race men are resilient to a threat that threatens to be invisible: a threat that draws much of its strength from its obfuscation and deniability. Derrick Bell (1993, p. 198) argues that 'we can only delegitimate it if we can accurately pinpoint it', despite the threat of the 'post-racial', this is what Black mixed-race men show they are able to do. In a sense then, as I suggested in Chapter 1, what we are talking about is a sense of 'post-racial' double consciousness. Double consciousness enables Black mixed-race men to be cognizant of the ways in which the white gaze threatens to construct and distort their identities. From this consciousness, comes the possibilities to respond.

Drawing upon performativity theory (Butler, 2011; Tate, 2005, 2015a, 2015b; Youdell, 2000), in this book, I have argued that in holding a fluid, complex and multiplicitous sense of self, Black mixed-race men are able to engage in processes of hybridisation that are resistant to the ubiquitous threat of identity erasure. This, I argue, is the second step in Black mixed-race men's PRR. At the level of the everyday, Black mixed-race men open up a third space of hybridity in which identities and meanings are negotiated and renegotiated (Bhabha, 1996; Tate, 2005). Discourses are manipulated, modified and reconstituted as Black mixed-race men create identifications that are neither entirely bound by those constitutive discourses nor entirely bereft of their meanings. As Homi Bhabha might put it, the identifications of Black mixed-race men demonstrated in this study are best understood as a 'yoking together' of that which is already known (Bhabha, 1990, p. 212). Black mixed-race men's identities are always in a process of hybridity, a bricolage-like assemblage of identifications in order to constitute the self (Hall, 1996): a self that is resistant to the apparent constraints of 'post-racial' Black/white dichotomised white supremacy. As they ceaselessly move between notions of sameness and difference, Black mixed-race men draw upon a range of counter-hegemonic representations in order to occupy positions of *an-other Black*, *an-other mixed-race*, and *an-other Black mixed-race*. These are positions of *the same but different* (Tate, 2005). In negotiating these positionalities, it became clear that the Black mixed-race men in this study drew upon discourses of race, culture, ethnicity, nationality, ancestry, sexuality and gender in order to defiantly understand and perform the totality of the self (Hall, 1996). Thus, as Black mixed-race men strive to recognise the particularities of their identifications, hybridity is an always ongoing process. I began to unpack this in Chapter 1 where I showed just how profound Black mixed-race men's sense of double consciousness was.

'Post-Racial' Double Consciousness, Multiplicity and Hybridity

In Chapter 2, I showed how an acute sense of double consciousness (Gilroy, 1993) manifests as an integral component in Black mixed-race men's PRR, enabling the effective engagement in negotiating identity positionings. Unpersuaded by 'post-racial' logic, this double consciousness engendered an awareness of the white gaze's threat of erasure and the potential for the over-determination of Black mixed-race men as the Black criminal monster. This sense of double consciousness, predicated on a rejection of the 'post-racial', was a theme I returned to throughout the book. As I showed its manifestation at the intersection of gender, through racial symbolism, in the face of microaggressions, and in peer and friendship groups, 'post-racial' double consciousness represents a fundamental component of Black mixed-race men's PRR.

It was in Chapter 2 that I began to show Black mixed-race men to be capable of holding multiple racial identifications simultaneously and interchangeably. Most commonly, the men spoke of a 'Black mixed duality'. The fluidity and multiplicity of the men's sense of self meant that they rejected official identity categories that increasingly seek to rupture Blackness and mixedness. Whilst such conceptualisations were demonstrative of agency, of course, this should not be regarded as absolute; indeed, few, if any, felt able to truly access whiteness. Thus, it is worth reiterating that identifications are never constituted in abstraction from a social world defined by white supremacy. Nevertheless, Black mixed-race men held, cultivated, and drew upon positive counter-hegemonic representations of Blackness and mixedness that – cultivated among families, friends and communities (Joseph-Salisbury, 2018a) – oftentimes ran counter to the dominant white supremacist anti-Black discourse. The ability to draw upon positive representations strengthens Black mixed-race men's *capacity to withstand and/or recover quickly from racist and racialised difficulties.*

It was also in Chapter 2 that I gave consideration to the apparent threat posed by racial mismatch. As I suggested, literature on mixedness has considered disjuncture between one's sense of self (internal) and the way the individual is read by others (external) to be problematic for the individual (Appiah, 2010; Campbell & Troyer, 2007; Cheryan & Monin, 2005; Rockquemore & Laszloffy, 2005). Thus, racial mismatch would likely pose a threat to Black mixed-race men's resilience. The respondents in this study added support to Aspinall and Song's (2013) work that has troubled this axiomatic assumption that racial mismatch is inherently problematic.

For the Black mixed-race men in this study, seeing one's identity as fluid and multiplicitous enhanced the 'post-racial' resilience needed to withstand this potential threat. Moreover, this PRR was further enhanced by the demonstrable ability to see through the 'post-racial' myth and recognise the work of the racial. It was for those Black mixed-race men who were susceptible to being misread as white that the biggest threat was posed. The clear desire to not be white shows a pride in Black mixedness that is counter-hegemonic and resistant to the logic of white supremacy. Even those men who faced the greatest threat were able to negotiate and renegotiate their positionalities in order to affirm identifications that refused fragmentation (Khanna, 2004). In these instances, Black mixed-race men engage in identity work to subvert dark skin and mono-raciality as markers of authentic Blackness. In so doing, Black mixed-race men not only reposition themselves but redefine the contours of Blackness. By way of example, the reader may recall the identity work of Claude (UK), who, sought to utilise his knowledge of African history as a marker of authentic Blackness that placed a challenge to what he saw as narrow definitions based on dark skin. Hybridity, and PRR, is therefore enhanced by one's ability to draw upon a range of cultural capitals. Chapter 2 showed that, through the utilisation of PRR, at the quotidian level, Black mixed-race men are able to cultivate multiplicitous identities that resist threats of erasure. As I showed throughout, but particularly in Chapter 3, the intersection of gender is significant in the ways that Black mixed-race men cultivate PRR.

Black Mixed-Race Men, Gender, Masculinities and PRR

Black mixed-race men in the study showed themselves to be cognizant of the ways popular culture constructs Black men as sexually attractive: this was something they felt that they were able to play into and manipulate. For many of the participants, the performative act of 'getting girls' (Pascoe, 2011) produced forms of cultural capital that were convertible into homophilic peer popularity. To put it more plainly, popular notions of the cool and sexually attractive Black man were used to bolster Back mixed-race men's PRR.

Interestingly, a small number of the participants felt that sexual attractiveness as a form of capital was particularly accessible to Black mixed-race men. They reasoned that, on account of their mixedness and/or lighter skin tone, they were deemed to be more attractive than their mono-racial Black peers. However, those participants were keen to impress that this was not totalising and should not be overstated. As the majority of participants argued, 'white girls just see Black'. Across the internal–external dialectic, the Black mixed-race men in this study articulated complex and nuanced understandings of their positionalities as they considered the multiple intersections of Blackness, mixedness, light skin and masculinity. As they did so, the participants once again demonstrated an ability to see beyond 'post-racial' logic in order to understand and critique the racialised structures that simultaneously advantage and disadvantage them: this is the PRR that enables Black mixed-race men to *remain in or spring back into shape, amidst threats that are deniable: elasticity.*

Sexual attractiveness is not the only discourse that surrounds Black mixed-race men, of course. Seeing through the 'post-racial', the partici-pants in this study were acutely aware of the threat posed by pervasive anti-Black stereotypes of hypermasculinity, violence and criminality (Joseph-Salisbury, forthcoming-a; Yancy, 2017). The awareness of this erasure-threatening discourse did not render the participants docile, however. Instead, the men reported being able to manipulate and modify that discourse for their own ends. In many cases, performances of masculine toughness enhanced the men's *capacity to withstand and/or recover quickly from racist and racialised difficulties*: to be seen as tough — offered protection from racist bullying, and, in some cases, translated into peer group popularity (Warikoo, 2011). This was not absolute, however. Often, the men's awareness of the racial work at play meant that they were able to utilise different performances selectively and con-textually. In some instances, Black mixed-race men rejected the imposi-tion of masculine toughness and sought to cultivate hybrid Black mixed-race masculine identities that were different from the Black tough stereotype: this allowed many of the men to cultivate the stereotype-defying identity of 'intelligent' (or, academically engaged) Black mixed-race man.

Through their accounts in Chapter 3, the men highlighted apparently contradictory discourses that implicate them and showed an ability to grapple with those contradictions. Whilst, particularly under the white gaze, Blackness attributed a sense of hypermasculinity to the men, in a few cases, light skin, it was argued, was regarded as a marker of femininity (particularly under the gaze of Black peers). Black mixed-race men were able to identify and negotiate these processes and there-fore cultivate the PRR to resist being torn asunder. As I argued in Chapter 3, and throughout, at the intersection of race and gender, Black mixed-race men occupy very particular positions that cannot easily be understood through existing explanatory frameworks: this points at a need for further disaggregated work in Critical Mixed Race Studies.

Whilst Chapter 3 primarily complicated notions of masculinity based upon race, by centring the accounts of two participants who identified as gay and queer, I was able to trouble axioms of race and masculinity. Drawing upon the accounts of Jake, and particularly Trent, I was able to further destabilise heterosexuality as the norm. In so doing, the chapter helped to move towards a fuller picture of the diverse and multi-dimensional lives of Black mixed-race men. Speaking of the complex interplay between Blackness and sexuality, Trent identified the threats of erasure that representations of monolithic heterosexual Blackness posed to his sense of self. In so doing, Trent pierced the 'post-racial' façade and was therefore able to open up a third space of hybridity in which he identified as a Black man who was also queer. Trent's PRR is in his refusal to be limited or bound by popular racialised conceptions of identification. As he explored the nuances and seeming contradictions in the stereotypes imposed upon his identities – Black (tough) and gay (soft) – Trent argued that stereotypes of Black masculine toughness protected him from the homophobic bullying that is so commonplace for many homosexual young men.

Particularly in Chapter 3, but throughout the book, participant insights underline the need to complicate understandings of hegemonic masculinities and to move away from notions of a monolithic Black masculinity (Joseph-Salisbury, forthcoming-a; Newman, 2017; Sims and Joseph-Salisbury, forthcoming). In so doing, the men's insights in this chapter urge scholars to extend the theoretical terrain of Critical Mixed Race Studies and Critical Studies of Men and Masculinities.

Black Mixed-Race Men, Racial Symbolism and PRR

In *Black Skins, Black Masks*, Shirley Anne Tate (2005) theorises of hybridity as a process that occurs at the everyday level, in and through talk. Continuing in this tradition, and contributing to hybridity theory, this book has further mapped out some of the ways in which hybridity occurs at the quotidian level. One particular way in which I've done this is through a focus on racial symbolism. As we have seen in Chapter 4, through stylization Black mixed-race men cultivate forms of cultural capital that enable the negotiation of hybrid identities. In 'post-racial' contexts, where race is rendered invisible, racial symbolism acts as a particularly salient metonym. Through 'post-racial' double consciousness, the racialisation of symbols was something that Black mixed-race men were acutely aware of. Thus, participants resisted, modified and manipulated racial symbols as meanings were constantly negotiated and renegotiated. Racial symbols are utilised in the realm of hybridity. In terms of dress, for instance, participants were aware that not only does dress have racial meaning, but race and dress interact to produce particular meanings and performances.

Through 'post-racial' double consciousness many Black mixed-race men understood that whilst certain clothing might be accessible to white men, the interaction of race and masculinity would see them, as Black mixed-race men, interpellated as the archetypal Black criminal man (Yancy, 2017). As the men showed an ability to understand and manipulate existing discourses through stylization, this logic extended to styles of speech, hair and music. The men shared a sense that in certain situations – in contact with school authorities or employment, for instance – dressing, speaking and stylising one's self in ways that were 'stereotypically white' proved to be advantageous. However, in terms of Black peer groups, Black mixed-race men used racial symbolism that they saw as embodying Blackness to accentuate a Black performance. Through these 'balancing acts' (Warikoo, 2011), the Black mixed-race men in this study displayed high levels of agency as they negotiated hybrid positionalities through and against racial symbolism. The ability to do so, although somewhat constrained by racial markers such as skin (Yancy, 2017), is demonstrative of Black mixed-race men's PRR at the quotidian level.

Again, as was the case in terms of the discussion of masculinity in Chapter 3, although active in manipulating racial discourses, the men were deeply critical of the racial ideologies underpinning much of the symbolism. This was particularly evident in relation to speech where the men critiqued the ways in which white speech codes were valorised and black speech codes pathologised. Similarly, in terms of music, a number of the men were critical of notions that music should be considered 'Black' or 'white'. Nevertheless, the ability to utilise speech and music tastes as performative forms of cultural capital allowed Black mixed-race men to hold fluid conceptions of self that bolstered their 'post-racial' resilience in the face of threats of marginalisation and exclusion.

As existing literature has shown, hairstyles manifest as a significant marker of identity generally and a marker of racial identity particularly (Mercer, 1994). What existing literature has not fully explored is what hair means to Black mixed-race men and how hair manifests as a site of racial symbolism. As I argued, for some, Black hairstyles, most notably Afro hair, offered a space for speaking back to anti-Black discourse: a symbol of defiance. There was a sense that, like speech codes, Black hairstyles offered a source of cultural capital for Black mixed-race men as they were able to gain popularity among peers. However, this was never absolute as the positives were haunted by negatives of hypervisibility and white surveillance. In the school context in particular, Black mixed-race men were disciplined for their hairstyles. Given the post-racial metonymic nature of racial symbolism, for Black mixed-race men, disciplining Black hairstyles was tantamount to disciplining Blackness. Nevertheless, by identifying the 'post-racially' obfuscated racial processes, and modifying one's hair to meet one's aims, Black mixed-race men were able to negotiate hybrid identities. Music also enabled the negotiation of identities, as the men demonstrated an acute awareness of the ways in which music tastes come to be racialised, they were able to utilise knowledge of specific genres as a source of cultural capital that could be converted into friendships and popularity.

Whilst Chapter 4 in no way exhausted forms of cultural capital, it did highlight how racial symbolism has the potential to enhance Black mixed-race men's PRR. The first step in the cultivation of this resilience was of course in Black mixed-race men's recognition of the processes that racialise symbols. From here they were able to resist, speak back to, modify and/or manipulate. Much of what the men were up against could be understood through the conceptual lens of racial microaggressions.

Black Mixed-Race Men, PRR and Racial Microaggressions

In a context in which few readily profess to being racist (Bonilla-Silva, 2006), racial microaggressions illuminate the seemingly innocuous and invisible forms of racism as they are enacted at the level of everyday interaction (Pérez Huber & Solórzano, 2015; Pierce, 1988). 'Post-racial' logic suggests that the microaggression is an isolated incident bereft of social context. However, as I noted, racial microaggressions do not occur in isolation or abstraction from social context but rather are validated by a macroaggression of systemic and systematic white supremacy (Pérez Huber & Solórzano, 2015). In turn, the repetition and normalisation of racial microaggressions act to perpetuate the system of white supremacy. Black mixed-race men are acutely aware of the wider context in which racial microaggressions occur.

For Black mixed-race men, racial microaggressions take on a number of forms. The Black/white racial dichotomy and the legacy of the one-drop rule mean that in many cases Black mixed-race men are interpellated as Black and subject to anti-Black racial microaggressions. There were, however, a number of instances in which Black mixed-race men were subject to mixed-race specific microaggressions. Thus, Black mixed-race men were subject to a threat of dual-pathology: as Black and as mixed-race, as the 'nigger' and the 'half-breed'. Whether subject to microassaults, microinsults, or microinvalidations, Black mixed-race men drew on PRR in order to *remain in or spring back into shape*.

I showed in Chapter 5 that it is in the ability to identify the larger racial processes/structures that Black mixed-race men are able to cultivate the PRR to withstand and delegitimise the threat posed by racial microaggressions (Bell, 1993). From this point, the rejection of the 'post-racial', Black mixed-race men were able to respond in a number of ways. Through hybridity, for instance, Black mixed-race men refused their negative racist interpellation, in order to reposition themselves as different from the imaginary 'nigger half-breed' of the white gaze, or to produce an identification that was multiplicitous and refused erasure.

Through PRR, Black mixed-race men drew upon positive representations in order to know that they are not that which the white gaze imagines. As discussed in Chapter 3 (and 5), toughness was another response that bolstered the men's PRR. This was not only an external combative but an internal emphasis on not being impacted upon by microaggressions. In some instances, by critiquing their white aggressors as ignorant and/or stupid, Black mixed-race men spoke back in order to invalidate racial microaggressions and present a counter-narrative that destabilised white supremacy and renegotiated racial positionalities.

Black mixed-race men in the study recalled instances in which interlocutors were unable to comprehend them having a white parent. Instances such as this reaffirmed the notion that, through the white gaze, Black mixed-race men were part of a homogeneous Black monolith. These encounters were potentially upsetting for Black mixed-race men and posed a real threat to their PRR. However, the men were able to identify the racialised assumptions underpinning these instances and again, through processes of hybridity, sought to reposition themselves as, for instance, *an-other Black who has a white mum*.

In Chapter 5, I ultimately found that Black mixed-race men were not only able to identify racial microaggressions but were aware of the links between the microaggressions and the macroaggression. In identifying the threats, and knowing that they are not the pathological figment of the white imaginary, Black mixed-race men are well placed to remain resilient enough to engage in processes of hybridity that refuse erasure.

Black Mixed-Race Men PRR and Peer Groups

The fluid and multiplicitous self-conceptions that Black mixed-race men hold came to be an important component at the quotidian level of everyday interaction with peer groups. Based upon perceptions of race (and gender) homophily, the majority of the Black mixed-race men in this study formed peer groups and friendships with Black men. Many of the participants felt that they shared interests and understandings with Black men in ways that were not often the case with white peers. Although not always explicitly invoked, race, it emerged, persisted as the defining factor in friendships. Thus, despite the 'post-racial', Black mixed-race men had an evident awareness of the way race shaped their lives and their relationships.

The Black masculine peer group was deemed to be highly functional for many of the men. The group enhanced the tough performatives that I first discussed in Chapter 3 and thus acted as a protection from racism and a source of capital for attracting girls and forming homo-philic friendships. To precipitate this functionality, it was argued, mix-edness was given little recognition for the sake of Black unification. We may recall Trent's (UK) remarks there that 'you're not gonna stop trying to wonder what Blackness you are. You're just gonna club together'. Black mixed-race men and their Black peers manipulated the stereotype of the Black hypermasculine gang for their own ends. This was their collective hybrid identification that manifested as a form of cultural capital to boost their individual and collective PRR. Many of the men formed these peer groups because they had experienced, or were aware of the threat of, white anti-Black racism. Thus, once again, lived experiences shattered any clinging to the illusion of the 'post-racial'.

Whilst peer groups have external utility (Alexander, 1996), and a display of unity, there were, of course, internal negotiations. Some Black mixed-race men reported experiencing discrimination as the gov-ernmentality of the Black peer group threatened to marginalise them. However, I showed that Black mixed-race men engage in identity work that enables them to negotiate their positionalities, present a challenge to the regime of dark skin as Black authenticity, and redefine the bor-ders of Blackness. This process of hybridity, as they draw upon a range of cultural capitals, is integral to Black mixed-race men's PRR. I sug-gested that Black peer groups were not solely defined along lines of dark skin or mono-raciality but were contestable along lines of class, race, gender, sexuality and ancestry. Indeed, many of these vectors seemed to trump mixedness in importance. In showing the ways in which Black mixed-race men are able to gain acceptance, Chapter 5 really contributes to the field of Critical Mixed Race Studies that has — based upon studies that have drawn on samples predominantly made up of women and girls — argued that Black mixed-race populations are often marginalised and unable to gain acceptance from Blacks. In this regard then, Chapter 6 importantly highlights particularities to Black mixed-race men who are able to draw upon racialised masculinity, performed through toughness, to cultivate a sense of strategic sameness.

This strategic sameness occurs not only in Black peer groups, I argued. In some instances, Black mixed-race men challenged the racial homophily of peer groups and, especially where Black mixed-race men were an isolated Black presence in the higher sets, as racist streaming often dictates (Carter, 2012; Gillborn, 2008), they were able to draw upon similarities to cultivate friendships across racial lines, with white peers. In these instances, Black mixed-race men were again able to engage in identity work (Khanna & Johnson, 2010) in order to gain acceptance. Whilst these friendships were often seen as pragmatic, it is the multiplicitous conception of the racial self that acts as the 'post-racial' resilience for Black mixed-race men's ability to do so. This was particularly apparent in those instances where men felt the need and ability to move between peer groups and across seemingly stubborn racial boundaries. There was a sense that the ability to move between groups might not be as accessible to mono-racial Black men. Thus, the men felt they were particularly well placed to engage in processes of hybridity (Tutwiler, 2016). Not only this but, for a few of the men, it was their experiences of being racialised as mixed-race, and at times marginalised, that compelled them to refuse racialised boundaries.

There were examples of Black mixed-race men who did feel they were marginalised in the context of school peer groups. However, these men are perhaps best seen not as victims but as active and agentic in speaking back and redefined meanings. For one Black mixed-race man, this involved forming a peer group with others who were rendered outside of the racial borders, and for another, this meant forming a peer group based on his chosen sport; sporting identity took primacy over racial identity. In each case, what we see is the profound *capacity to withstand and/or recover quickly from racist and racialised difficulties that are denied.*

Black Mixed-Race Men and 'Post-Racial' Resilience

Collectively and individually the chapters contribute to the development of a Critical (Mixed) Race theory of 'post-racial' resilience. As I have argued, occurring at multiple levels, 'post-racial' resilience is the ability of Black mixed-race men to refuse identity erasure in the face of ubiquitous threats. Black mixed-race men are able to resist and reject 'post-racial' logic in order to identify the racialised threats they face. Black mixed-race men also hold fluid and multiplicitous conceptions of self that allow them to engage in processes of hybridity in order to resist being torn asunder. These processes, as each chapter contributes to showing, occur as race and gender intersect, through racial symbolism and forms of cultural capital, as Black mixed-race men deal with racial microaggressions, and as Black mixed-race men form friendships and peer groups in the context of the school. Importantly, this book has shown that 'post-racial' resilience is a Transatlantic phenomenon and that there is a litany of consistencies in Black mixed-race men's experiences across national contexts. Ultimately, this book is a speaking back to the dominance of pathological discourses on Black mixed-race men. Black mixed-race men are post-racially resilient.

Bibliography

Agard, J. (2004). *Half-caste and other poems*. London: Hodder Children's Books.

Alcoff, L. M. (1999). Philosophy and racial identity. In M. Bulmer & J. Solomos (Eds.), *Ethnic and racial studies today* (pp. 29–44). London: Routledge.

Alexander, B. K. (2003). Fading, twisting, and weaving: An interpretive ethnography of the Black barbershop as cultural space. *Qualitative Inquiry*, *9*(1), 105–128.

Alexander, C. E. (1996). *The art of being black: The creation of black British youth identities*. Oxford: Clarendon Press.

Alexander, E. (1994). "Coming out Blackened and Whole": Fragmentation and reintegration in Audre Lorde's *Zami* and *The Cancer Journals*. *American Literary History*, *6*(4), 695–715.

Alexandre, S. (2012). *The properties of violence: Claims to ownership in representations of lynching*. Jackson, MS: University Press of Mississippi.

Ali, S. (2003). *Mixed-race, post-race: Gender, new ethnicities and cultural practices*. Oxford: Berg Publishers.

Ali, S. (2007). Gendering mixed-race, deconstructing mixedness. In J. M. Sims (Ed.), *Mixed heritage – Identity, policy and practice* (pp. 7–10). London: Runnymede Trust.

Alibhai-Brown, Y. (2001). *Mixed feelings: The complex lives of mixed race Britons*. London: Women's Press.

Alibhai-Brown, Y., & Montague, A. (1992). *The colour of love: Mixed race relationships*. London: Virago.

Alim, H. S., & Smitherman, G. (2012). *Articulate while black: Barack Obama, language, and race in the U.S.* Oxford: Oxford University Press.

Allen, Q. (2010). Racial microaggressions: The schooling experiences of Black middle-class males in Arizona's secondary schools. *Journal of African American Males in Education*, *1*(2), 125–143.

Allwood, E. H. (2015). British fashion's new identity politics. *DAZED*. Retrieved from http://www.dazeddigital.com/fashion/article/24624/1/british-fashion-s-new-identity-politics. Accessed on December 13, 2017.

Andrews, K. (2014). From the 'Bad Nigger' to the 'Good Nigga': An unintended legacy of the Black Power movement. *Race & Class*, *55*(3), 22–37.

Andrews, K. (2016). Black is a country: Black people in the West as a colonised minority. In K. Andrews & L. Palmer (Eds.), *Blackness in Britain* (pp. 50–63). London: Routledge.

Anzaldua, G. (1987). *Borderlands: La Frontera: The New Mestiza*. San Francisco, CA: Aunt Lute Books.

Apel, D. (2004). *Imagery of lynching: Black men, white women, and the mob*. Jackson: Rutgers University Press.

Appiah, K. A. (2010). *The ethics of identity*. Princeton, NJ: Princeton University Press.

Aristotle. (1934). *Rhetoric. Nichomachean ethics. Aristotle in 23 volumes*. Cambridge, MA: Harvard University Press.

Aspinall, P. J. (2009). 'Mixed race', 'mixed origins' or what? Generic terminology for the multiple racial/ethnic group population. *Anthropology Today*, *25*(2), 3–8.

Aspinall, P. J. (2013). The social evolution of the term "Half-Caste" in Britain: The paradox of its use as both derogatory racial category and self-descriptor. *Journal of Historical Sociology*, *26*(4), 503–526.

Aspinall, P. J., & Song, M. (2013). *Mixed race identities*. Basingstoke: Palgrave Macmillan.

Auer, P. (2013). *Code-switching in conversation: Language, interaction and identity*. London: Routledge.

Baldwin, J. (1964). *The fire next time*. London: Penguin Books Ltd. (originally published 1963).

Bardack, N. R., & McAndrew, F. T. (1985). The influence of physical attractiveness and manner of dress on success in a simulated personnel decision. *The Journal of Social Psychology*, *125*(6), 777–778.

BBC News. (2010). Mixed race people are 'more attractive' and successful. *BBC News*, April 14. Retrieved from http://news.bbc.co.uk/1/hi/wales/8618606.stm Accessed on December 13, 2017.

BBC News. (2016). Black MP Dawn Butler 'mistaken for cleaner' in Westminster. *BBC News*, February 29. Retrieved from http://www.bbc.co.uk/news/uk-england-london-35685169. Accessed on December 13, 2017.

BBC Sport. (2016). Joe Marler: England prop avoids sanction for 'Gypsy boy' comment. *BBC Sport*, March 16. Retrieved from http://www.bbc.co.uk/sport/rugby-union/35827133. Accessed on December 13, 2017.

Beckles-Raymond, G. (2016). Mixed race masquerades: Myths of multiracial harmony in Britain. In T. F. Botts (Ed.), *Philosophy and the mixed race experience* (pp. 55–74). London: Lexington.

Bell, D. A. (1993). *Faces at the bottom of the well: The permanence of racism*. New York, NY: Basic Books.

Benjamin, R. (2016). Innovating inequity: If race is a technology, postracialism is the genius bar. *Ethnic and Racial Studies*, *39*(13), 2227–2234.

Bhabha, H. (1984). Of mimicry and man: The ambivalence of colonial discourse. *Discipleship: A Special Issue on Psychoanalysis*, *28*, 125–133.

Bhabha, H. K. (1990). The third space: Interview with Homi Bhabha. In J. Rutherford (Ed.), *Identity: Community, culture, difference* (pp. 207–221). London: Lawrence and Wishart.

Bhabha, H. K. (1996). Culture's in-between. In S. Hall & P. D. Gay (Eds.), *Questions of cultural identity* (pp. 53–60). London: Sage.

Bhabha, H. K. (2012). *The location of culture*. London: Routledge.

Billson, J. M. (1996). *Pathways to manhood: Young Black males struggle for identity*. New Brunswick: Transaction Publishers.

Black, L. N. (2015). *"Light Skin Guys Be Like" — On the boundaries of blackness (a response)*. Retrieved from http://www.nicholeblack.com/light-skin-guys-be-like-on-the-boundaries-of-blackness-a-response/. Accessed on December 13, 2017.

Blyth, E., & Milner, J. (1993). Exclusion from school: A first step in exclusion from society? *Children & Society*, *7*(3), 255–268.

Bojadžijev, M. (2016). Is there a post-racism? On David Theo Goldberg's conjunctural analysis of the post-racial. *Ethnic and Racial Studies*, *39*(13), 2235–2240.

Bonilla-Silva, E. (2002). "We are all Americans": The Latin Americanization of race relations in the United States. *Race and Society*, 5, 3–16.

Bonilla-Silva, E. (2004). From bi-racial to tri-racial: Towards a new system of racial stratification in the USA. *Ethnic and Racial Studies*, *27*(6), 931–950.

Bonilla-Silva, E. (2006). *Racism without racists: Color-blind racism and the persistence of racial inequality in the United States*. Lenham: Rowman & Littlefield Publishers.

Bonilla-Silva, E. (2015). Getting over the Obama hope hangover: The new racism in 'post-racial' America. In K. Murji & J. Solomos (Eds.), *Theories of race and ethnicity* (pp. 57–73). Cambridge: Cambridge University Press.

Botts, T. F. (2016). Editors introduction: Towards a mixed race theory. In T. F. Botts (Ed.), *Philosophy and the mixed race experience* (pp. 1–17). London: Lexington Books.

Bourdieu, P. (1973). Cultural reproduction and social reproduction. In R. Brown (Ed.), *Knowledge, education and cultural change*. London: Routledge.

Bourdieu, P. (1977). *Outline of a theory of practice*. Cambridge: Cambridge University Press.

Boyles, A. S. (2015). *Race, place, and suburban policing: Too close for comfort*. Oakland, CA: University of California Press.

Brown, A. L., & Donnor, J. K. (2011). Toward a new narrative on Black males, education, and public policy. *Race, Ethnicity and Education*, *14*(1), 17–32.

Brown, D. L., & Tylka, T. L. (2010). Racial discrimination and resilience in African American young adults: Examining racial socialization as a moderator. *Journal of Black Psychology*, *37*(3), 259–285.

Brunsma, D. L. (2006). Public categories, private identities: Exploring regional differences in the biracial experience. *Social Science Research*, *35*(3), 555–576.

Brunsma, D. L., & Rockquemore, K. A. (2001). The new color complex: Appearances and biracial identity. *Identity: An International Journal of Theory and Research*, *1*(3), 225–246.

Bunning, K. R., Unzueta, M. M., Huo, Y. J., & Molina., L. E. (2009). The interpretation of multiracial status and its relation to social engagement and psychological well-being. *Journal of Social Issues*, *65*(1), 35–49.

Burgess, S., & Wilson, D. (2005). Ethnic segregation in England's schools. *Transactions of the Institute of British Geographers*, *30*(1), 20–36.

Butler, J. (1990). *Gender trouble and the subversion of identity*. London: Routledge.

Butler, J. (1997). *Excitable speech: A politics of the performative*. London: Psychology Press.

Butler, J. (1999). Bodies that matter. In J. Price & M. Shildrick (Eds.), *Feminist theory and the body: A reader* (pp. 235–245). Edinburgh: Edinburgh University Press.

Butler, J. (2005). *Giving an account of oneself.* New York: Fordham University Press.

Butler, J. (2011). *Gender trouble: Feminism and the subversion of identity.* London: Routledge.

Byrd, A., & Tharps, L. (2002). *Hair story: Untangling the roots of black hair in America.* New York, NY: St Martin's Press.

Byrd, C. M. (1997). Kweisi Mfume just doesn't get it! *Interracial voice.* Retrieved from http://www.interracialvoice.com/editor10.html. Accessed on December 13, 2017.

Byrne, B. (2000). *Troubling race. Using Judith Butler's work to think about racialised bodies and selves.* Queer Development, IDS seminar series, June 23, 2000. Retrieved from https://www.ids.ac.uk/files/dmfile/byrne.pdf. Accessed on December 13, 2017.

Caballero, C. (2004). *"Mixed race projects": Perceptions, constructions and implications of mixed race in the UK and USA.* Thesis, Bristol, University of Bristol.

Caballero, C., Edwards, R., & Smith, D. (2008). Cultures of mixing: Understanding partnerships across ethnicity. Twenty-first century society. *Journal of the Academy of Social Sciences, 3*(1), 49–63.

Campbell, M. E., & Troyer, L. (2007). The implications of racial misclassification by observers. *American Sociological Review, 72*(5), 750–765.

Carter, P. L. (1999). *Balancing "Acts": Issues on identity and cultural resistance in the social and educational behaviors of minority youth.* PhD thesis, New York, NY, Columbia University.

Carter, P. L. (2003). "Black" cultural capital, status positioning, and schooling conflicts for low-income African American youth. *Social Problems, 50*(1), 136–155.

Carter, P. L. (2005). *Keepin' it real: School success beyond black and white.* Oxford: Oxford University Press.

Carter, P. L. (2012). *Stubborn roots: Race, culture, and inequality in US and South African schools.* Oxford: Oxford University Press.

Cashmore, E. (2008). Tiger Woods and the new racial order. *Current Sociology, 56*(4), 621–634.

Castagno, A. D. (2012). *"Founding Mothers:" White mothers of biracial children in the multiracial movement (1979–2000).* PhD thesis, Middletown, Wesleyan University.

Caughy, M. O. B., O'Campo, P. J., Randolph, S. M., & Nickerson, K. (2002). The influence of racial socialization practices on the cognitive and behavioral competence of African American preschoolers. *Child Development, 73*(5), 1611–1625.

Chambers, E. (2016). *Roots and culture: Cultural politics in the making of Black Britain.* London: I.B. Tauris.

Cheryan, S., & Monin, B. (2005). Where are you really from?: Asian Americans and identity denial. *Journal of Personality and Social Psychology, 89*(5), 717.

Clark, M., & Ayers, M. (1992). Friendship similarity during early adolescence: Gender and racial patterns. *The Journal of Psychology, 126*(4), 393–405.

Coates, T. N. (2015). *Between the World and me.* New York, NY: Spiegel & Grau.

Collins, P. H. (2004). *Black sexual politics: African Americans, gender, and the new racism.* London: Routledge.

Connell, R. (1989). Cool guys, swots and wimps: the interplay of masculinity and education. *Oxford Review of Education, 15*(3), 291–203.

Connell, R. (1996). Teaching the boys: New research on masculinity, and gender strategies for schools. *The Teachers College Record, 98*(2), 206–235.

Connell, R. (2005). *Masculinities.* Berkley, CA: University of California Press.

Connell, R., & Messerschmidt, J. W. (2005). Hegemonic masculinity rethinking the concept. *Gender & Society, 19*(6), 829–859.

Cooper, F. R. (2009). Our first unisex President?: Black masculinity and Obama's feminine side. *Suffolk University Law School Faculty Publications,* Paper *52.* Retrieved from http://lsr.nellco.org/suffolk_fp/52.

Critcher, C. R., & Risen, J. L. (2014). If he can do it, so can they: Exposure to counterstereotypically successful exemplars prompts automatic inferences. *Journal of Personality and Social Psychology, 106*(3), 359.

Cross, W. E. Jr (1971). The Negro-to-Black conversion experience. *Black World, 20*(9), 13–27.

Cross, W. E. Jr (2001). Encountering Nigrescence. In J. G. Ponterotto, J. M. Casas, L. A. Suzuki, & C. M. Alexander (Eds.), *Handbook of multicultural counseling* (pp. 30–44). Thousand Oaks, CA: Sage Publications.

Curington, C. V., Lin, K.-H., & Lundquist, J. H. (2015). Positioning multiraciality in cyberspace: Treatment of multiracial daters in an online dating website. *American Sociological Review, 80*(4), 764–788.

Dalmage, H. M. (2000). *Tripping on the color line: Black-white multiracial families in a racially divided world.* New Brunswick: Rutgers University Press.

Dalmage, H. M. (2004). *The politics of multiracialism: Challenging racial thinking.* New York, NY: State University of New York Press.

Daniel, G. R. (2014). Editor's note. *Journal of Critical Mixed Race Studies, 1*(1), 1–5.

Daniel, G. R., Kina, L., Dariotis, W. M., & Fojas, C. (2014). Emerging paradigms in critical mixed race studies. *Journal of Critical Mixed Race Studies, 1*(1), 6–65.

Davenport, L. D. (2016). The role of gender, class, and religion in biracial Americans' Racial labeling decisions. *American Sociological Review, 81*(1), 57–84.

Davis, A. Y. (2003). Race and criminalization: Black Americans and the punishment industry. In E. McLaughlin & J. Muncie (Eds.), *Criminological perspectives: Essential readings.* London: Sage.

Davis, A. Y. (2011). *Women, race, & class.* New York, NY: Vintage.

Davis, F. (1994). *Fashion, culture, and identity.* Chicago, IL: University of Chicago Press.

DeAngelis, T. (2009). Unmasking 'racial micro aggressions'. *Monitor on Psychology, 40*(2), 42–47.

de Boise, S. (2015). I'm not homophobic, "I've Got Gay Friends": Evaluating the validity of inclusive masculinity. *Men and Masculinities, 18*(3), 318–339.

Delgado, R. (1982). Words that wound: A tort action for racial insults, epithets, and name-calling. *Harvard Civil Rights-Civil Liberties Law Review, 17*, 133.

Delgado, R., & Stefancic, J. (2012). *Critical race theory: An introduction.* New York, NY: NYU Press.

Derrida, J. (1981). *Dissemination,* Translated from French by Barbara Johnson. London: The Athlone Press.

Deutsch, N. L. (2008). *Pride in the projects: Teens building identities in urban contexts.* New York, NY: NYU Press.

DeVerteuil, G. (2015). *Resilience in the post-welfare inner city: Voluntary sector geographies in London, Los Angeles and Sydney.* Bristol: Policy Press.

Dobratz, B. A., & Shanks-Meile, S. L. (2000). *The white separatist movement in the United States: "White power, white pride!".* Baltimore, MD: JHU Press.

Donnor, J. K., & Brown, A. L. (2011). The education of Black males in a 'post-racial' world. *Race Ethnicity and Education, 14*(1), 1−5.

Downs, R. (2014). Understanding Drake's meme appeal. This week in Drake, *Vice.* Retrieved from http://noisey.vice.com/en_uk/blog/understanding-drakes-meme-appeal. Accessed on December 13, 2017.

Doyle, J. M., & Kao, G. (2007). Friendship choices of multiracial adolescents: Racial homophily, blending, or amalgamation? *Social Sciences Research, 36*(2), 633−653.

Du Bois, W. E. B. (1994). *The souls of black folk.* Oxford: Oxford University Press.

Dumas, M. J. (2014). 'Losing an arm': Schooling as a site of black suffering. *Race Ethnicity and Education, 17*(1), 1−29.

Dunsmuir, L. (2013). Many Americans have no friends of another race: Poll. *Reuters,* August 8. Retrieved from https://www.reuters.com/article/us-usa-poll-race/many-americans-have-no-friends-of-another-race-poll-idUSBRE97704320130808. Accessed on December 13, 2017.

Dyer, R. (1997). *White: Essays on race and culture.* London: Routledge.

East, E. M., & Jones, D. F. (1919). *Inbreeding and outbreeding: Their genetic and sociological significance.* Philadelphia, PA: JB Lippincott.

Edwards, T. (2006). *Cultures of masculinity.* London: Routledge.

Elliot-Cooper, A. (2016). From slavery to Serco. In K. Andrews & L. A. Palmer (Eds.), *Blackness in Britain.* London: Routledge.

Ellis, A. J. (2011). *If we must die: From bigger Thomas to Biggie smalls.* Detroit: Wayne State University Press.

Entwistle, J., & Wilson, E. (2001). Introduction: Body dressing. In J. Entwisle & E. Wilson (Eds.), *Body dressing.* New York, NY: Bloomsbury.

Erasmus, Z. (2011). Oe! My hare gaan huistoe': Hair-styling as black cultural practice. *Agenda, 13*(32), 11−16.

Fanon, F. (2008). *Black skin, white masks.* New York, NY: Grove press.

Farley, R. (2004). Identifying with multiple races: A social movement that succeeded but failed. In M. Krysan & A. E. Lewis (Eds.), *The changing terrain of race and ethnicity* (pp. 123−148). New York, NY: Russell Sage Foundation.

Fatimilehin, I. A. (1999). Of jewel heritage: Racial socialization and racial identity attitudes amongst adolescents of mixed African−Caribbean/White parentage. *Journal of Adolescence, 22*(3), 303−318.

Feagin, J. R., & Van Ausdale, D. (2001). *The first R: How children learn race and racism*. Lanham, MD: Rowman & Littlefield Publishers.

Finkelstein, J. (1991). *The fashioned self*. Cambridge, MA: Polity Press.

Fleras, A. (2016). Theorizing micro-aggressions as Racism 3.0: Shifting the discourse. *Canadian Ethnic Studies, 48*(2), 1–19.

Fletcher, M. E. (1930). *Report on an investigation into the colour problem in Liverpool and other ports*. Liverpool: Liverpool Association for the Welfare of Half-Caste Children.

Ford, R., Jolley, R., Katwala, S., & Mehta, B. (2012). *The melting pot generation. How Britain became more relaxed on race*. London: British Future.

Foucault, M. (1991). Governmentality. In M. Foucault et al. (Ed.), *The Foucault effect: Studies in governmentality*. Chicago, IL: University of Chicago Press.

Freeman, J. B., Penner, A. M., Saperstein, A., Scheutz, M., & Ambady, N. (2011). Looking the part: Social status cues shape race perception. *PLoS One, 6*(9), e25107.

Freitas, A., Kaiser, S., Joan Chandler, D., Carol Hall, D., Kim, J. W., & Hammidi, T. (1997). Appearance management as border construction: Least favorite clothing, group distancing, and identity not! *Sociological Inquiry, 67*(3), 323–335.

Gans, H. J. (1979). Symbolic ethnicity: The future of ethnic groups and cultures in America. *Ethnic and Racial Studies, 2*(1), 1–20.

Garber, M. (2015). The history of 'Thug': The surprisingly ancient and global etymology of a racially charged epithet. *The Atlantic*, April 28.

Garside, K., & Arron, S. (2008). Lewis Hamilton subject of racist abuse ahead of the Brazilian Grand Prix. *The Telegraph*, October 30.

Gaskins, P. F. (1999). *What are you?: Voices of mixed-race young people*. New York: Henry Holt and Co.

Gellman, E. S. (2012). *Death blow to Jim Crow: The National Negro Congress and the rise of Militant Civil Rights*. Chapel Hill, NC: University of North Carolina Press.

Gillborn, D. (2003). *Race, ethnicity and education: Teaching and learning in multi-ethnic schools*. London: Routledge.

Gillborn, D. (2005). Education policy as an act of white supremacy: Whiteness, critical race theory and education reform. *Journal of Education Policy, 20*(4), 485–505.

Gillborn, D. (2008). *Racism and education: Coincidence or conspiracy?* Abington: Routledge.

Gilroy, P. (1993). *The black Atlantic: Modernity and double consciousness*. Cambridge, MA: Harvard University Press.

Gilroy, P. (2013). *There ain't no black in the Union Jack*. London: Routledge.

Glenn, E. (2009). *Shades of difference: Why skin color matters*. Redwood city: Stanford University Press.

Goff, P. A., Jackson, M. C., Di Leone, B. A. L., Culotta, C. M., & DiTomasso, N. A. (2014). The essence of innocence: Consequences of dehumanizing Black children. *Journal of Personality and Social Psychology, 106*(4), 526.

Goffman, E. (1990). *The presentation of self in everyday life*. London: Penguin Books.

Goldberg, D. T. (2009). Racial comparisons, relational racisms: Some thoughts on method. *Ethnic and Racial Studies, 32*(7), 1271–1282.

Goldberg, D. T. (2015). *Are we all postracial yet?* Cambridge, MA: John Wiley & Sons.

Goldberg, D. T. (2016). Vanishing points: Reflecting on my respondents. *Ethnic and Racial Studies, 39*(13), 2278–2283.

Grant, M. (1916). The passing of the great race. *Geographical Review, 2*(5), 354–360.

Halberstam, J. (1998). *Female masculinity*. Durham: Duke University Press.

Hall, J. R. (1992). The capital (s) of cultures: A nonholistic approach to status situations, class, gender, and ethnicity. In M. Lamont & M. Fournier (Eds.), *Cultivating differences: Symbolic boundaries and the making of inequality* (p. 257). Chicago, IL: University of Chicago Press.

Hall, N., Grieve, J., & Savage, S. (2013). *Policing and the legacy of Lawrence*. London: Routledge.

Hall, R. E. (1995). Dark skin and the cultural ideal of masculinity. *Journal of African American Men, 1*(3), 37–62.

Hall, S. (1990). Cultural identity and diaspora. In J. Rutherford (Ed.), *Identity, community, culture and difference* (pp. 222–237). London: Lawrence and Wishart.

Hall, S. (1993). Encoding, decoding. In S. During (Ed.), *The cultural studies reader* (pp. 90–103). London: Routledge.

Hall, S. (1996). Who needs identity? In S. Hall & P.d. Gay (Eds.), *Questions of cultural identity* (pp. 1–17). London: Sage.

Hamilton, L. (2014). Lewis Hamilton: Being F1's first black driver is important. *BBC Sport*, May 23. Retrieved from http://www.bbc.co.uk/sport/formula1/27526301. Accessed on December 13, 2017.

Harker, J. (2011). For black Britons, this is not the 80s revisited. It's worse. *The Guardian*, 11 August 2011.

Harrell, E. (2007). *Black victims of violent crime*. US Department of Justice, Office of Justice Programs, Bureau of Justice Statistics.

Harris, C. A., & Khanna, N. (2010). Black is, black ain't: Biracials, middle-class blacks, and the social construction of blackness. *Sociological Spectrum, 30*(6), 639–670.

Harris, D. R., & Sim, J. J. (2002). Who is multiracial? Assessing the complexity of lived race. *American Sociological Review, 67*(4), 614–627.

Harris, H. E. (2010). *Obama effect: Multidisciplinary Renderings of the 2008 campaign*. New York, NY: State University of New York Press.

Harris, J. C. (2017). Multiracial college students' experiences with multiracial microaggressions. *Race Ethnicity and Education, 20*(4), 429–445.

Harvey, A. R. (1995). The issue of skin color in psychotherapy with African Americans. *Families in Society, 76*(1), 3–10.

Hearn, J. (2004). From hegemonic masculinity to the hegemony of men. *Feminist Theory, 5*(1), 49–72.

Henriques, F. (1975). *Children of conflict: A study of interracial sex and marriage*. New York, NY: Dutton.

Herman, M. (2004). Forced to choose: Some determinants of racial identification in multiracial adolescents. *Child Development, 75*(3), 730–748.

Hewitt, R. (1986). *White talk, black talk: Inter-racial friendship and communication amongst adolescents.* Cambridge, MA: Cambridge University Press.

Hill, M. E. (2002). Skin color and the perception of attractiveness among African Americans: Does gender make a difference? *Social Psychology Quarterly, 65*(1), 77–91.

Ho, A. K., Sidanius, J., Levin, D. T., & Mahazarin, R. B. (2011). Evidence for hypodescent and racial hierarchy in the categorization and perception of biracial individuals. *Journal of Personality and Social Psychology, 100*(3), 492–506.

Hochschild, J. L., & Powell, B. M. (2008). Racial reorganization and the United States Census 1850–1930: Mulattoes, half-breeds, mixed parentage, Hindoos, and the Mexican race. *Studies in American Political Development, 22*(1), 59–96.

Holland, S. P. (2012). *The erotic life of racism.* Durham: Duke University Press.

Holland, S. P., Cohen, C. J., Johnson, E. P., & Henderson, M. G. (2005). *Black queer studies: A critical anthology.* Durham: Duke University Press.

hooks, b. (1990). *Yearning: Race, Gender, and Cultural Politics.* Boston, MA: South End Press.

hooks, b. (1992). *Black looks: Race and representation.* Brooklyn, NY: South End Press.

hooks, b. (2004). *We real cool: Black men and masculinity.* New York, NY: Psychology Press.

hooks, b. (2014). *Teaching to transgress.* London: Routledge.

Hope, J. (2010). Brits believe mixed-race people are the 'most attractive and successful'. *Daily Mail*, April 15. Retrieved from http://www.dailymail.co.uk/science-tech/article-1265949/Mixed-race-people-attractive-finds-British-study.html. Accessed on December 13, 2017.

Hopkins, I. (2013). Is George Zimmerman white or Hispanic? That depends. *Salon*, July 16. Retrieved from http://www.salon.com/2013/07/16/is_george_zimmerman_white_or_hispanic/. Accessed on December 13, 2017.

Howard, T. C., & Flennaugh, T. (2011). Research concerns, cautions and considerations on Black males in a 'post-racial' society. *Race Ethnicity and Education, 14*(1), 105–120.

Hunter, M. (2007). Color and the changing racial landscape. In T. D. Gupta, C. E. James, R. C. A. Maaka, G.-E. Galabuzi, & C. Andersen (Eds.), *Race and racialization: Essential readings.* Toronto: Canadian Scholars Press.

Hylton, K. (2012). Talk the talk, walk the walk: Defining Critical Race Theory in research. *Race Ethnicity and Education, 15*(1), 23–41.

Ifekwunigwe, J. O. (1999). *Scattered belongings: Cultural paradoxes of race, nation and gender.* London: Routledge.

Ifekwunigwe, J. O. (2004). *'Mixed race' studies: A reader.* New York, NY: Psychology Press.

Iwunze, C. (2009). *The factors responsible for low educational achievement among African-Caribbean youths.* London: Author House.

Jackson, K. F. (2009). Beyond race: Examining the facets of multiracial identity through a life-span developmental lens. *Journal of Ethnic and Cultural Diversity in Social Work, 18*(4), 293–310.

Jenkins, R. (2014). *Social identity*. London: Routledge.

Johnson, A., & Joseph-Salisbury, R. (2017). Racial microaggressions and the native informant. In J. Arday (Ed.), *Dismantling racial inequality within the academy: Race and higher education*. Basingstoke: Palgrave.

Johnston, M. P., & Nadal, K. L. (2010). Multiracial microaggressions: Exposing monoracism in everyday life and clinical practice. In D. W. Sue (Ed.), *Microaggressions and marginality: Manifestation, dynamics and impact*. New York, NY: Wiley and Sons.

Jolivétte, A. (2012). *Obama and the biracial factor: The battle for a new American majority*. Chicago, IL: University of Chicago Press.

Jones, J. (2004). His fair lady weds my Nigger son. *The Journal of Speculative Philosophy, 18*(4), 311–316.

Jones, V. (2015). The black-white dichotomy of race: Influence of a predominantly white environment on multiracial identity. *Higher Education in Review, 12*, 1–22.

Joseph-Salisbury, R. (2013). *Black mixed-race male identity in the UK*. MA dissertation. Leeds, The University of Leeds.

Joseph-Salisbury, R. (2016a). No, Bill Clinton, we're not 'all mixed race' — And you of all people should know that. *The Independent*, February 15. Retrieved from http://www.independent.co.uk/voices/no-bill-clinton-were-not-all-mixed-race-and-you-of-all-people-should-know-that-a6875411.html. Accessed on December 13, 2017.

Joseph-Salisbury, R. (2016b). Black mixed-race British males and the role of school teachers: New theory and evidence. In K. Andrews & L. Palmer (Eds.), *Blackness in Britain*. London: Routledge.

Joseph-Salisbury, R. (2016c). Facebook CEO Mark Zuckerberg is right, Black lives matter. *The Voice*, March 8. Retrieved from http://www.voice-online.co.uk/article/facebook-ceo-mark-zuckerburg-right-black-lives-matter. Accessed on December 13, 2017.

Joseph-Salisbury, R. (2017c). Of course Stormzy's neighbours thought he was a burglar — They can't imagine a black man becoming successful. *The Independent*, February 14. Retrieved from http://www.independent.co.uk/voices/stormzy-burglary-flat-met-police-broken-down-door-successful-black-man-a7580341.html. Accessed on December 13, 2017.

Joseph-Salisbury, R. (2018a). Black mixed-race men, perceptions of the family, and the cultivation of 'post-racial' resilience. *Ethnicities, 18*(1), 86–105.

Joseph-Salisbury, R. (2018b). Black mixed-race male experiences of the British secondary school curriculum. *The Journal of Negro Education, 8*(4), 449–462.

Joseph-Salisbury, R. (forthcoming-a). Wrangling with the Black Monster: Young Black mixed-racemen and masculinities. *Gender and Society*.

Joseph-Salisbury, R. (forthcoming-b). Black mixed-race men and the Black monster: Challenging the axiom of self-fulfilling prophecies. In S. Blackman, D. Conrad, & L. I. Brown (Eds.), *Achieving inclusive education in the Caribbean and beyond*.

Joseph-Salisbury, R., & Andrews, K. (2017). Locating black mixed-raced males in the black supplementary school movement. *Race, Ethnicity and Education, 20*(6), 752–765.

Joseph, R. L. (2012). *Transcending blackness: From the new millennium mulatta to the exceptional multiracial.* London: Duke University Press.

Kaiser, S., Rabine, L., Hall, C., & Ketchum, K. (2004). Beyond binaries: Respecting the improvisation in African-American style. In C. Tulloch (Ed.), *Black style.* London: V&A Publications.

Kamiya, G. (1997). Cablinasian like me: Rejection of orthodox racial classifications points the way to a future where race will no longer define us. *Salon.* Retrieved from http://www.political-economy.net/human_geography/activities/u4-tiger_woods-article.pdf. Accessed on December 13, 2017.

Kamunge, E., Joseph-Salisbury, R., & Johnson, A. (forthcoming [2018]). Changing our fate in the fire now. In A. Johnson, R. Joseph-Salisbury, & E. Kamunge (Eds.), *The Fire Now: Anti-racist scholarship in times of explicit racial violence.* London: Zed Books.

Kennedy, R. (2012). *Interracial intimacies: Sex, marriage, identity, and adoption.* London: Vintage.

Khanna, N. (2004). The role of reflected appraisals in racial identity: The case of multiracial Asians. *Social Psychology Quarterly, 67*(2), 115–131.

Khanna, N. (2010). "If you're half Black, you're just Black": Reflected appraisals and the persistence of the one-drop rule. *The Sociological Quarterly, 51*(1), 96–121.

Khanna, N. (2011a). *Biracial in America: Forming and performing racial identity.* Lanham, MD: Lexington Books.

Khanna, N. (2011b). Ethnicity and race as 'symbolic': The use of ethnic and racial symbols in asserting a biracial identity. *Ethnic and Racial Studies, 34*(6), 1049–1067.

Khanna, N., & Johnson, C. (2010). Passing as Black racial identity work among biracial Americans. *Social Psychology Quarterly, 73*(4), 380–397.

Kilson, M. (2001). *Claiming place: Biracial young adults of the post-civil rights era.* Westport, CT: Greenwood Publishing Group.

Korgen, K. O. (1998). *From black to biracial: Transforming racial identity among Americans.* Westport, CT: Greenwood Publishing Group.

Kupers, T. A. (2005). Toxic masculinity as a barrier to mental health treatment in prison. *Journal of Clinical Psychology, 61*(6), 713–724.

Labov, W. (1969). The logic of non-standard English. *Georgetown monographs on language and linguistics, 22*(1), 1–31.

Ladson Billings, G. (2011). Boyz to men? Teaching to restore Black boys' childhood. *Race Ethnicity and Education, 14*(1), 7–15.

Lamont, M., & Lareau, A. (1988). Cultural capital: Allusions, gaps and glissandos in recent theoretical developments. *Sociological Theory, 6*(2), 153–168.

Lamont, M., & Molnár, V. (2002). The study of boundaries in the social sciences. *Annual Review of Sociology, 28*, 167–195.

Lamont, M., Welburn, J. S., & Fleming, C. (2013). Responses to discrimination and social resilience under neo-liberalism: The United States compared.

In P. A. Hall & M. Lamont (Eds.), *Social resilience in the neoliberal age* (pp. 129—157). Cambridge: Cambridge University Press.

Lawler, S. (2014). *Identity: Sociological perspectives.* Cambridge, MA: Polity Press.

Lee, J., & Bean, F. D. (2004). America's changing color lines: Immigration, race/ethnicity, and multiracial identification. *Annual Review of Sociology, 30,* 221—242.

Lemelle, A. J. Jr (2010). *Black masculinity and sexual politics.* Abingdon: Routledge.

Lentin, A. (2016). Racism in public or public racism: Doing anti-racism in 'post-racial' times. *Ethnic and Racial Studies, 39*(1), 33—48.

Leonardo, Z. (2004). The color of supremacy: Beyond the discourse of 'white privilege'. *Educational Philosophy and Theory, 36*(2), 137—152.

Leonardo, Z. (2009). *Race, whiteness, and education.* London: Routledge.

Leonardo, Z. (2013). The story of schooling: Critical race theory and the educational racial contract. *Discourse: Studies in the Cultural Politics of Education, 34*(4), 599—610.

Lewis, M. B. (2010). Why are mixed-race people perceived as more attractive? *Perception, 39*(1), 136—138.

Lipsitz, G. (1995). "Swing Low, Sweet Cadillac": White supremacy, antiblack racism, and the new historicism. *American Literary History, 7*(4), 700—725.

Lloyd, M. (2007). *Judith Butler: From norms to politics.* Cambridge, MA: Polity Press.

Long, E. (1772). *Candid reflections upon the judgment lately awarded by the Court of King's Bench, in Westminster-Hall, on what is commonly called the Negroe-cause.* London: T. Lowndes.

Long, L., & Joseph-Salisbury, R. (2018). Black mixed-race men's perceptions and experiences of the police. *Ethnic and Racial Studies.* Retrieved from https://www.tandfonline.com/doi/abs/10.1080/01419870.2017.1417618

Lopez, N. (2003). Disentangling race-gender work experiences: Second generation Caribbean young adults in New York City. In P. Hondagneu-Sotelo (Ed.), *Gender and US immigration: Contemporary trends* (pp. 174—193). Berkley, CA: University of California Press.

Lorde, A. (2003). The master's tools will never dismantle the master's house. In L. Reina (Ed.), *Feminist postcolonial theory: A reader* (pp. 25—28). Oxon: Routledge.

López, I. H. (2003). White Latinos. *Harvard Latino Law Review, 6,* 1—7.

López, I. H. (2010). Post-racial racism: Racial stratification and mass incarceration in the age of Obama. *California Law Review, 98*(3), 1023—1074.

Mac an Ghaill, M. (1988). *Young, gifted, and Black: Student-teacher relations in the schooling of Black youth.* Milton Keynes: Open University Press.

Mac an Ghaill, M. (1994a). The making of Black English masculinities. In H. B. Michael Kaufman (Ed.), *Theorizing masculinities* (pp. 183—199). London: Sage.

Mac an Ghaill, M. (1994b). *The making of men: Masculinities, sexualities and schooling.* Buckingham: Open University Press.

MacLin, O. H., & Malpass, R. S. (2001). Racial categorization of faces: The ambiguous race face effect. *Psychology, Public Policy, and Law, 7*(1), 98.

Mahtani, M. (2001). Racial remappings: The potential of paradoxical space. *Gender, Place and Culture: A Journal of Feminist Geography, 8*(3), 299–305.

Mahtani, M. (2002a). Interrogating the hyphen-nation: Canadian multicultural policy and 'mixed race' identities. *Social Identities, 8*(1), 67–90.

Mahtani, M. (2002b). Tricking the border guards: Performing race. *Environment and Planning D: Society and Space, 20*(4), 425–440.

Mahtani, M. (2014). *Mixed Race Amnesia*. Vancouver: UBC Press.

Majors, R., & Billson, J. M. (1993). *Cool pose: The dilemma of Black manhood in America*. London: Simon and Schuster.

Malagon, M. C., Huber, L. P., & Velez, V. N. (2009). Our experiences, our methods: Using grounded theory to inform a critical race theory methodology. *Seattle Journal of Social Justice, 8*(1), 253–272.

Mancini, J. K. (1980). *Strategic styles: Coping in the inner city*. Lebanon: University Press of New England.

Matthews, J. (2007). Eurasian persuasions: Mixed race, performativity and cosmopolitanism. *Journal of Intercultural Studies, 28*(1), 41–54.

McBride, D. A. (1998). Can the queen speak? Racial essentialism, sexuality and the problem of authority. *Callaloo, 21*(2), 363–379.

McDermott, L. A., & Pettijohn, T. (2011). The influence of clothing fashion and race on the perceived socioeconomic status and person perception of college students. Poster presented at the 23rd Annual Association for Psychological Science Convention, Washington, DC.

McGill, R. K., Way, N., & Hughes, D. (2012). Intra-and interracial best friendships during middle school: Links to social and emotional well-being. *Journal of Research on Adolescence, 22*(4), 722–738.

McIntosh, P. (1990). Unpacking the knapsack of white privilege. *Independent School, 49*(2), 31–36.

McPherson, M., Smith-Lovin, L., & Cook, J. M. (2001). Birds of a feather: Homophily in social networks. *Annual review of sociology, 27*, 415–444.

Mead, G. H. (1934). *Mind, self and society form the standpoint of a social behaviourist*. Chicago, IL: University of Chicago Press.

Mengel, L. M. (2001). Triples – The social evolution of a multiracial panethnicity: An Asian American Perspective. In D. Parker & M. Song (Eds.), *Rethinking 'mixed race'* (pp. 99–116). London: Pluto Press.

Mercer, K. (1994). *Welcome to the jungle*. London: Routledge.

Mercer, K. (2000). Black hair/style politics. In K. Owusu (Ed.), *Black British culture and society: A text reader*. London: Routledge.

Mercer, K. (2004). Foreword. In C. Tulloch (Ed.), *Black style*. London: V&A Publications.

Meredith, P. (1998). Hybridity in the third space: Rethinking bi-cultural politics in Aotearoa/New Zealand, *Te Oru Rangahau Maori Research and Development Conference*, July 7–9, 1998.

Mills, C. (2007). White ignorance. In S. Sullivan & N. Tuana (Eds.), *Race and epistemologies of ignorance* (pp. 11–38). New York, NY: State University of New York Press.

Mills, C. W. (1997). *The racial contract*. Ithaca, NY: Cornell University Press.

Mirza, H. S. (1997). *Black British feminism: A reader.* London: Psychology Press.

Mirza, H. S. (1999). Black masculinities and schooling: A black feminist response. *British Journal of Sociology of Education, 20*(1), 137–147.

Modica, M. (2015). *Race among friends: Exploring race at a suburban school.* New Brunswick: Rutgers University Press.

Morley, D., & Street, C. (2014). *Mixed experiences: Growing up mixed race – Mental health and well-being.* London: Jessica Kingsley Publishers.

Morning, A. (2005). Multiracial classification on the United States census. Myth, reality, and future impact. *Revue européenne des migrations internationales, 21*(2), 111–134.

Morning, A. (2012). Multiraciality and census classification in global perspective. In R. Edwards et al. (Eds.), *International perspectives on racial and ethnic mixedness and mixing.* Oxon: Routledge.

Morris, T. L., Gorham, J., Cohen, S. H., & Huffman, D. (1996). Fashion in the classroom: Effects of attire on student perceptions of instructors in college classes. *Communication Education, 45*(2), 135–148.

Mowatt, R. (2008). The king of the damned: Reading lynching as leisure. *Policy Futures in Education, 7*(2), 185–199.

Murray, M. S., Neal-Barnett, A., Demmings, J. L., & Stadulis, R. E. (2012). The acting White accusation, racial identity, and anxiety in African American adolescents. *Journal of anxiety disorders, 26*(4), 526–531.

Mutua, A. D. (2006). *Progressive Black masculinities?* London: Routledge.

Mwakikagile, G. (2007). *Relations between Africans, African Americans and Afro-Caribbeans: Tensions, indifference and harmony.* Dar Es Salaam: New Africa Press.

Nadal, K. L., Sriken, J., Davidoff, K. C., Wong, Y., & McLean, K. (2013). Microaggressions within families: Experiences of multiracial people. *Family Relations, 62*(1), 190–201.

Nagel, J. (1994). Constructing ethnicity. *Social Problems, 41*(1), 152–176.

Nakashima, C. L. (1992). An invisible monster: The creation and denial of mixed-race people in America. In M. P. Root (Ed.), *Racially mixed people in America.* Newbury Park: Sage Publications.

Nero, C., Johnson, E. P., & Henderson, M. G. (2005). Why are gay ghettos white? In *Black queer studies* (pp. 228–245). Durham: Duke University Press.

Newman, A. (2017). Desiring the standard light skin: black multiracial boys, masculinity and exotification, *Identities* [online]. Retrieved from https://www.tandfonline.com/doi/abs/10.1080/1070289X.2017.1377420?journalCode=gide20

Nishimura, N. J. (1998). Assessing the issues of multiracial students on college campuses. *Journal of College Counseling, 1*(1), 45–53.

Noels, K. A., Leavitt, P. A., & Clément, R. (2010). "To See Ourselves as Others See Us": On the implications of reflected appraisals for ethnic identity and discrimination. *Journal of Social Issues, 66*(4), 740–758.

Noguera, P. A. (2009). *The trouble with black boys: And other reflections on race, equity, and the future of public education.* Hoboken, NJ: John Wiley & Sons.

Obama, B. (2004). *Dreams from my father: A story of race and inheritance.* New York, NY: Three Rivers Press.

Omi, M., & Winant, H. (1994). *Racial formation in the United States: From the 1960s to the1990s*. New York, NY: Routledge.

Palmer, L. (2016). Introduction. In K. Andrews & L. A. Palmer (Eds.), *Blackness in Britain* (pp. 9−23). London: Routledge.

Paludi, M. A. (2013). *Women and management: Global issues and promising solutions*. Santa Barbra, CA: ABC-CLIO.

Paludi, M. A., & Coates, B. E. (2011). *Women as transformational leaders: From grassroots to global interests*. Santa Barbra, CA: ABC-CLIO.

Parekh, B. C. (2000). *The future of multi-ethnic Britain: Report of the Commission on the Future of Multi-Ethnic Britain*. London: Profile Books.

Pascoe, C. J. (2011). *Dude, you're a fag: Masculinity and sexuality in high school, with a new preface*. Berkley, CA: University of California Press.

Passel, J. S., Wang, W., & Taylor, P. (2010). One-in-seven new US marriages is interracial or interethnic. *Pew Social & Demographic Trends*. Retrieved from http://www.pewsocialtrends.org/2010/06/04/marrying-out/

Patel, T. (2009). *Mixed-up Kids? Race, identity and social order*. Dorset: Russell House Publishers.

Pateman, C., & Mills, C. W. (2007). *Contract and domination*. Cambridge, MA: Polity.

Penner, A., & Saperstein, A. (2013). Engendering racial perceptions: An intersectional analysis of how social status shapes race. *Gender & Society*, *27*(3), 319−344.

Perlmann, J , & Waters, M. C. (2002). *The new race question: How the census counts multiracial individuals*. New York, NY: Russell Sage Foundation.

Peterson-Lewis, S., & Bratton, L. M. (2004). Perceptions of "acting Black" among African American teens: Implications of racial dramaturgy for academic and social achievement. *The Urban Review*, *36*(2), 81−100.

Pettersson, T. (2013). Belonging and unbelonging in encounters between young males and police officers: The use of masculinity and ethnicity/race. *Critical Criminology*, *21*(4), 417−430.

Pérez Huber, L., & Solorzano, D. G. (2015). Racial microaggressions as a tool for critical race research. *Race Ethnicity and Education*, *18*(3), 297−320.

Phillips, D. (2007). Ethnic and racial segregation: a critical perspective. *Geography Compass*, *1*(5), 1138−1159.

Pierce, C. M. (1969). Is bigotry the basis of the medical problems of the ghetto? In J. C. Norman (Ed.), *Medicine in the ghetto*. New York, NY: Appleton-Century-Crofts.

Pierce, C. M. (1974). Psychiatric problems of the Black minority. In S. Arieti & G. Caplan (Eds.), *American handbook of psychiatry* (2nd ed., pp. 512−523). New York, NY: Basic Book.

Pierce, C. M. (1980). Social trace contaminants: Subtle indicators of racism in TV. In S. B. Withey & R. P. Abeles (Eds.), *Television and social behaviour: Beyond violence and children: A report of the Committee on Television and Social Behavior Social Science Research Council* (pp. 249−257). Hillsdale, MI: L. Erlbaum Associates.

Pierce, C. M. (1988). Stress in the workplace. In A. F. Coner-Edwards & J. Spurlock (Eds.), (eds.), *Black families in crisis: The middle class* (pp. 27−34). New York, NY: Brunner/Mazel.

Pitcher, B. (2014). *Consuming race.* London: Routledge.

Pitts, L. Jr (1997). Is there room in this sweet land of liberty for such a thing as a "Cablinasian". *Baltimore Sun,* April 29. Retrieved from http://articles.baltimoresun.com/1997-04-29/news/7901011331_1_black-plessy-collard-greens. Accessed on December 13, 2017.

Plato. (1968). *Laws. Plato in twelve volumes* (Vol. 11). Cambridge, MA: Harvard University Press.

Platt, L. (2012). A descriptive account of those self-identifying as of mixed ethnicity in Great Britain. In R. Edwards, et al. (Eds.), *International perspectives on racial and ethnic mixedness and mixing.* London: Routledge.

Preves, S. E. (2003). *Intersex and identity: The contested self.* New Brunswick: Rutgers University Press.

Profit, W., Mino, I., & Pierce, C. (2000). Black stress. In G. Fink (Ed.), *Encyclopedia of stress* (Vol. 1 (A-D), pp. 324−330). San Diego, CA: Academic Press.

Provine, W. B. (1973). Geneticists and the biology of race crossing. *Science, 182*(4114), 790−796.

Pullum, G. (1999). African American Vernacular English is not standard English with mistakes. In R. S. Wheeler (Ed.), *The workings of language: From prescriptions to perspectives* (pp. 36−58). Westport, CT: Praeger Publishers.

Puwar, N. (2004). *Space invaders: Race, gender and bodies out of place.* Oxford: Berg Publishers.

Qureshi, S. (2004). Displaying Sara Baartman, the 'Hottentot Venus'. *History of Science, 42*(2), 233−257.

Quillian, L., & Redd, R. (2009). The friendship networks of multiracial adolescents. *Social Science Research, 38*(2), 279−295.

Rankine, C. (2015). *Citizen: An American Lyric.* London: Penguin UK.

Rhamie, J. (2007). *Eagles who soar: How black learners find the path to success.* Stoke-on-Trent: Trentham Books.

Rivkin, S. G. (1994). Residential segregation and school integration. *Sociology of Education, 67*(4), 279−292.

Roberts, S., & Baker, P. (2010). Asked to declare his race, Obama checks 'black'. *New York Times.* April 2. Retrieved from http://www.nytimes.com/2010/04/03/us/politics/03census.html. Accessed on December 13, 2017.

Rockquemore, K. A., & Laszloffy, T. A. (2005). *Raising biracial children.* Lanham, MD: Altamira Press, Rowman and Littlefield.

Rockquemore, K. A., Brunsma, D. L., & Delgado, D. J. (2009). Racing to theory or retheorizing race? Understanding the struggle to build a multiracial identity theory. *Journal of Social Issues, 65*(1), 13−34.

Roediger, D. R. (2008). *How race survived US history: From settlement and slavery to the Obama phenomenon.* Brooklyn, NY: Verso Books.

Rollock, N. (2012). The invisibility of race: Intersectional reflections on the liminal space of alterity. *Race Ethnicity and Education, 15*(1), 65−84.

Rondilla, J. L., & Spickard, P. (2007). *Is lighter better?: Skin-tone discrimination among Asian Americans*. Lanham, MD: Rowman & Littlefield Publishers.

Root, M. P. (1990). Resolving "other" status: Identity development of biracial individuals. *Women & Therapy, 9*(1–2), 185–205.

Root, M. P. (1996). *The multiracial experience: Racial borders as a significant frontier in race relations*. Thousand Oaks, CA: Sage.

Root, M. P. (2003). Multiracial families and children: Implications for educational research and practice. In J. A. Banks & C. A. M. Banks (Eds.), *Handbook of research on multicultural education* (pp. 110–124). San Francisco, CA: Jossey-Boss.

Roth, W. M. (2008). Bricolage, métissage, hybridity, heterogeneity, diaspora: Concepts for thinking science education in the 21st century. *Cultural Studies in Science Education, 3*(4), 891–916.

Russell, K., Wilson, M., & Hall, R. E. (1992). *The color complex: The politics of skin color among African Americans*. New York, NY: Anchor Publishing.

Salih, S. (2007). On Judith Butler and Performativity. In M. M. Jenkins & K. E. Lovaas (Eds.), *Sexualities and communication in everyday life: A reader* (pp. 55–68). London: Sage.

Scheff, T. J. (1990). Socialization of emotion: Pride and shame as causal agents. In T. D. Kemper (Ed.), *Research agendas in the sociology of emotions* (pp. 281–304). Albany, NY: State University of New York Press.

Sebba, M. (2007). Caribbean Creoles and British Black English. In D. Britain (Ed.), *Language in the British Isles*. Cambridge: Cambridge University Press.

Sebba, M., & Tate, S. (1986). You know what I mean? Agreement marking in British Black English. *Journal of Pragmatics, 10*(2), 163–172.

Sebba, M., & Wooton, T. (1998). We, they and identity. In P. Auer (Ed.), *Codeswitching in conversation: Language, interaction and identity* (pp. 262–289). London: Routledge.

Senna, D. (1998). Mulatto millennium. In C. C. O'Hearn (Ed.), *Half + half: Writers growing up biracial and bicultural*. New York, NY: Pantheon.

Sewell, T. (1997). *Black masculinities and schooling. How Black boys survive modern schooling*. Stoke-on-Trent: Trentham Books.

Sharpley-Whiting, T. D. (1999). *Black Venus: Sexualized savages, primal fears, and primitive narratives in French*. Durham: Duke University Press.

Shih, M., Bonam, C., Sanchez, D., & Peck, C. (2007). The social construction of race: Biracial identity and vulnerability to stereotypes. *Cultural Diversity and Ethnic Minority Psychology, 13*(2), 125–133.

Simien, J. (dir.) (2014a). *Dear White People*. Code Red, Duly Noted, Homegrown Pictures: Lions Gate.

Simien, J. (2014b). *Dear white people*. London: Simon and Schuster.

Sims, J. P. (2012). Beautiful stereotypes: The relationship between physical attractiveness and mixed race identity. *Identities, 19*(1), 61–80.

Sims, J. P. (2014). *Doing race: Physical appearance, identity and the micro-politics of racial ambiguity*. PhD thesis. University of Wisconsin-Madison.

Sims, J. P. (2016). Reevaluation of the influence of appearance and reflected appraisals for mixed-race identity: The role of consistent inconsistent racial perception. *Sociology of Race and Ethnicity*, 569–583.

Sims, J. P., & Joseph-Salisbury, R. (forthcoming). "We were all just the black kids": Black mixed-race men and the importance of Black male peer groups for identity development.

Sinyangwe, S. (2012). The significance of mixed-race: Public perceptions of Barack Obama's race and its effect on his favorability. *Stanford Undergraduate Research Journal, 11*(2012), 87–94.

Small, S., & King-O'Riain, R. (2014). Global mixed race: An introduction. In R. King-O'Riain et al. (Eds.), *Global mixed race*. London: New York University Press.

Smith, V. (2013). *Not just race, not just gender: Black feminist readings*. London: Routledge.

Soja, E. W. (1996). *Thirdspace: Journeys to Los Angeles and other real-and-imagined places*. Oxford: Blackwell.

Solorzano, D. G., & Yosso, T. J. (2002). Critical race methodology: Counter-storytelling as an analytical framework for education research. *Qualitative Inquiry, 8*(1), 23–44.

Song, M. (2003). *Choosing ethnic identity*. Cambridge: Polity Press.

Song, M., & Aspinall, P. (2012). 'Mixed-race' young people's differential responses to misrecognition in Britain. In R. Edwards et al. (Eds.), *International perspectives on racial and ethnic mixedness and mixing*. Oxon: Routledge.

Song, M. (2015). Does a recognition of mixed race move us towards post-race? In K. Murji & J. Solomos (Eds.), *Theories of race and ethnicity* (pp. 74–93). Cambridge: Cambridge University Press.

Spell, S. A. (2017). Not just black and white: How race/ethnicity and gender intersect in hookup culture. *Sociology of Race and Ethnicity, 3*(2), 172–187.

Spencer, J. M. (2000). *The new colored people: The mixed-race movement in America*. New York, NY: NYU Press.

Spickard, P. (2001). The subject is mixed race: The boom in biracial biography. In D. Parker & M. Song (Eds.), *Rethinking 'mixed race'* (pp. 76–98). London: Pluto Press.

Stockdill, B. C., & Danico, M. Y. (2012). The Ivory Tower paradox: Higher education as a site of oppression and resistance. In B. C. Stockdill & M. Y. Danico (Eds.), *Transforming the Ivory Tower: Challenging racism, sexism, and homophobia in the academy* (pp. 1–30). Hawaii: University of Hawaii Press.

Stonequist, E. V. (1937). *The marginal man: A study in personality and culture conflict*. New York, NY: Russell and Russell.

Stubblefield, A. (2005). *Ethics along the color line*. Ithaca, NY: Cornell University Press.

Sue, D. W. (2010). *Microaggressions in everyday life: Race, gender, and sexual orientation*. Hoboken, NJ: John Wiley & Sons.

Sue, D. W., Capodilupo, C. M., Torino, G. C., Bucceri, J. M., Holder, A., Nadal, K. L., & Esquilin, M. (2007). Racial microaggressions in everyday life: implications for clinical practice. *American psychologist, 62*(4), 271–286.

Sue, D. W., Capodilupo, C. M., & Holder, A. (2008). Racial microaggressions in the life experience of Black Americans. *Professional Psychology: Research and Practice, 39*(3), 329–336.

Sullivan, S. (2006). *Revealing whiteness: The unconscious habits of racial privilege.* Bloomington: Indiana University Press.

Sundstrom, R. R. (2016). Responsible multiracial politics: Chasing mixed-race ghosts. In T. F. Botts (Ed.), *Philosophy and the mixed race experience* (pp. 21–54). London: Lexington Books.

Tate, S. A. (2005). *Black skins, black masks: Hybridity. Dialogism, performativity.* Aldershot: Ashgate Publishing.

Tate, S. A. (2012). *Black beauty: Aesthetics, stylization, politics.* Aldershot: Ashgate Publishing, Ltd.

Tate, S. A. (2013). Racial affective economies, disalienation and 'race made ordinary'. *Ethnic and Racial Studies, 37*(13), 2475–2490.

Tate, S. A. (2015a). *Skin Bleaching in Black Atlantic Zones: Shade Shifters.* London: Palgrave Macmillan.

Tate, S. A. (2015b). Performativity and 'raced' bodies. In K. Murji & J. Solomos (Eds.), *Theories of race and ethnicity* (pp. 180–198). Cambridge: Cambridge University Press.

Tate, S. A. (2016). 'I can't quite put my finger on it': Racism's touch. *Ethnicities, 16*(1), 68–85.

Tate, S. A. (2017). *The Governmentality of black beauty shame: Discourse, iconicity and resistance.* Basingstoke: Palgrave.

Tate, S. A., & Page, D. (2018). Whitcliness and institutional racism: Hiding behind (un)conscious bias. *Ethics and Education, 13*(1),141–155.

Tatum, B. D. (2003). *"Why are all the Black kids sitting together in the cafeteria?": And other conversations about race.* New York, NY: Basic Books.

Tharps, L. L. (2014). The case for Black with a capital B. *New York Times,* November 18. Retrieved from http://www.nytimes.com/2014/11/19/opinion/the-case-for-black-with-a-capital-b.html?smid=tw-share&_r=2. Accessed on December 13, 2017.

Thicknesse, P. (1788). *Memoirs and anecdotes of Philip Thicknesse: Late Lieutenant Governor of Land Guard Fort, and unfortunately father to George Touchet.* Baron Audley.

Tikly, L., Caballero, C., Haynes, J., & Hill, J. (2004). *Understanding the educational needs of mixed heritage pupils.* London: DfES.

Tizard, B., & Phoenix, A. (2002). *Black, white or mixed race?: Race and racism in the lives of young people of mixed parentage.* London: Psychology Press.

Townsend, S. S., Markus, H. R., & Bergsieker, H. B. (2009). My choice, your categories: The denial of multiracial identities. *Journal of Social Issues, 65*(1), 185–204.

Topix. (2007). Lewis Hamilton IS NOT BLACK!. Retrieved from http://www.topix.com/forum/formula1/lewis-hamilton/TIK3163VH30IUICNT. Accessed on December 13, 2017.

Tuan, M. (1998). *Forever foreigners or honorary whites?: The Asian ethnic experience today.* London: Rutgers University Press.

Tulloch, C. A. (2004). *Black Style*. London: V & A Publications.

Tutwiler, S. W. (2016). *Mixed-race youth and schooling: The fifth minority*. Abingdon: Routledge.

Twine, F. W. (2010). *A White Side of Black Britain: Interracial Intimacy and Racial Literacy*. Durham: Duke University Press.

Uzogara, E. E., et al. (2014). A comparison of skin tone discrimination among African American men: 1995 and 2003. *Psychology of men & masculinity, 15*(2), 201–212.

Valluvan, S. (2016). What is 'post-race' and what does it reveal about contemporary racisms? *Ethnic and Racial Studies, 39*(13), 2241–2251.

Van Thompson, C. (2004). *The tragic Black buck: Racial masquerading in the American literary imagination*. New York, NY: Peter Lang.

Vasquez, J. M. (2010). Blurred borders for some but not 'others': Racialization, 'flexible ethnicity,' gender, and third-generation Mexican American identity. *Sociological Perspectives, 53*(1), 45–72.

Vest, J. L. (2016). Being and not being, knowing and not knowing. In T. F. Botts (Ed.), *Philosophy and the mixed race experience* (pp. 93–116). London: Lexington Books.

Warikoo, N. K. (2011). *Balancing acts: Youth culture in the global city*. Berkley, CA: University of California Press.

Warmington, P. (2012). 'A tradition in ceaseless motion': Critical race theory and Black British intellectual spaces. *Race Ethnicity and Education, 15*(1), 5–21.

Warmington, P. (2014). *Black British intellectuals and education: Multiculturalism's hidden history*. London: Routledge.

Waters, M. C. (1999). Explaining the comfort factor: West Indian immigrants confront American race relations. In M. Lamont (Ed.), *The cultural territories of race: Black and white boundaries* (pp. 63–96). Chicago, IL: Chicago University Press.

Waters, M. C. (1990). *Ethnic options: Choosing identities in America*. Berkley, CA: University of California Press.

Waters, M. C. (2010). Optional ethnicities. In M. L. Andersen & P. H. Collins (Eds.), *Race, class, and gender: An anthology* (pp. 201–209). Boston: Wadsworth Cengage Learning.

Werbner, P., & Modood, T. (2005). *Debating cultural hybridity: Multi-cultural identities and the politics of anti-racism*. London: Zed Books.

Weitz, R. (2004). *Rapunzel's daughters: What women's hair tells us about women's lives*. New York, NY: Farrar, Straus and Giroux.

Whitehead, S. M. (2002). *Men and masculinities: Key themes and new directions*. Cambridge, MA: Polity Press.

Williams, K. M. (2004). Linking the civil rights and multiracial movements. In H. Dalmage (Ed.), *Politics of multiracialism: Challenging racial thinking* (pp. 77–97). New York, NY: State University of New York Press.

Williams, D. (2011). *Mixed Matters: Mixed-race pupils discuss school and identity*. London: Troubador Publishing Ltd.

Williams, J. C., Phillips, K. W., & Hall, E. V. (2014). Double jeopardy? Gender bias against women of color in science, tools for change. Retrieved from http://www.uchastings.edu/news/articles/2015/01/double-jeopardy-report.pdf. Accessed on December 13, 2017.

Williamson, J. (1980). *New people: Miscegenation and mulattoes in the United States*. New York, NY: Free Press.

Winant, H. (1994). *Racial conditions. Politics, theory, comparisons*. Minneapolis, MN: University of Minnesota Press.

Wise, T. (2013). *Colorblind: The rise of post-racial politics and the retreat from racial equity*. San Francisco, CA: City Lights Books.

Woody, E. L. (2002). Constructions of masculinity in California's single-gender academies. In A. Datnow & L. Hubbard (Eds.), *Gender in policy and practice: Perspectives on single-sex and coeducational schooling* (pp. 280–303). New York, NY: Routledge Falmer.

Yancy, G. (2008). *Black bodies, white gazes: The continuing significance of race*. Lanham, MD: Rowman and Littlefield.

Yancy, G. (2017). *Black bodies, white gazes*. Lanham, MD: Rowman and Littlefield.

Youdell, D. C. (2000). *Schooling identities: An ethnography of the constitution of pupil identities*. PhD thesis, Institute of Education, University of London.

Youdell, D. (2004). Identity traps or how Black students fail. In D. Gillborn & G. Ladson-Billings (Eds.), *The RoutledgeFalmer reader in multicultural education* (pp. 84–102). London: RoutledgeFalmer.

Zack, N. (1994). *Race and mixed race*. Philadelphia, PA: Temple University Press.

Zilanawala, A., Sacker, A., & Kelly, Y. (2016). Mixed ethnicity and behavioural problems in the Millennium Cohort Study. *Archives of disease in childhood*. Retrieved from pp.archdischild-2015-309701

Index

www.ingramcontent.com/pod-product-compliance
Lightning Source LLC
Chambersburg PA
CBHW052001270326
41929CB00015B/2748